D1253963

BOOKS BY PETER GUNN

My Dearest Augusta

WITHDRAWN

Augusta Leigh. Sketch by Sir George Hayter

My Dearest Augusta

A Biography of Augusta Leigh,
Lord Byron's Half-Sister
PETER GUNN

There should always be some foundation
of fact for the most airy fabric, and pure
invention is but the talent of a liar.

*Lord Byron, letter to John Murray,
2nd April, 1817*

NEW YORK

Atheneum

1968

Copyright © 1968 by Peter Gunn
All rights reserved
Library of Congress catalog card number 68–27656
Printed in the United States of America by
The Murray Printing Company, Forge Village, Massachusetts
Bound by H. Wolff, New York
First American Edition

49,288

PR
4382
.G8
1968

Author's Note

I wish gratefully to acknowledge help given to me on various matters. My thanks are due to Major Roger Mortimer, the Hon. David Erskine, Mr. Peter Quennell, the Keeper of Printed Books, Bodleian Library, Mr. John G. Murray, the Earl of Lytton, Mr. Malcolm Elwin, the Trustees of the British Museum, and the Nottingham City Librarian and Curator of Newstead Abbey. In addition, I acknowledge my indebtedness to those whose work on Byron has made this book possible, and whose published copyright material I have used or quoted: *Lord Byron's Wife* © Malcolm Elwin 1962; *The Late Lord Byron* © Doris Langley Moore 1961; *Byron: A Biography* © Leslie Marchand 1957; The Earl of Lytton: extracts from the Lovelace Papers first published in the Earl of Lovelace's *Astarte*, Ethel Colburn Mayne's *Life of Lady Byron*, *The Late Lord Byron*, and *Lord Byron's Wife*; John Murray: extracts from *Byron: A Self-Portrait* edited by Peter Quennell, and *Lord Byron's Correspondence* edited by John Murray. Furthermore, I am much indebted to Mr. James Michie of The Bodley Head for his care and courtesy in bringing to my notice infelicities, and worse, in points of style.

Cambridge, November 1967   PETER GUNN

Contents

Illustrations

My Dearest Augusta

I

Family Portraits

IN JANUARY 1779 the rumours concerning Amelia, Marchioness of Carmarthen, which had hitherto been confined to the drawing-rooms, became open knowledge through the gossip columns of *The Town and Country Magazine*. Each month the readers of this miscellany were regaled with the 'foibles and indiscretions of the gay and polite' on a series entitled 'Histories of the Tête-à-Tête', and the January number now revealed the amorous adventures of the 'Boisterous Lover and the Capricious Marchioness'. Written in the exaggerated cant phrasing of the time, the account is lively enough, and the attempt to veil the personages involved by the use of dashes is mere pretence. It is highly probable, from the corroborative evidence provided, that the facts related were true in the main, since the persons and certain events and details would have been widely known.

According to the columnist, her ladyship was distinguished by reason of 'the *éclat* she has made in the brilliant vortex of dissipation'. In giving some account of her upbringing, he states that her father, 'the late earl of H', had himself superintended her studies; her progress, as it is related, was so rapid as to suggest that the Earl was hard put to it to find her worthy preceptors. 'French, Italian, dancing and music composed the smallest share of her learning; history, the belles lettres, and the whole circle of the sciences, were unfolded to her; and her genius and avidity for knowledge seemed to outstrip the attention of her masters:·she constantly anticipated their lessons, and was usually found to be as well acquainted with the subjects which were taught her, as the teachers themselves.' To the intellectual endowments of this aristocratic young paragon were added 'one of the most angelic faces and elegant figures' that ever graced a drawing-room or enlivened a rout.

On 16th May, 1778, shortly before the occurrence of the main events chronicled in *The Town and Country Magazine*, Robert d'Arcy, fourth Earl of Holdernesse, Warden of the Cinque

Ports, died in the south of France, where he had gone in the hope of restoring his failing health. Lord Holdernesse, who appears to have been an intelligent and cultivated man, had had a career of distinguished public service; he had represented his country as ambassador at the courts of Venice and The Hague, and served as a secretary of state from 1751 until 1761; a few years later he was appointed by George III as governor to his eldest sons, the Prince of Wales and Prince Frederick. Ill health had obliged him in 1776 to relinquish this last post to the Duke of Montagu, 'one of the weakest and most ignorant men living', with Bishop Richard Hurd as tutor, who thus had the responsibility of educating the future Prince Regent; and thenceforth the Earl watched over the education of his precocious only child, Amelia. Lady Holdernesse, the daughter of the Sieur Francis Doublet of Groeneveldt, a member of the States-General of Holland, was 'the lovely Dutch girl' who had married Robert d'Arcy in 1742. In mature age she appears to have been a devout and capable woman, who for many years was in attendance at the court of Queen Charlotte. On the Earl's death his titles became extinct, with the exception of that deriving from the barony of Conyers, which had been granted to an ancestor, Sir William Conyers, in 1509, and which now descended to his daughter, who in 1773 at the age of nineteen had married Francis, Marquis of Carmarthen, the heir to the fourth Duke of Leeds. From her father's estate Amelia, Marchioness of Carmarthen and Baroness Conyers in her own right, was to receive the substantial annual income of £4000 during her lifetime.

The tone of aristocratic eighteenth-century society, while perhaps not so indulgent as that of the Restoration, was still generously permissive; so long as some respect was shown to appearances, marital infidelity was discreetly countenanced, if not openly condoned. The young and high-spirited Lady Carmarthen, remarkable both for her beauty and her intelligence, was not overlong in displaying her independence of any such slight restraints as society imposed. Yet she had married the Marquis for love. He alone of the many eligible suitors had touched her heart; and when he seemed first insensible of her charms, it was she who sought the help of a near relation to unfold to the young man three years older than herself the

12

secret of her feelings. Her persistence found its reward; in fact, if we are to believe the anonymous chronicler, after the marriage 'the young lord seemed to be convinced of his felicity, and for some time their hours glided away in a constant rotation of reciprocal fondness'. Three children were born to them: George, who was to succeed his father as sixth Duke of Leeds in 1799; Francis Godolphin Osborne; and Mary, who afterwards married Lord Pelham, later the second Earl of Chichester.

'But alas! the dissipation and frivolity of the age now began their baneful influence upon his lordship: cloyed even with transcendent bliss, he sought for extraneous pleasures; domestic enjoyments had lost their zest, and he found more pastime at a masquerade, or a hazard table, than in the arms of captivating beauty.' At this stage the gossip-writer, carried forward on the wave of his own rhetoric, does less than justice to the Marquis in describing in this fashion his public activities. In fact, his duties often required his presence in Yorkshire, where he was Lord-Lieutenant of the East Riding; in 1774 he entered the House of Commons, and remained there until in 1776 he was raised to the peerage as Baron Osborne, although he was still usually known by his courtesy title. In the House of Lords he showed himself an opponent to the policies of Lord North, but Horace Walpole had a poor opinion of his merits—'he was a light variable young man, of very moderate parts, and less principle'. However, the columnist has his own explanation for this early promotion of the Marquis to the Upper House, in ignorance, perhaps of the similar example of his great-grandfather in 1690.

Amelia (he states) suffered much from her husband's neglect, and, moved by feelings of wounded pride, resentment, jealousy, and even revenge, eventually took to herself a lover from among the circle of her own domestics, thus, we are told, 'planting the antlers on his lordship's brow'. A dismissed lady's maid divulged her secret to her husband, and the Marquis was about to begin proceedings for a divorce, when Lord Holdernesse, who was still living, used his influence with the King to secure a barony for his son-in-law as the price of his silence. After a trip abroad, the Carmarthens appeared again in society as an apparently united and loving couple.

Then, in the summer of 1778, about the time of the death of

13

her father, Lady Carmarthen first met Captain John Byron. 'Mad Jack' or 'Johnny' Byron was the eldest son of Admiral the Hon. John Byron and nephew to the fifth Lord Byron, 'the Wicked Lord'. Born in 1756, John was educated at Westminster, from which he went on to a French military academy, where he acquired a thorough knowledge of the French language and more than a passing acquaintance with the manners of pre-revolutionary French society. His father having bought him a commission in the Guards, he saw some active service in America after the outbreak of the War of American Independence in 1775; but wearying of the profession of arms and perhaps dreaming of other conquests in London drawing-rooms, he returned to England in 1778. If he was not under a cloud of some sort, it seems strange that at a time when officers were badly needed for the extended war he was allowed to dispose of his commission, which he apparently did. Handsome, arrogant and unscrupulous—it is said that he extracted money from his mistresses to pay his gambling debts—he brought to the pursuit of his pleasures all the unrestrained recklessness of the Byrons. Clearly Captain Byron was at twenty-two (as was said later of his son) 'mad—bad—and dangerous to know'.

During the summer, when Lord Carmarthen was absent from London on a prolonged visit to Yorkshire, his wife was frequently seen at Ranelagh, Vauxhall and other public places. We are not informed when or where precisely Amelia met Jack Byron, but on the occasion of their making a '*partie carrée*' with another couple on an outing to Coxheath (then open country used for military manoeuvres), she was observed to make him 'the constant butt of her wit and pleasantry'. This Beatrice and Benedict episode led to further and warmer meetings, and the liaison was soon conducted brazenly, without any attempt at concealment. So widely was the affair noised abroad that it reached the ears of Lord Carmarthen in Yorkshire. He had written to his wife that he would be staying in the country for another fortnight, but now he anticipated his departure and arrived back in London three days after this letter was posted. The couple were out of town picnicking at Barrowhedges, when the Marquis reached London. He immediately set out in pursuit of them. They were warned, however, in time, and made good their escape.

14

The husband, subject to outbursts of fury and self-pity in turn, gave orders that the doors should be locked against the Marchioness, and vowed that she should never again enter his house. Thereupon he took steps to bring about a divorce. Her ladyship, we are told, 'heard her doom with great coolness and philosophy, saying it was what she had long expected, and was perhaps the most lucky incident of her life'. The next day she sent for her clothes and jewels, and in a note requested that her husband should make her a present of the last carriage he had given her. This he did, after first ordering the coachmaker to obliterate the coat of arms on the doors. Captain Byron and Lady Carmarthen then openly lived together in the latter's town house in Grosvenor Square or alternately at Aston Hall near Doncaster, another of her properties. In mid-1779 the Marquis secured the passage of a bill of divorcement through Parliament, and he subsequently remarried. On 9th June in the same year the marriage took place between Captain John Byron and Lady Amelia d'Arcy; a little more than a month later, on 19th July, Lady Amelia Byron gave birth to a daughter in Grosvenor Square.

The momentous events which were absorbing the energies of the nation seem to have had small effect on the affairs of John Byron; possibly he was a Whig in politics and had seen enough of English behaviour in the American colonies to feel some sympathy for the aspirations of the revolted colonists. With greater likelihood he was simply too engrossed in his own pleasures, and in the means to pay for them; for Amelia's income was insufficient to meet the cost of their style of living, and over them soon hung a constant fear of duns. In February 1778 France had come to the aid of the American insurgents in their struggle with the home country; in 1779 the allies were joined by Spain and in the following year England declared war on Holland. The French and Spanish fleets appeared in the Channel; Captain Paul Jones had landed and spiked the guns in Whitehaven harbour, and later in 1779 was to force two English men-of-war to surrender off Flamborough Head. Eleven days before Byron's marriage to Amelia his father, as admiral in command of the English squadron in West Indian waters, had sent back dispatches in which he gave an account of an ineffectual action off Grenada against the French fleet

15

under the Comte d'Estaing. In October the Admiral was home (he had been succeeded in command by Rodney), and on the 15th he had a long audience of the King, who, the papers reported, detained him at court till half past five. Whether it was immediately after this prolonged interview that the Admiral remonstrated with his profligate son, we do not know; but then or some time later he publicly signified his disapproval of his son's scandalous mode of life by disinheriting him.

The profligacy and the utter contempt for the world's opinion which were such marked features of members of three generations of the family (they perhaps reached their culmination in the poet), may possibly suggest the presence of some common element in their heredity. The Byrons claimed as the founder of their house a certain Ralph de Burun, who accompanied William on his conquest of England and who is shown in the Doomsday Book as the holder of extensive lands in Nottinghamshire. To his descendants, with the title of Lords of Horestan Castle, came considerable possessions in Derbyshire, and later in the reign of Edward I the estates of Rochdale in Lancashire. On the dissolution of the monasteries Henry VIII disposed for the sum of £810 to 'our beloved servant John Byron of Colewyke all the house and site, ground and soil, of the late Monastery or Priory of Newstede within the Forest of Sherewode in our said County of Notingham'. The Priory of Newstead was founded by Henry II about 1170 and dedicated to God and the Virgin as a house of the Canons Regular of the Augustinian Order, known as the Austin or Black Canons from the colour of their habit. Sir John Byron converted the monastic quarters round the square cloister into a spacious mansion, using for this purpose the stonework from two walls of the adjoining abbey church. The ornate tomb of his successor of the same name, who was knighted by Queen Elizabeth in 1579 and was known familiarly as 'Little Sir John of the Great Beard', may be seen today in Newstead Abbey. Little Sir John apparently had extravagant tastes, and maintained a large establishment which included a private troop of players; for on his death Gilbert, Earl of Shrewsbury, wrote to his heir counselling him to retrench: 'I do therefore advise you, that so soon as you have, in such sort as shall be fit, finished yr father's funerals, to dispose and disperse that great household, reducing them to the number of forty or fifty, at the most, of all sort . . .'

During the Civil War the Byrons were cavaliers to a man. No fewer than seven Byron brothers were said to have fought at Edgehill, the eldest of them, another John, having raised his own regiment of horse for the King, who had knighted him for his political and military services. In October 1643 Charles raised this Sir John to the peerage as Baron Byron of Rochdale in the county of Lancaster. The splendid portrait of the first Lord Byron, painted by William Dobson and now in the collection of Lt-Colonel J. Leicester-Warren, shows admirably the characteristics of these Royalist Byrons: the backward tilt of the head gives the suggestion of superb arrogance; the black hair worn long is parted to show a low forehead; the eyes are dark, vulturine, beneath their hooded lids; the prominent nose ends in somewhat coarse nostrils; a thick moustache hides the upper lip, but the lower lip is full above a pointed beard; a livid scar on the left cheek and a wart on the chin complete this realistic portrait of a man headstrong, hot-blooded, not given to niceties of thought, but generous, brave and loyal in the service of his sovereign. Lord Byron was one of the seven persons excluded by Parliament from all pardon in 1648, but he had already followed Charles II into exile, where he became superintendent to the household of the Duke of York, later James II. He had no children; and it appears that he had to undergo treatment ironically similar to that meted out to other husbands by later Byrons, for (if we are to believe Pepys) he was cuckolded in the person of his second wife Eleanor, and that by no less a dignitary than his sovereign Charles II. (She was the latter's seventeenth mistress, if the score was accurately kept.) At John Byron's death in 1652 he was succeeded by his brother Richard.

On the return of Charles II from his exile he was accompanied by the second Lord Byron, who was reinstated in the house and estate of Newstead Abbey, sequestrated by Parliament; but it seems that he had to pay for this privilege. His memorial in Hucknall Torkard parish church records the steadfastness of the Byrons to the royal cause, and tells how they 'suffered much for their loyalty, and lost all their present fortune; yet it pleased God to bless the honest endeavours of the said Richard Lord Byron that he repurchased part of their ancient inheritance'. William, his only surviving son, who succeeded to the barony, had married in 1661 Elizabeth, daughter of John, Viscount Chatworth in the peerage of Ireland, whose lands of Annesley Hall adjoined the Newstead estate. He in turn was followed by another William, the fourth Lord Byron, who thrice married, his last wife being Frances, the younger daughter of Lord Berkeley of Stratton, the family whose London property was around Berkeley Square and Stratton Street. It has been said that the eccentricity, profligacy and recklessness of behaviour of the Byrons from this time forth owes something to the Berkeley strain. (The elder Berkeley daughter married John Trevanion of Carhays, Cornwall; and a daughter of this marriage, Sophia, married her cousin Admiral John Byron, the son of the fourth Lord, thus giving an additional tincture of Berkeley blood to his son 'Mad Jack', and through him to the latter's children, Augusta and her half-brother, George, the poet.) William, fourth Lord Byron, had six children (all by his third wife), two of whom appear to have died at an early age; the eldest, another William, born in 1722, became the fifth, 'the Wicked Lord'; his brother John, later the Admiral, was born in 1723; then followed a daughter, Isabella, who subsequently married the fourth Earl of Carlisle (a child of this marriage being the fifth Lord Carlisle, who befriended the orphan Augusta and became legal guardian to George Gordon, the poet and sixth Lord Byron); the last surviving child was a son, who married a Miss Kennedy in 1773.

In order to understand something of the hereditary Byronic influences (since heredity does account for much) in the lives of both Augusta Byron and her half-brother, it is perhaps worth while to look beyond their immediate parents to their grandfather the Admiral and to their grand-uncle William, 'the Wicked Lord'. William Byron inherited the title in 1736 at the age of fourteen and later entered the Royal Navy; serving as lieutenant on the *Victory* under Admiral Balchen, he was fortunate in not being on board when the vessel was wrecked off the coast of Alderney. He seems to have retired early from a naval career, for he married in 1747 a Norfolk heiress, Elizabeth Shaw of Besthorpe Hall, and spending much time in London when not at Newstead, he quickly gained for himself the reputation of a rake. Much noise was made of his extravagances and of his unsuccessful attempt to carry off the actress, Miss Bellamy. He was by way of being a connoisseur—at least he spent a great deal of money on 'very rare and costly articles of vertu or art' in the London salerooms, ordering horses to his carriage and setting out from Newstead at a moment's notice, should an advertisement of some desired purchase catch his eye. In 1749 he built a miniature castle or casino among the woods overlooking the lake, and here he entertained his guests with musical concerts and lavish parties. It was these in later years, when his evil reputation had made him the object of fantastic speculation, that gave rise to the popular tales of his orgies. The statues of nymphs struggling in the arms of satyrs and centaurs, which he placed in the grounds, would have added spice to these reports. It was presumably about the same time that he built the two forts by the lake, where he staged naval engagements with small cannon between the forts and armed vessels, the estate servants (among them the faithful Joe Murray) being mustered to serve as attacking crews and defenders on the battlements.

The resources at his disposal were quite insufficient to meet such reckless expenditure, so he began the systematic spoliation of his estate that was to cause his heir much vexatious litigation and pressing anxiety. When Horace Walpole visited Newstead Abbey in 1760, he was charmed with its architecture (as one would expect of the architect of Strawberry Hill)—'there is grace and gothic indeed'; but he was appalled at the dereliction of the park: 'the present Lord has lost large sums and paid part in old oaks, five thousand pounds worth of which have been cut near the house'. As his debts mounted, he felled further trees; the great 'Druid' oak near the gatehouse on the main road was only spared by the timely intervention of a nature-loving purchaser. The deer from the park followed the oaks; two thousand seven hundred of them were slaughtered and sold for next to nothing in Mansfield market. Finally in 1784 he leased (quite illegally) the coal mines of the Rochdale estate for the paltry sum of £60 a year. As an old man he dined alone, his pistols laid on the table as part of the dinner service, and into such poverty had he fallen that (as Joe Murray afterwards reported) 'one and the same Bottle of Claret was kept by me by his Lordship's order the cork drawn and when the cloth was removed his Lordship cried aloud, "Joe, put the claret on the table" . . . The Claret was daily removed . . . and re-appeared on each successive day but never touched.'

An incident, when he was in his early forties, created a great stir at the time and gave colour to the popular characterisation of him as 'the Wicked Lord'. Some Nottinghamshire gentle-men, neighbouring landlords, formed a London dining club, which met once a month at the fashionable Star and Garter Tavern in Pall Mall. Lord Byron was a member of this con-vivial group, and seated near him on the evening of 26th January, 1765, was his second cousin and neighbour, William Chaworth of Annesley Hall, who seems to have been an intractable individual, loud-spoken, irascible, quick to take offence. After dinner, flushed with the claret in which they had liberally indulged, a quarrel arose between them over the trivial subject of how best to preserve game. Peace was restored for the moment by others present, but Lord Byron thought that he had heard words from Mr Chaworth which implied a challenge. When the party retired, the latter was waiting for Lord Byron at the head of the stairs and the altercation was renewed. They asked a waiter to find them an empty room; this he did and, bringing a single candlestick, left them. Chaworth had the advantage of his opponent, as his weapon was the sword, Byron's being habitually the pistol. In the semi-darkness Chaworth drew his sword and lunged at his adversary, the blade becoming caught up in his waistcoat. The facts were never seriously disputed. According to Chaworth's own account, he saw Byron's sword 'half drawn, and, *knowing the man*, immediately, or as quick as he could, whipped out his sword, and had the first thrust.' Thinking that he had wounded or even killed Byron, he came up close to him, whereupon the latter shortened his sword and ran him through the belly.

Chaworth lingered until the following day, but, though cross-examined by his friends, he maintained that the fight had been fair, that he was a fool to have fought in a dark room, and that he was thankful not to have another's life on his conscience. The coroner's jury returned a verdict of wilful murder, and Lord Byron was lodged in the Tower, to stand trial before his peers in the House of Lords. The trial, when it took place on 16th and 17th April in Westminster Hall, attracted so much public interest that tickets of admission fetched the price of six guineas. Lord Byron defended himself clearly and straightforwardly, admitting the irregularity of fighting in a dimly lighted room, but claiming that the fight itself had been fairly conducted. The verdict was more favourable than in the coroner's court, four peers voting 'Not guilty', and one hundred and nineteen 'Not guilty of murder, but guilty of manslaughter'. Byron, claiming the benefit of a statute of Edward VI, was then discharged by simply paying his fees, and retired to Newstead. Afterwards he kept the sword with which he killed Chaworth in his bedroom at the Abbey. However, the notoriety caused by the trial made London uncongenial to him, and thenceforth he went up only on pressing business, travelling on such occasions under the name of Waters.

Debts and quarrels with his neighbours turned him increasingly with the years into a sombre recluse, but he continued to think he could retrieve his position in society by the marriage of his only son William to an appropriate heiress. On the latter's coming of age in October, 1770, all the county echoed to the cannonade from Newstead, where a fully-rigged ship had been brought overland from the coast, and discharged its twenty-one guns on the lake in honour of William's majority. Shortly after there occurred an event which put the seal on 'the Wicked Lord's' latent misanthropy. He had chosen as William's bride a Miss Danvers, a young lady of considerable fortune; but on the very eve of the wedding the prospective bridegroom gave proof of his being a true Byron in lacking respect for others' opinions by eloping to Gretna Green with his first cousin, Juliana Elizabeth, daughter of Admiral John Byron. From this time 'the Wicked Lord' became more embittered and eccentric. He vowed that if his heir should come into the estate his inheritance would be not worth having. His incalculable behaviour encouraged the mythopoeic imagination of the countryside. Whether such tales as his throwing his wife into the pond, or his shooting his coachman for some trivial offence, bundling the corpse into the carriage with Lady Byron, and then driving on, are true or not, he did make life so unbearable for her that she left him. He found solace with a servant, Elizabeth Hardstaff, who became known to all as 'Lady Betty'; she and Joe Murray tended to his wants until his death. Murray would assist his master as a whipper-in, when his lordship staged races with the crickets which he had trained to course over his recumbent body. His grandson said that he used to beat them with a wisp of straw if they became too familiar.

His son died in 1776, leaving as heir to the title another William, who died of wounds in Corsica at the siege of Calvi in 1794. Since his brother the Admiral had died in 1786 and the latter's son 'Mad Jack' Byron, in 1791, the heir to the barony for the last years of 'the Wicked Lord's' life was the 'little boy that lives at Aberdeen', as he was called, and for whose welfare the old man took not the slightest concern. The only member of his family he would tolerate in his presence in his latter days was his niece, Frances, a daughter of the Admiral, who was married to General Charles Leigh. When death released him from his misery on 21st May, 1798, there was not enough money in hand to bury him; it was not until 16th June that the lawyers could decide how the funeral expenses were to be met, and 'the Wicked Lord' was lowered into the family vault in the Church at Hucknall Torkard.

The other prominent element in the Byronic heredity, that of sexual promiscuity, is particularly evident in 'the Wicked Lord's' brother, John Byron, the second son of the fourth Lord, who was born at Newstead on 8th November, 1723. Even in that indulgent age John Byron achieved a niche to himself in the gallery of gallantry. He, as well as his son, figures in the gossip columns of *The Town and Country Magazine;* in the number for December, 1773, appears the 'Tête-à-Tête' entitled 'The Memoirs of the Nautical Lover and Miss Betty G—n'. If we are to credit the stories told of him here, he early evinced a character of courageous determination and an amatory prowess that remained with him through life. At the age of sixteen he was removed from school for sleeping with his bed-maker, and entered the Royal Navy as a midshipman. In Plymouth he lodged with a personable young widow, and it was only the sailing of his ship that prevented her marrying him. But, as the chronicler puts it, 'new objects created new ideas, and he forgot his charming widow, and intended bride, in the arms of a beautiful Italian at Leghorn'. He accompanied Commodore Anson in his voyages in the South Seas; his ship the *Wager* was wrecked on the rocky coast of Patagonia in 1741, and the incredible hardships he and his companions survived (on one occasion they were forced to make a meal of a favourite dog), before they were released five years later by the Spanish authorities, are related in *The Narrative of the Honourable John Byron*, written by himself and published in 1768. After his return to England in 1746 he appears to have had several amorous successes before he married his cousin Sophia Trevanion in 1748. Sophia Byron, an educated and amiable woman, who was a friend of Mrs Thrale and a favourite of Dr Samuel Johnson, bore nine children, the eldest of whom was John, later 'Mad Jack'.

In 1756, on the outbreak of the Seven Year's War, 'Hardy' Byron, as he was affectionately known, was at sea again, and served with distinction until 1763, when, upon the Treaty of Paris, he retired once more to life in the west country. But the respite was short, for the following year he was appointed as commodore to sail in the *Dolphin* on a voyage of discovery in the South Seas. He discovered some islands, but somehow mysteriously missed Australia, thereby leaving the honour of its charting to Captain Cook in 1769. Even in these remote parts he added to his reputation for amorous adventures. 'We cannot suppose', write the columnist, 'that in the course of three years absence from his native country, the spirit of discovery precluded every other desire, or that the females of the southern hemisphere, many of whom are described as beautiful and attracting, did not exercise those passions in our hero, which have so often agitated him at home . . . We find that the queens and princesses of the islands were ever partial to Englishmen; and we may reasonably suppose the commodore did not escape their notice; and that nature and politeness prompted him to return their civilities.'

Once more back in England he published the account of his early adventures in *The Narrative* in 1768, and then in the following year he was appointed Governor of Newfoundland. By this time he had encountered so many storms at sea that he gained for himself the nickname of 'Foulweather Jack'. 'He had no rest at sea, nor I on shore', is his grandson's comment. After his term as governor he once more retired to the country and lived a life of liberal hospitality among his neighbours, spiced with some gallantries which were the staple of society gossip. It is probably because of his irregularities that Mrs Thrale referred to poor Sophia as 'wife to the Admiral *pour ses péchés*'. (He was promoted rear-admiral in 1775 and vice-admiral on his appointment to the West Indian squadron in 1778. He finally retired the next year and died, as we have seen, in 1786.)

The story of his liaison with Miss Betty G—n, with which the readers of *The Town and Country Magazine* were entertained, would relate to the period of his late forties or even early fifties. Betty, the daughter of a local farmer, was a charming fresh-skinned, fair-haired girl with a 'captivating' figure, who had been well educated, and was, before her appointment as lady's maid to Mrs Byron, the constant companion of the vicar's daughter. 'The nautical lover' was said to 'have urged his suit so forcibly' that the girl was swept off her feet and into his bed, where she was unfortunate enough to be discovered by her mistress, who promptly dismissed her. The Commodore, as he was then, was not the man to cast her off, and he forthwith found her lodgings in London in a house near Golden Square, where he often visited her. Sophia Byron, suspecting this, tracked them down in their retreat, and raised such a storm that even 'Foulweather Jack' was obliged to shorten sail and ride it out. When the wind dropped he found her lodgings elsewhere. There he continued to pay her visits, treating her with such consideration that, despite many tempting offers from other quarters for 'temporary gratifications', she is reported to have remained ever faithful to her 'nautical lover'.

The two characteristics of carelessness to public opinion and sexual promiscuity were united and raised to a high degree in the Admiral's son, 'Mad Jack' Byron; he had other vices of his own—gambling and dissipation among them—so that society was possibly not wrong in regarding him as an eminent example of incorrigible profligacy. His son was later, after his death, at pains to contradict the rumours that he was brutal and maltreated his wife and that she had died of a broken heart: 'So far from being "brutal", he was, according to the testimony of all those who knew him, of an extremely amiable and joyous character, but careless and dissipated . . . It is not

24

by "brutality" that a young Officer in the Guards seduces and carries off a Marchioness . . . It is true that he was a very handsome man, which goes a great way.' Although there were plenty of circles in London and in the country where society would receive the wayward couple, yet John Byron must have longed to return to the pleasures he had tasted in Paris. Moreover, his creditors were once more on his trail, and constant flitting was not to his taste. But the war between England and the revolted American colonies, allied with continental Europe, dragged on, so that escape to France was not possible. Finally in November, 1782, a peace treaty with the United States was signed, and early next year the continent was open again to English visitors, although the definitive Treaty of Versailles was not ratified until 3rd September, 1783.

It is to be supposed that the Byrons were some of the first to avail themselves of the newly opened frontiers, for we find them settled in Paris, where the gay round of pleasures was resumed. The English branch of Byron was apparently acknowledged as collateral relations by the French family of de Gontaut, Ducs de Biron. On 26th January, 1784, was born to Amelia Byron in Paris her only surviving child by her second marriage, Augusta Mary; but Amelia herself did not survive the birth of her daughter. We do not know who looked after the baby girl on her mother's death; perhaps she was taken, with her nurse, by her aunt Frances, wife of General Charles Leigh, who may have moved in by this time to the house the Leighs owned at Valenciennes; or perhaps she was taken in by her uncle, Captain George Anson Byron, who had married Henrietta Dallas in 1779 and was then living at Chantilly. Nor have we any knowledge of how affected Captain Byron was by his wife's unexpected demise. Nevertheless, it is clear that France without her was a luxury he could not afford. The winds were blowing cold over Paris; he was inextricably in debt and his wife's four thousand pounds had ceased with her death. There was nothing else for it: leaving his year-old baby daughter behind him, 'Mad Jack' was once more in England in the spring of 1785—not in London, where his creditors knew him too well. He travelled down to the West Country instead and installed himself in the fashionable watering-place of Bath, to re-equip himself with an heiress.

II

A Child in Strange Houses

1788 - 1802

If the pressing nature of Captain John Byron's debts caused him inner concern, there was nothing in the external elegance of his person and the amiability of his manners to reveal it. Not yet thirty, strikingly handsome, with the easy distinction gained in Parisian salons, his graceful dancing must have found many admirers among the young ladies of Bath to whom he was introduced at Lindsay's or Hayes's. In no time at all he had achieved the purpose of his visit. One of these admiring young women, a Miss Catharine Gordon of Gight, who was staying in Bath for the season with her Duff relations, lost her heart to him and the couple were married on the 13th May, 1785, at the parish church of St Michael. He had found his 'Golden Dolly' (as his son would have said), but to a man as discriminating in feminine attractiveness as John Byron this provincial Scottish girl, with her dumpy figure, awkward movements and heightened complexion must have been a sad falling off from the attractive Amelia d'Arcy. However, she had the charm of youth (she was just twenty), was of ancient lineage and the possessor of an estate of a value exceeding twenty-five thousand pounds. This last consideration was paramount in his mind; and although the sum itself was not large (in fact, he ran through most of it within eighteen months of his marriage), it was better to take what was so willingly offered, especially since there were apparently no embarrassing questions asked or settlements demanded. Indeed it does seem incredible to us who know the sequel that Catharine Gordon's relations did nothing to prevent her marrying so precipitately or, at least, did not tie her money up in some way to stop this notorious spendthrift from getting his hands on it. But Catharine Gordon had a will of her own, and she was wildly in love with her enchanting husband; and she could hardly have known the true extent of his debts, for the payment of which

out the entire Byron story.) On 22nd January, 1788, Catharine Byron gave birth to a son, who was born with a caul and—which had incalculable consequences on his subsequent career—with a malformation of the right foot. There is no record that John Byron was present at his son's birth or at his christening at Marylebone parish church on 29th February, when he was given the names George Gordon, the Duke of Gordon and Colonel Duff of Fetteresso standing as godfathers —clearly sponsors of Mrs Byron's choosing.

That 'Mad Jack' was in England early in January we know from the evidence of his running up debts in that month at Dover. However, fear of the debtor's prison soon necessitated his hiding in the country; he only returned into London on a Sunday, when the laws against debtors were relaxed. A London lawyer, Mr Watson, writing on behalf of Mrs Byron to the commissioners in Edinburgh for money urgently needed to pay the household bills and doubtless to subsidise John Byron, described in a graphic phrase the latter's melancholy position—constantly threatened with duns, he was 'obliged to be at hide and seek'. His debts at this time were calculated to be in the region of £1300. Catharine herself wrote to Watson on 20th March, demanding the reason for the arbiters' 'keeping Mr Byron in suspense'; and a few days later she again appealed for aid, omitting most punctuation in her stress of mind: 'I must leave London . . . and pray how am I to leave it without a farthing in short you may tell them if they delay sending me any money a week after you receive this I shall be reduced to the greatest misery.' It seems that some money was forthcoming, and the family moved out of London; but their movements for the next year are most uncertain. Probably late in 1789, and certainly by early 1790, Mrs Byron had taken a small house in Queen Street, Aberdeen, and moved there with her baby son. 'Mad Jack' gave himself in the summer a well-earned holiday by the sea, as we learn from a letter written on 4th August, 1789, to George Anson Byron by the heir-apparent to the title, his nephew, the eighteen-year-old William:

'Your brother took a small house at Sandgate Castle this summer where I stayed some time with him and we had a very fine Lugger all the time so that we were at sea a great deal

31

and in France but since he has been very near taken up and put into prison at Boulogne [he appears to have owed a debt of £90 there to a Viscount de Hoyle] but now he has gone down to Scotland and I am sure I wish he may make a long stay as it is by much the safest place for him.' The nephew seems to have enjoyed John Byron's sparkling company and to have had a genuine affection for him.

At some time in the year following her half-brother's birth Augusta's grandmother, Lady Holdernesse, hearing of the Byron family's straitened circumstances (whether Mrs Byron appealed to her or not is unknown), took the four-year-old girl to live with her. The cause of the long-lived quarrel between the two women has not been revealed—there would be reason enough in the dissimilarity of temperament between the staid, aristocratic, devout old Lady Holdernesse and the harassed, vulgar, tempestuous Catharine Byron to account for it; but Augusta from that time onward was not to see her half-brother George for twelve years. The paths of John Byron's two children diverged; little George to a life of genteel poverty in Aberdeen, with a mother whose lack of all self-control led to scenes of violent reproach and obloquy followed by equally unrestrained and impassioned embraces; Augusta to the privileged tranquillity of great houses and the companionship of her other half-brothers and -sisters, George, Francis and Mary Henrietta Osborne, the children of the fifth Duke of Leeds, and her second cousins, the Howards, the sons and daughters of the Earl of Carlisle.

It is unlikely that after her departure with Lady Holdernesse Augusta ever saw her father again, but she was old enough to have memories of him, and that those remembrances were pleasant there is the evidence of Byron himself in a letter written from Genoa in 1823 just before he sailed for Greece. He was anxious to correct some references to his father in a recently published essay in French, which stated that 'the vices and brutality' of Captain Byron had been the cause of his first wife's death. After categorically denying this, he wrote —and we may smile at the son's loyal gloss on his father's behaviour towards his own mother: 'His second wife, my respected mother, had, I assure you, too proud a spirit to bear the ill-usage of any man, no matter who he might be; and

32

this she would have soon proved.' But there is no reason to doubt the sincerity of the passage which followed: 'He died some years before the age of forty, and whatever may have been his faults, they were certainly not those of harshness and grossness. If the notice should reach England, I am certain that the passage relative to my father will give much more pain to my sister . . . even than to me; and this she does not deserve, for there is not a more angelic being upon earth. Augusta and I have always loved the memory of our father as much as we loved each other, and this at least forms a presumption that the stain of harshness was not applicable to it. If he dissipated his fortune, that concerns us alone, for we are his heirs; and till we reproach him with it, I know no one else who has a right to do so.' It appears that Byron's loyalty to his father, in this last remark, overstrains the truth: 'Mad Jack' did not dissipate his own fortune (since he had none) but those of his two wives.

Augusta, protected as she was in the comfortable circles of her well-placed connections, would have had little news of Baby George and the penurious household in Aberdeen. She was in her eighth year when the intelligence arrived that her father had died in France. 'Mad Jack' was incorrigible to the last. He seems to have paid two visits to Aberdeen in search of funds; on the first occasion he was foolish enough to try to live with his wife in the little house in Queen Street, but the baby's crying and, more especially, his wife's alternating moods (at one time the adoring mistress, the next a vociferous termagant) drove him to take a room of his own at the other end of the street. From there he would address her notes beseeching the necessary guinea. She was not the only one whom he was importuning; his sister Frances, the wife of General Charles Leigh, was continually appealed to and managed to spare him occasional sums. With a remittance from her he now escaped to France. However, in the summer of 1790 he was back in Aberdeen for the last time, to extract enough money from the wife who could not stop herself adoring him, in order that he might return to France. As usual his 'personal appeal' was successful; the infatuated woman secured for him a loan of £300, further diminishing her small income by the annual interest of £15 which she paid on the

33

capital. Then Mad Jack was off, and his wife and son, now in his third year, never saw him again.

Installed in a house owned by the Leighs in Valenciennes, he did not allow the progress of the revolution to disturb his pleasures. His unashamed letters to his sister Frances mark the stages of the dénouement of the tragicomedy that was Johnny Byron's life. On 1st December, 1790, he wrote: 'As for me, here I am, and in love with whom? A new actress who is come from Paris, she is beautiful and played last night in *L'Epreuve Villageoise* . . . As for Madame Schoner—she fairly told me, when drunk, that she liked me, and I really do not know what to do . . . No duns appear, as Fanny bites them all, and I am never at home. We are all well here, and Josephine in the best order—as she gets no money and plenty of abuse, it is the only way to treat her.' He gives an account of his going to the theatre in the Leighs' box to the play *Raoul de Créqui*: 'Everybody cried "Bis" and "Vive le Roi" and "Vive la Nation" for me, what with the Juice of the Grape, and remembering our Ancestors were French, I cried as much as anybody . . . For my Amours, these are all finished and everybody says "Je suis très amoureux but très inconstant. Un clou chasse l'autre" and I believe I have had one third of Valenciennes, particularly a Girl at l'Aigle Rouge, and Inn here[.] I happened to [be] there one day when it rained so hard . . . She is very handsome and very tall, and I am not yet tired.'

As for his wife and son in Scotland—well, out of sight, out of mind. Catharine Byron, almost destitute, appealed to him to secure a loan of £30 for her from his sister, but he fobbed her off with some excuse, so that in the end the frantic woman herself addressed Mrs Leigh, whom she did not know, in a pathetic letter, with the plaintive refrain, 'I will pay you honestly in May'. It appears that Mrs Leigh was touched by her sister-in-law's plight and sent her financial help. But affairs in Valenciennes were quite as desperate. On 16th February, 1791, John Byron wrote to Frances Leigh a begging letter which contains his only reference to his son:

'Have you received any letters from me by way of Boulogne? I have sent two. For God's sake send me some, as I have a great deal to pay. With regard to Mrs Byron, I am glad she

34

writes to you. She is very amiable at a distance; but I defy you and all the Apostles to live with her for two months, for if anybody could live with her, it was me. Mais jeu de Mains, jeu de Vilains. For my son, I am happy to hear he is well; but for his walking, 'tis impossible, as he is club-footed.'

As the spring of 1791 turned to summer his letters to his sister became more tragically appealing: 'I am really without a shirt . . . I have not a sou . . . I have but one coat to my back, and that in rags . . . I would rather be a galley slave . . . I have not a shirt to my back, not a coat, as the one I had here is totally used.' On 21st June he dictated his will from his sick bed to two French lawyers. In this document, which was lodged at Doctors' Common on 17th August, there is no mention of his wife or of Augusta. The lack of a sense of mundane reality, a sense that was never strong in John Byron, is nowhere better illustrated than in the unreal provisions of this will. The operative paragraph runs:

'I give and bequeath to Mrs Leigh, my sister, the sum of £400 sterling, to be paid out of the effects of my deceased father and mother. I appoint my son Mr George Byron, heir to my real and personal estate, and charge him to pay my debts, legacies and funeral expenses.

'I appoint the said Mrs Leigh, my sister, executrix of this my will.'

The providential end came on 2nd August, his devoted sister present at his bedside. When the news came in a letter from Mrs Leigh to Mrs Byron, she was hysterical with grief; her distracted cries could be heard by the neighbours in Queen Street. For Catharine Byron in her uncontrollable fashion had adored her engaging ne'er-do-well husband, who had brought her in so short a time to the verge of poverty and left her at the age of twenty-six a widow with a lame son now three and a half. Byron many years later told Medwin: 'I was not so young when my father died, but that I perfectly remember him; and had very early a horror of matrimony, from the sight of domestic broils . . . He seemed born for his own ruin, and that of the other sex.'

Mrs Byron replied to her sister-in-law in a letter which by its directness reveals the depth of her anguish: 'You wrong me very much when you suppose I would not lament Mr

35

Byron's death. It has made me very miserable, and the more so that I had not the melancholy satisfaction of seeing him before his death. If I had known of his illness I would have come to him. I do not think I shall ever get the better of it;—necessity, not inclination, parted us, at least on my part, and I flatter myself that it was the same with him; and notwithstanding all his foibles, for they deserve no worse name, I ever sincerely loved him . . . You say he was sensible to the last. Did he ever mention me? Was he long ill, and where was he buried? . . .

'George is well. I shall be happy to let him be with you sometimes, but at present he is my only comfort, and the only thing that makes me wish to live. I hope, if anything should ever happen to me, you will take care of him. I was not well before, and I do not think I shall ever recover the severe shock I received. It was so unexpected. If I had only seen him before he died! Did he ever mention me? I am unable to say more . . .'

'Notwithstanding all his foibles' John Byron was capable of inspiring love, and it was this quality above all that was transmitted to his children. There is no reason to suspect that Augusta's childhood was unhappy; from Lady Holdernesse, a kind, practical woman, she experienced nothing but kindness; but among these Osbornes and Howards this shy girl would remember that she was a Byron—she and 'Baby' George, whom she did not see but of whom she heard from time to time through her aunt Frances Leigh. But parental love she never experienced. Her life followed the routine of other aristocratic families. The 'season' was spent in London at Lady Holdernesse's house in Hertford Street; and there would be visits and parties with the children of relatives and friends, and perhaps courtesy calls on the young princesses, since Lady Holdernesse kept up her court connections, and she would not miss an important Drawing-Room. The summer would be passed in Derbyshire, where Lady Holdernesse had taken a house near the village of Eckington, north of Chester-field, in that beautiful countryside which was just beginning to be disfigured with coal-pits. There would be carriage drives to the Peak district or to the lovely Dovedale, to Matlock Bath and to the house of neighbouring magnates, among them the Devonshires at Chatsworth and the Rutlands at Haddon Hall.

But not once did she drive over to nearby Newstead Abbey, where 'the Wicked Lord' lived—or, rather, continued to exist—in misanthropic seclusion.

There were journeys north into Yorkshire to stay with the Howards at Castle Howard, Vanburgh's early essay in architecture, the house set in most delightful grounds, with long drives of lime-trees and little classical temples and gazebos. The fifth Earl of Carlisle, a prodigious dandy and friend of George Selwyn and Charles James Fox, was a man of taste, and had furnished Castle Howard with his collection of statues, pictures and *objets de virtu*. He was always a good friend to Augusta and she repaid his kindness by a loyal attachment to him when later he was unfairly attacked by Byron. For the youngest of his three daughters, a girl about her own age, Lady Gertrude Howard, she had a particular liking—her 'sentimental friend'; she and her youngest brother, Lord Frederick Howard (who was afterwards killed at Waterloo, 'the young gallant Howard', 'the best of his race'), were Augusta's special favourites in this large family. Besides Castle Howard, she went to stay at Kiveton, near Worksop in Nottinghamshire, with the Duke of Leeds who, after his divorce from Augusta's mother, had married in 1788 Catherine Anguish and by her had two further children, Lord Sydney Godolphin Osborne, who was five years Augusta's junior, and, younger still, Lady Catherine Anne Sarah. Of her own Osborne half-brothers and sister, George, Marquis of Carmarthen, was nine years her senior, Lord Francis Godolphin seven, and Lady Mary Henrietta Juliana five years older than she. Mary was perhaps the closest to Augusta of all her relations; she had adopted towards her from the first a big-sisterly attitude of affectionate patronage. And furthermore there were visits to her uncle and aunt, General Charles and Frances Leigh, where she went riding with her cousin George and formed for him a romantic attachment, which the difference in their ages (he was four years older) perhaps helped to foster.

We have a pen-portrait of Augusta, as she was in her fifteenth year, in a letter from Lady Mary Osborne, written in August, 1798, to a friend, whom she asked to pass it on to Augusta's aunt, the unmarried Sophia Maria Byron, the youngest of 'Foulweather Jack's' children: 'This child of mine is a great dear and the greatest comfort to me from her cheerfulness and goodness which together makes her society very agreeable to me, with whom she is perfectly at ease. With every other creature in the world she is (more or less) shy to a degree beyond all shyness I ever saw before, and yet shy as she is at this minute, she is *impudent* comparatively speaking to what she was when I first knew her. Her manner is very genteel and gentle, and with her very pretty face and expressive countenance, makes her tout ensemble very striking and interesting at first sight. She grows handsomer every day as she grows less thin. She is taller than the Duchess of Leeds tho' not so tall as I am. Her head is very small and she has a very fine head of dark brown hair . . . which with her long neck and falling shoulders becomes her much and gives her whole bust an air *dégagé*. The upper part of her face is very handsome, her eyes being beautiful and her nose pretty and retroussé. Her mouth is very large—her worst feature—but a very fine set of teeth make up for this disadvantage. She has a fine complexion and fine colour, but is rather freckled. She is as light as a feather . . .

'[Augusta] has a great turn for music, being very fond of it, having an admirable ear and a pretty voice. She has been several times to the play, her favourite amusement, and her taste is remarkably good and *nice* in everything, and memory astonishing when she *wishes* to fix anything on it. She has been very happy lately, having had so much of Carmarthen company and of Lady Carmarthen in the house. Next to me Lady Carmarthen [Charlotte, daughter of the Marquess Townshend, married George Osborne in 1797] is the person she is most at ease with. She has been excessively kind to her and is very fond of her, as are likewise both my Brothers and she worships them quite . . .' [Staying with the Osbornes,] 'she was very happy . . . and almost broke her heart to come away . . . All this makes a very nice child, does it not? Pray tell this all to Miss Byron, as it must please her to know her niece is so amiable and so happy. Somebody who saw Augusta for the first time lately was struck with her likeness to Lady Elizabeth Garnier. She is like all the Carlisles but most to Lady Elizabeth Howard, not so regularly handsome but with much expression and a better figure.'

Kindly treated as Augusta was, she could not but feel a

stranger in these great houses, in which the inmates lived their sheltered lives revolving about the family centres which their position in society fixed for them. These pivotal points, which brought security to their existence, were not hers; and when she at times felt herself an outsider, an intruder present only on sufferance, her self-pity, looking for sympathy, would turn her thoughts and feelings towards little George, her Byron brother whom she was not allowed to see. Mrs Byron's uncouth behaviour had early placed her and her son beyond the pale. In 1794, when Augusta was ten years old, the news arrived that young William Byron, who had cruised so merrily in the Channel with her father on board the lugger, had been killed fighting in Corsica. Within two years William's father also died, still unreconciled with his half-mad parent, 'the Wicked Lord', and the heir-presumptive to the barony of Rochdale became George Byron, 'the little boy in Aberdeen'. These events would have kindled an interest in the new status of her half-brother, even if her own position had not already disposed her to regard him affectionately. Augusta was fourteen, a shy, hesitant, somewhat sentimental girl, when in 1798 she heard that the miserable earthly existence of the fifth Lord Byron was over, and that George Byron, aged ten, was the new lord. But what pleasure the girl might have had in communicating now with her ennobled half-brother was denied her. This unnatural silence was not to be broken for a further three years; and the deprivation of an outlet for her own emotions and her natural feelings towards young Byron was to have unforeseen consequences.

Early in 1801 the wedding took place of Lady Mary Osborne and Lord Pelham, the heir to the Earl of Chichester. By this time Lady Holdernesse's health was failing. We have evidence of the esteem in which the old lady was held by Queen Charlotte—as well as a curious insight on the dietary habits of the age—in a letter from Princess Elizabeth to Lady Mary Pelham. Writing on behalf of the Queen, she informs her correspondent that Her Majesty 'understands that the physical people have allowed Lady Holdernesse anything She likes, She has ordered two Pigs which have been born and bred at Frogmore [where the Princess supervised the breeding of a "small succulent Chinese variety"] to be sent up by tomorrow

39

morning's early stage for her. She flatters herself that dear Lady Holdernesse will like them; you may laugh, Lady Mary, but I am not a little proud of receiving this commission from Mama, for the farm is my Hobby Horse . . .' In the same year Lady Holdernesse died, and thus Augusta at seventeen was bereft of the care and devotion which had been hers for thirteen years. Pious and limited as she was in many ways, Lady Holdernesse had provided her with a home and background and had loved her in her rather staid, undemonstrative fashion. She had always told Augusta that she would make her 'residee legatoo' (as she expressed it), and she was true to her word, leaving her in trust with the Duke of Leeds a capital sum of £7000 which henceforth ensured her pin-money.

After Lady Holdernesse's death Augusta went to stay with the Pelhams, and thereafter she spent part of the year with them and the rest either in the country or at the town houses of the Duke of Leeds or Lord Carlisle, or at Windsor with General the Hon. and Mrs Harcourt. But her grandmother's death brought about another more important change in her life. On 18th October, 1801, she received an extraordinary letter of condolence from Mrs Byron: 'As I wish to bury what is passed in *oblivion*, I shall avoid all reflections on a person now no more; my opinion of yourself I have suspended for some years; the time is now arrived when I shall form a very *decided* one. I take up my pen now, however, to condole with you on the melancholy event that has happened, to offer you every consolation in my power, to assure you of the inalterable regard and friendship of myself and son. We will be extremely happy if ever we can be of any service to you, now or at any future period. I take it upon me to answer for him; although he knows so little of you, he often mentions you to me in the most affectionate manner, indeed the goodness of his heart and amiable disposition is such that your being his sister, had he never seen you, would be a sufficient claim upon him and ensure you every intention in his power to bestow . . .

'Your brother is at Harrow School, and, if you wish to see him, I have now no desire to keep you asunder.'

That Mrs Byron should have had a poor opinion of Lady Holdernesse was no news to Augusta; that she had suspended her judgement of her stepdaughter for some years and was now about to arrive at a 'very *decided* one' was something of a surprise. What this curious way of conveying condolence did suggest was that Mrs Byron was not at all clear in her own mind the form their future relation would take. In the summer of 1799 Hanson, the solicitor, had called on the Earl of Carlisle to try to interest the reluctant peer in the affairs of the young Lord Byron. Lord Carlisle was 'anything but disposed to interfere', since Mrs Byron and her son were total strangers to him. He knew by report too much that was offensive in the behaviour of Mrs Byron to relish the idea of being involved in any business matters to do with her or her son. Although his mother was the Hon. Isabella Byron, daughter of the fourth Lord Byron, and he was therefore Captain John Byron's first cousin, Lord Carlisle's family feeling did not extend to the latter's son by that vulgar and tempestuous Scotswoman. Hanson, however, managed to persuade him, so impressed was he by the boy's promise, to become the nominal guardian on the understanding that this entailed nothing more than advice. In the same year a petition was drawn up to the King and Mrs Byron was awarded from the Civil List a provision of £300 for her son's education. In July Hanson took Byron to meet his guardian in Grosvenor Place: yet the boy's shyness was such that, though Lord Carlisle spoke kindly to him, he quickly asked Hanson that they might take their leave. In the following month Byron was placed at Dr Glennie's school at Dulwich, and his mother during the winter took lodgings at Sloane Terrace to be near him. Here she made such a nuisance of herself, descending on the school at any hour, taking Byron away with her and keeping him, that Dr Glennie was obliged to remonstrate with her. He then felt the stinging lash of her vituperative tongue. Glennie appealed to Hanson, who brought the matter to Lord Carlisle, and Mrs Byron was forbidden to take the boy out without written authority of his lordship. On receiving a further prohibition from visiting the school she broke into 'such audible fits of temper as it was impossible to keep from reaching the ears of the scholars and the servants'. Byron's sensitive feelings were mortified by these fishwife displays; he was overheard by the sympathetic Glennie, on a boy's saying to him, 'Byron, your mother is a fool', to reply resignedly, 'I know it'.

Lord Carlisle often regretted having taken on this charge, and Augusta, being so much in his presence and hearing the accounts of Mrs Byron's tantrums, felt deeply for the injured pride of 'Baby' Byron, subject to the gaucheries of this voluble lady. In Mrs Byron's eyes Augusta was in the enemy's camp, the confidante, if not the outright ally, of the overbearing earl who was so resistant to her having her own way. However, there was another consideration which caused her now to address the girl in this ambiguous manner: Byron had few acquaintances, save his Harrow school-friends, among the aristocracy, whereas Augusta moved in some of the highest circles in the land. Her potential usefulness on this account was not lost on the canny Mrs Byron. Augusta, notwithstanding the threatening judgement suspended over her, was delighted that she would be able to see Byron again after so many years. It is not known whether she saw him while he was at Dulwich, but in April 1801, with Lord Carlisle's approval, he was deposited in Dr Drury's care at Harrow; and it may have been during his Christmas holidays, which he spent with the homely Hansons at Earl's Court, that brother and sister met. In January, 1802, Augusta at eighteen was a graceful, distinguished-looking girl; Byron a handsome, rather too plump boy of fourteen. Pryse Lockhart Gordon describes Byron at this time as 'a fine, lively, restless lad, full of fire and energy, and passionately fond of riding . . . though he was a spoiled child, and had too much of his own way . . .' To Augusta he was to be more than she had ever dared hope—he was brilliant, her own brother, a Byron.

III
'Baby' Byron and Love
1802 - 1809

THE EARLIEST letters between Augusta and Byron have
not survived, but there is no reason to doubt that a correspondence, entered into on both sides with delighted anticipation, did exist from 1802. There were so many points in
common in their characters and situations, needing just such
an outlet, that it was a natural consequence of their meeting,
and, once established, there followed a connection which from
the beginning contained something much more than the
ordinary relation of kinship. Both were inordinately shy,
highly sensitive and, in an important sense, deprived persons;
and the recognition of the ties of blood only served to heighten
their knowledge that they were so much alike—yet, through
no fault of their own, so completely strangers. The discovery
of each other, therefore, was in the nature of a self-discovery,
which reinforced the awareness that they were individual
persons who were at one and the same time harmoniously
complementary to an extraordinary degree. Augusta was
enchanted with 'Baby' Byron, and he too was fascinated by
the possession of an older sister whose shyness did not hide
from him that she had achieved a social ease and grace, a
savoir faire, that with him was conspicuously lacking. And, once
the shyness was overcome, followed the welcome realisation
(or was it precisely the means by which the tension itself was
relaxed?) that they shared a sense of ironic humour, of
mockery, an ability to resolve a tense situation in laughter.
Further, with Augusta (right from the start) there was a
serious concern for the welfare of this lame boy, whose moods
were so unpredictable, with sullen, menacing silences followed
by *farouche* outbursts of passion. His character needed understanding; and her affection for him, and the fact that she too
was a Byron, gave Augusta just this. The letters that have
come down to us reveal the intensity of their need to love and

43

to be loved; the expressions of affection were there from the outset; the future was to confirm them with a poignant profundity.

It is a matter of some interest to biographers of Byron to note that the girls who influenced most the early ideal element in his poetry were all relatives. His first love had been for his distant cousin Mary Duff, whom he met at Banff in his eighth year. Another early love, Mary Parker, was the daughter of Charlotte Augusta Byron, a younger sister of Captain John Byron, and married to Christopher Parker of the Royal Navy. It was for this cousin that Byron made his 'first dash into poetry' about the year 1800. Mary Parker died of tuberculosis in 1802. Augusta had gone to visit the sick girl shortly before she died, and on accidentally mentioning Byron's name Augusta was astonished to see Margaret colour 'through the paleness of mortality to the eyes'. The third of his boyhood romances was with another distant cousin, Mary Chaworth, a descendant of the Chaworth killed by 'the Wicked Lord'. It was unrequited love for Mary that caused him to stay away from Harrow (for the second time) in 1803.

On 13th February, 1803, Augusta wrote to Hanson enquiring if he knew the reason for Byron's refusal to return to Harrow from Bath, where he was staying with his mother for the school holidays. Byron at fifteen was already displaying a characteristic self-will. He had quarrelled with his house-master, Henry Drury, the son of the headmaster, and had indeed refused to go back to school. Mrs Byron explained her predicament to Hanson: 'Byron *positively* refuses to return to Harrow to be Henry Drury's *Pupil* as he says he has been used *ill* for some time past . . . You may perhaps be surprised that I don't force him to return but he is rather too old and has too much sense for that.' It was finally agreed that he should go to a Mr Evans' house, and he went back in mid-February, but by the spring a fresh dispute with Drury occasioned a fiery letter from Byron to his mother: 'Mr Henry Drury has behaved himself to me in a manner I neither *can* nor will *bear* . . . Better let him take away my life than ruin my *Character*.' On receiving this long indignant letter Mrs Byron wrote frantically to Harrow from Nottingham on 6th May in what Byron termed her *furioso* style: 'I send you a letter from Byron—I would not be surprised if he was to come here for Godsake see to settle the Business and if he will leave Harrow he must go to some other School I will not have his education interrupted and I have at present no Home or House to receive him, it is extremely *vexatious* and very odd that the Doctor cannot make his son behave with *Propriety* to the Boys.' Dr Drury himself stepped in at this stage and made peace; he had a fine sense of the boy's worth and a firmness and tact which allowed him to guide Byron on a silken cord where the use of rougher means would have been disastrous. Called by Lord Carlisle about this time to report progress, Drury expressed his admiration for his charge: 'He has talents, my lord, which will add lustre to his rank'. A laconic 'Indeed!' was the incredulous nobleman's response to this information.

Committed as Augusta now was to the pursuit of Byron's welfare, these distant rumblings of thunder from Harrow, Bath and Nottingham filled her mind with anxious concern. Although the correspondence has not been preserved, it seems that she had heard directly or, more likely, by letter from Byron of his growing differences with his impossible mother. Mrs Byron's opinion of her son in a letter to Hanson, however, reveals another aspect of the picture: 'God only knows, he is a turbulent, unruly boy that wants to be emancipated from all restraint, his sentiments are however noble.' In her anxiety, Augusta, when Byron did not write or when Mrs Byron's short explosions on paper were unsatisfactory, had recourse to Hanson, the much harried solicitor and family agent. She apologised for troubling him: 'The very great interest I of course feel in all that concerns him will I trust plead my excuse for plaguing you with these Enquiries—Be as good as not to mention to Mrs B. having heard from me on this subject.' In the summer holidays of 1803 Byron, dismayed at the boredom of Southwell, where his mother had taken Burgage Manor, rode over and settled in with the factor at Newstead Abbey, which had recently been let to Lord Grey de Ruthyn. From here he saw much of Mary Chaworth, the heiress to the adjoining property of Annesley Hall, now engaged to a neighbouring fox-hunting squire, John Musters. The inevitable happened; Byron fell desperately in love, and refused for the second time to return to Harrow; nor could he be persuaded until he had been snubbed by Mary (he overheard her say to her maid, 'Do you think I could care anything for that lame boy?'). He finally went back to school only in January, 1804, not long after his sixteenth birthday.

Absorbed in 'love, desperate love, the *worst* of all *maladies*', as Mrs Byron suitably expressed it, Byron had not communicated with Augusta, but she would have heard enough to cause her extreme disquiet. Then, on 12th March, she could bear the silence no longer and wrote a formal note to Hanson: 'Miss Byron presents her compliments to Mr Hanson and would be particularly obliged to him, if he could call upon her at the Duchess of Leeds, 60 Lower Grosvenor Street, on Wednesday before 2 o'clock . . . Miss Byron hopes her request will not put Mr Hanson to inconvenience . . .

'She feels particularly anxious to have some conversation with him about Lord Byron whom she has not seen this Twelve-month.'

Hanson apparently came to Lower Grosvenor Street, and, returning to his office, wrote to Byron, with the result that the latter, immediately on his arrival at Southwell from Harrow, sent off the affectionate letter, which is the first of his many letters to Augusta to have survived:

'Burgage Manor, March 22d, 1804

'Although, My ever Dear Augusta, I have hitherto appeared remiss in replying to your kind and affectionate letters; yet I hope you will not attribute my neglect to a want of affection, but rather to a shyness naturally inherent in my Disposition. I will now endeavour as amply as is in my power to repay your kindness, and for the Future I hope you will consider me not only as *a Brother* but as your warmest and most affectionate *Friend*, and if circumstances should require it your *protector*. Recollect, My Dearest Sister, that you are the *nearest relation* I have in *the world by the ties of Blood* and affection. If there is anything in which I can serve you, you have only to mention it; Trust to your Brother, and be assured he will never betray your confidence. When you see my Cousin and future Brother George Leigh, tell him that I already consider him as my Friend, for whoever is beloved by you, my amiable Sister, will always be equally Dear to me . . . Write to me Soon, my Dear

46

Augusta, And do not forget to love me. In the meantime, I remain, more than words can express, your ever sincere, affectionate

Brother and Friend
Byron

'P.S. Do not forget to knit the purse you promised me, Adieu my beloved Sister.'

Pleased as she was to hear from Byron again, and in such affectionate terms, Augusta may perhaps have been just a little hurt at this passing reference to their cousin George Leigh, with whom she was already deeply in love. The propensity to marry cousins was strong among the Byrons: Admiral John ('Foulweather Jack') had married his cousin Sophia Trevanion; William, 'the Wicked Lord's' heir, had eloped with Juliana Elizabeth Byron; and Augusta was, but not for several years yet, to marry Colonel George Leigh. Byron, as we have already observed, was very strongly attracted as a boy and as a youth to girls closely related to him.

Augusta's near relatives, and equally George Leigh's parents, were opposed to the marriage, and the reason is not difficult to find. The Leighs had little money, and Augusta's had only her pin-money of £350 left her by Lady Holdernesse. In 1797, when George was still under twenty, General Leigh had purchased for him a majority in the 10th Dragoons, a regiment in the process of being changed to light hussars, and in particular favour with the Prince of Wales who was its colonel-in-Chief. 'Beau' Brummell was a captain in the Tenth. Leigh pinned his hopes on the patronage of the Prince—his father had since 1776 been attached to the Prince's court in one capacity or another—and as a keen horseman and follower of the turf he succeeded in obtaining an appointment in connection with the Prince's stud at Six Mile Bottom near Newmarket. Since the notorious 'Escape affair' in the autumn of 1789, when the Prince's horse, ridden by one of the leading jockeys of the time, Sam Chifney, had lost one race and quickly won another in circumstances which dissatisfied the Jockey Club and particularly Sir Charles Bunbury, its leading member, the Prince of Wales would no longer run his horses at Newmarket. However, he continued to maintain his stud at Six Mile Bottom.

George Leigh, having besides his equine expertise, charm and a good appearance, became one of the equerries to the Prince of Wales (as his father had been before him) and we catch several glimpses of him as a courtier in the racing reminiscences of 'The Druid': 'Brighton will never see such picturesque Watteau-like groups again, as those which were then presented by the Prince's court, for the evening promenade on the Steyne; the ladies with their high head-dresses and spreading "peacock tails" and the two Manners, Sir Bellingham Graham, and Colonels Mellish and Leigh, as esquires . . .' Lewes races were frequented by the Prince and his entourage of 'tandems, beautiful women and light hussars'. The racing friends of George Leigh included such rich enthusiasts as Lord Darlington (late the Duke of Cleveland), Lord Frederick Bentinck and Sir Harry Featherstonhaugh Fenbroom, men who had so much more money than he and who lived it up to the hilt. There were many unsavoury stories circulating of the low amours of Lord Darlington; it was said that a servant girl in Scotland, in attempting to evade his embraces, fell from a window and broke her back. It would be unreasonable to expect that a full-blooded young man—and we have no warrant to believe that George Leigh was anything but that— did not share in these escapades and the drinking bouts that customarily went on all night. Fulfilling his slight military duties, attending on the Prince, keeping an eye on the stud, and travelling around to race meetings, where he stayed at the great country houses of his friends—these were George Leigh's everyday occupations. In Augusta's eyes he could not have been more attractive; she waited more than three years to marry him; this speaks worlds for his early charm.

*

On receipt of another letter from Augusta, Byron replied at once from Southwell on 22nd March, 1804. 'I am as you may imagine a little dull here; not being on terms of intimacy with Lord Grey I avoid Newstead, and my sources of amusement are Books, and writing to my Augusta, which, wherever I am, will always constitute my Greatest pleasure.' He then went on to hint at the deep reasons which had caused him to sever all relations with Lord Grey, reasons which, appearing to attract while they repelled him, we may think were in some unspecified way sexual: 'I am not reconciled to Lord Grey, *and I never will*. He was once my Greatest Friend, my reasons for ceasing that Friendship are such as I cannot explain, not even to you, my Dear Sister (although were they to be made known to any body, you would be the first) but they will ever remain hidden in my own breast . . . He has forfeited all *title to my esteem*, but I hold him in too much *contempt* ever *to hate him* . . . As to your Future prospects, my Dear Girl, *may they be happy!* . . . Write to me soon. I am impatient to hear from you. God bless you, my amiable Augusta . . .'

A week later Byron wrote again to thank Augusta for the purse she had made him. 'You tell me that you are tired of London. I am rather surprised to hear that, for I thought the Gaieties of the Metropolis were particularly pleasing to *young ladies* . . . I shoot a good deal; but, thank God, I have not so far lost my reason as to make shooting my only amusement. There are indeed some of my neighbours whose only pleasures consist in field sports, but in other respects they are only one degree removed from the brute creation . . .' (These are clearly reflections on the pursuits of Lord Grey and John Musters.) 'I am an absolute Hermit; in a short time my Gravity which is increased by my solitude will qualify me for an Archbishoprick; I really begin to think that I should become a mitre amazingly well. . . . I am sure writing to you, my Dear Sister, must ever form my Greatest pleasure, but especially so at this time.' He wrote another bright and affectionate letter before returning to Harrow; but, once there, on his side the correspondence lapsed. At this time, surrounded by a worshipping set of young school favourites, whom he 'spoilt by indulgence', he was not at enmity with the world; he had, as he put it, ways and means of amusing himself very pleasantly.

In mid-June, having no word from Byron, Augusta had her usual recourse to Hanson: 'Pray write me a line and mention all you hear of my dear Brother: he was a most delightful correspondent while he remained in Nottinghamshire: but I can't obtain a single line from Harrow. I was much struck with his *general improvement;* it was beyond the expectations raised by what you had told me, and his letters gave me the most excellent opinion of both his Head and Heart.' However, back at Southwell in August for his summer holidays, Byron wrote to Augusta a letter which revealed the abysmal condition of his relations with his mother.

'My Dearest Augusta,—I seize this interval of my *amiable* mother's absence this afternoon, again to inform you . . . what is going on. For my own part I can send nothing to amuse you, excepting a repetition of my complaints against my tormentor, whose *diabolical* disposition (pardon me for staining my paper with so harsh a word) seems to increase with age, and to acquire new force with Time. The more I see of her the more my dislike augments; nor can I so entirely conquer the appearance of it, as to prevent her from perceiving my opinion; this, so far from calming the gale, blows it into a *hurricane*, which threatens to destroy everything, till exhausted by its own violence, it is lulled into a sullen torpor, which, after a short period, is again roused into a fresh and revived phrenzy, to me most terrible, and to every other Spectator astonishing. She then declares that she plainly sees I hate her, that I am leagued with her bitter enemies, viz. Yourself, Ld C[arlisle] and Mr H[anson], and, as I never Dissemble or contradict her, we are all *honoured* with a multiplicity of epithets, too *numerous*, and some of them too *gross*, to be repeated . . .

'Such Augusta is the happy life I lead . . . if I remained here a few months longer, I should become, what with *envy*, *spleen and all uncharitableness*, a complete *misanthrope*, but notwithstanding this,

'Believe me, Dearest Augusta, ever yours, etc. etc.,

Byron.'

These letters of Byron to Augusta, written in 1804, when he was a schoolboy of sixteen, are not all complaints about the dullness of Southwell and the sordid squalls with Mrs Byron; they are a compound of tenderness towards his sister, boastfulness and self-mockery, adolescent man-of-the-world advice, and a youthful assumption of a hard-boiledness which he was far from possessing. 'But really, after all (pardon me my dear Sister), I feel a little inclined to laugh at you, for love, in my humble opinion, is utter nonsense, a mere jargon of compliments, romance and deceit; now, for my part, had I fifty mistresses, I should in the course of one fortnight forget them all, and, if by any chance I recollected one, should laugh at it as a dream, and bless my stars for delivering me from the hands of the little mischievous Blind God. Can't you drive this cousin of ours out of your pretty little head (for as to *hearts* I think they are out of the question), or if you are so far gone, why don't you give old L'Harpagon (I mean the General) the slip, and take a trip to Scotland, you are now pretty near the Borders.' This letter was written in October, and in it he reports of his mother: 'I am sorry to say the old lady and myself don't agree like lambs in a meadow, but I believe it is all my own fault, I am rather too fidgety, which my precise mama objects to, we differ, then argue, and to my shame be it spoken fall out a *little*, however after a storm comes a calm. . . .' In these vigorous letters it is as if he were parodying his emotions for the pleasure he derived from expressing them in words; his delight in the flow of his ideas appears to compensate for the misery of the situation that he describes; the resources of the language he already commands with an unusual skill and verve.

However, two further letters in November were enough to warn Augusta of dangers ahead, if Byron continued his holidays alone with his mother at Southwell. On 2nd November he wrote: 'Now, Augusta, I am going to tell you a secret, perhaps I shall appear undutiful to you, but, believe me, my affection for you is founded on a more firm basis. My mother has lately behaved to me in such an eccentric manner, that so far from feeling the affection of a Son, it is with difficulty I can restrain my dislike. Not that I can complain of want of liberality; no, She always supplies me with as much money as I can spend . . . But with all this she is so hasty, so impatient, that I dread the approach of the holidays, more than most boys do their return from them. In former days she spoilt me; now she is altered to the contrary; for the most trifling thing she upbraids me in a most outrageous manner . . .' The proximate cause of these tempestuous disputes was Lord Grey de Ruthyn, with whom Mrs Byron demanded that Byron be reconciled, but the latter was adamant in his refusal. He appealed for Augusta's sympathy: 'You, Augusta, are the only relation I have who treats me as a friend; if you too desert me, I have nobody I can love but Delawarr'—this was a Harrow favourite.

The second letter, written on 11th November, was even more specific in describing the impossibility of his relations with Mrs Byron. 'I thought, my dear Augusta, that your opinion of my *meek mama* would coincide with mine; Her temper is so variable, and, when inflamed, so furious, that I dread our meeting . . . she flies into a phrenzy, upbraids me as if I was the most undutiful wretch in existence, rakes up the ashes of my *father*, abuses him, says I shall be a true Byrrone, which is the worst epithet she can invent. Am I to call this woman mother? . . . What example does she show me? I hope in God I shall never follow it . . . And can I, my dear Sister, look up to this mother, with that respect, that affection I ought? Am I to be eternally subjected to her caprice? I hope not— . . . "A talkative woman is like an Adder's tongue", so says one of the prophets . . .'

On receiving this appeal, Augusta decided to act at once. Her letter to Hanson is worth giving in full, as it shows the combination of sympathy, good sense and fine tact which were typical of her at twenty. Augusta's critics have used her later epistolary style as evidence of her feather-brained, inconsequential character; that this is essentially a false estimate of her the following letter is proof.

'Castle Howard, Nov. 18, 1804

'My dear Sir,—I am afraid you will think I presume almost too much upon the kind permission you have so often given me of applying to you about my Brother's concerns. The reason that induces me now to do so is his lately having written me several Letters containing the most extraordinary accounts of his Mother's conduct towards him and of complaints of the uncomfortable Situation he is in during the Holidays when with her. All this you will easily imagine has more *vexed* than *surprized* me. I am quite unhappy about him, and wish I could in any way remedy the grievances he confides to me. I wished, as the most likely means of doing this, to mention the subject to Lord Carlisle, who has always expressed the greatest interest about Byron and also shewn the greatest kindness. Finding that he did *not object* to it, I yesterday had some conversation with Lord C. on the subject, and it is partly by his advice and wishes that I trouble you with this Letter.

He authorized me to tell you that, if you would allow my Brother to spend the next vacation with you (which *he* seems *strongly* to wish), that it would put it into his power to see more of him and shew him more attention than he has hitherto, being withheld from doing so from the dread of having any concern whatever with Mrs Byron.

'I need hardly add that it is also MY first wish that this should be accomplished. I am sure you are of my opinion that it is now of the greatest consequence to Byron to secure the friendship of Lord C., the only relation he has who possesses the *Will* and *power* to be of use to him. I think the Letters he writes me *quite perfect* and he does not express one sentiment or idea I should wish different . . .

'I trust entirely to the interest and to the friendship you have ever so kindly expressed for my Brother, for *my Forgiveness*. Of course you will not mention to Mrs B. having heard from me, as she would only accuse me of wishing to estrange her Son from her, which would be very far from being the case further than his Happiness and comfort are concerned in it. My opinion is that *as* they cannot agree, they had better be separated, for such eternal Scenes of wrangling are enough to spoil the very best temper and Disposition in the universe . . .'

Augusta was successful in achieving both her objects: Byron spent his Christmas holidays with the Hansons in Chancery Lane, London, and while there dined with Lord Carlisle in Grosvenor Place. Byron wrote to Augusta telling her that the dinner with his 'formal guardy' (as he referred to him) had gone well and that on further acquaintance with the Howards he liked them very much. 'I think your friend Lady G. is a sweet girl. If your taste in *love* is as good as it is in *friendship*, I shall think you a *very discerning little Gentlewoman*. His Lordship too improves upon further acquaintance, Her Ladyship I always liked, but of the Junior part of the family Frederick is my favourite . . .' Augusta heard also from Lady Gertrude Howard that her father was 'very much pleased' with Byron.

Brother and sister met in London in April, 1805, where Byron spent a few days listening to 'our *Sapient* and *noble Legislators* of Both Houses on the Catholic Question', before returning to Harrow for his last term. Mrs Byron, hearing of Augusta's influence on Byron, tried to prevent their continued meetings, and in June wrote to her stepdaughter what Byron described as 'a decent specimen of the dowager's talents for epistles of the *furioso* style', but Augusta was not shaken in her loyalty to Byron by this intemperate letter. She had noticed a great change in her brother in the previous months. Many years later in his 'Detached Thoughts' Byron wrote: 'In the year 1804, I recollect meeting my sister at General Harcourt's in Portland Place. I was then *one* thing, and *as* she had always till then found me. When we met again in 1805 (she told me since), that my temper and disposition were so completely altered, that I was hardly to be recognized. I was not then sensible of the change, but I can believe it, and account for it.' On July 2nd he wrote to Augusta, who was still in London at the Carlisles', that he had just returned from Cambridge (where he had gone to enter himself at Trinity), and he invited her in mock inflated style to hear him declaim *Lear* at Harrow Speech Day. 'If you intend doing me the *honour* of attending, I would recommend you not to come without a Gentleman, as I shall be too much engaged all the morning to take care of you, and I should not imagine you would admire *stalking* about by yourself. . . . I don't know how you are to come, but for *Godsake* bring as few women with you as possible . . . I *beg, Madam*, you may make your appearance in one of his Lordship's most *dashing* carriages, as our Harrow *etiquette* admits of nothing but the most *superb* vehicles on our Grand *Festivals*. In the mean time, believe me, dearest Augusta . . .' However, although Byron was longing to show off his charming sister to his Harrovian admirers, it seems that he was disappointed, for she was apparently unable to be present.

Though Mrs Byron was irrational, she was no fool; becoming aware of Augusta's support for her son's intransigence, she tried to prevent their meeting by arranging to come to London at the beginning of the summer holidays. Byron countered this move by telling her that the holidays began later than they really did, and he appealed to Hanson to confirm this white lie when he wrote to her. Augusta and Byron then met in London in July, and Byron went down to Southwell at the end of the month or early in August, Augusta travelling north to Castle Howard. On 6th August Byron

54

wrote from that 'Garden of Eden', where he was alone with his 'diabolical' mother, whom he once described as 'certainly mad (to say that she was in her senses, would be condemning her as Criminal), her conduct is a *happy* compound of derangement and Folly.' 'I am', he wrote, 'at this moment *vis à vis* and *Tête à tête* with that aimiable personage, who is, whilst I am writing, pouring forth complaints against your *ingratitude*, giving me many oblique hints that I ought not to correspond with you, and concluding with an interdiction that if you ever after the expiration of my minority are invited to my residence, *she* will no longer condescend to grace it with her *Imperial* presence . . .' Augusta's sympathetic correspondence, he continues, 'must be some alleviation to my sorrows, which however are too ludicrous for me to regard them very seriously . . .' Escaping from 'this female Tisiphone' in September to stay with the Hansons at their country house at Farleigh, near Basingstoke, Byron went up to Trinity in October, 1805.

Augusta spent the second half of the year at Castle Howard. Whatever affection she had for the Howards—and the warmth of her feelings for this enlightened and kindly family was very strong—the attachments nearest her heart and uppermost in her thoughts were for Byron and George Leigh. The difficulties which beset her marriage with her cousin were as far from solution as ever. She was now in her twenty-second year and approaching her twenty-third. In December Byron wrote: 'I hope your everlasting negotiation with the Father of your *Intended* is near a conclusion in *some* manner; if you do not hurry a little, you will be verging into the *"Vale of Years"*, and, though you may be blest with Sons and daughters, you will never live to see your *grandchildren*.' (This is hardly consistent with his advice of June of that year, but consistency in these concerns was an indifferent matter to Byron. Then he wrote: '. . . Age brings experience and when you are in the flower of youth, between 40 and 50, shall then marry . . . the later one makes oneself miserable with the matrimonial clog, the better . . .')

Byron, up at Cambridge, and installed in fine rooms in Great Court, was ordering furniture and planning future decoration and laying in a stock of port, sherry, claret and madeira for immediate consumption. His letter of 6th November declaimed ecstatically on the virtues of his newly-found affluence and freedom from maternal restraint: 'As might be supposed I like a College Life extremely, especially as I have escaped the Trammels or rather *Fetters* of my domestic Tyrant Mrs Byron, who continued to plague me during my visit in July and September. I am now most pleasantly situated in *Super*excellent Rooms, flanked on one side by my Tutor, on the other by an old Fellow, both of whom are rather checks on my *vivacity*. I am allowed 500 a year, a Servant and Horse, so Feel as independent as a German Prince who coins his own Cash, or a Cherokee Chief who coins no Cash at all, but enjoys what is more precious, Liberty . . .'

Byron passed Christmas in London in lodgings at Mrs Massingberd's, No. 16 Piccadilly, where he wrote to Augusta on 20th December that he hoped to see her in town at the end of January, as he has some subjects to discuss with her which he did not wish to communicate in writing. The following day he sent her another long letter in which he disclosed the nature of these mysterious 'subjects'. First of all he pledged her to 'inviolable Secrecy'—'for if I ever find that it has transpired, all confidence, all Friendship between us has concluded'. After this rather sinister exordium, he ceased beating about the bush and came to the point: he was short of cash. '. . . like all other young men just let loose, and especially one as I am, freed from the worse than bondage of my maternal home, I have been extravagant, and consequently am in want of Money . . .' He was not writing to solicit money from her; he would refuse it, were it offered—rather 'starvation' than that; but would Augusta go joint security with him for a loan of 'a few Hundreds', since he as a minor could not enter into a bond with the money-lenders? He could not have recourse to his friends, as they were in a like predicament with himself—'to you therefore I appeal, and if I am disappointed, at least let me not be tormented with the advice of Guardians, and let silence rule your Resolution'—certainly she must not divulge the truth to 'that proud Grandee the Earl' or to 'that Chattering puppy Hanson'.

It would appear that others of Byron's letters to Augusta, written at this time, but now lost, disclosed the melancholy turn of his mind. He wrote to her at Castle Howard on 7th January, 1806, that her efforts to 'reanimate his sinking spirits' would fail, since she could not divine the cause whence they arose. 'You know me too well to think it is *Love;* and I have had no quarrel with Friend or enemy, you may therefore be easy, since no unpleasant consequences will be produced from the present Sombre cast of my Temper.' This is somewhat less than the truth, as he had indeed quarrelled with Hanson, who had reprimanded him for extravagance; and, although it was not 'love' in the way that Augusta would understand the word, he was deep in a 'passionate but pure' affair with a Trinity chorister named Edleston. In her anxious desire to help Byron Augusta now offered to lend him—or rather, to give him—some money herself. It seems that she did not refuse to stand joint security, for Byron in the letter of 7th January wrote that he would not accept her money and yet he feared she would not be in Town to settle the matter together with these '*sordid Bloodsuckers*' on the 20th of the month.

Augusta, deterred from seeking the advice of Lord Carlisle or Hanson by reason of Byron's threat should she disclose the matter to them; seeing her own offer of monetary help refused; and finally unable to be in London in time to put her name to the money-lenders' bond, was in a pitiable quandary. Her sympathies were all with 'Baby' Byron, but her intelligence warned her that the course he was taking in seeking finanicial aid at the exorbitant rate demanded by the money-lenders, after only one term of Cambridge and with three years to go before his majority, was reckless in the extreme. This, following his obscure hints of his melancholia, was enough to agitate one whose susceptibilities in any matter which affected her Byron were acute. What should she—what could she—do to save him from the consequences of a character which was (she considered) the bane of his heredity? For his character he was not responsible. Yet he must be prevented from bringing down ruin upon himself, even if the cost of this was the loss of his confidence and (dearest of all to her) his friendship. There was only one way open to her, and she took it—she went to Lord Carlisle. He advised her to consult Hanson. She then wrote to the solicitor and his reply to her letter only served to aggravate her perplexity and despair. On 5th February, when lectures recommenced at Cambridge, Byron remained in London.

Augusta returned to town on 12th February, and on the very evening of her arrival addressed a note to Hanson from Grosvenor Place:

'I shall feel particularly obliged to you to call upon me at Ld Carlisle's the *first* moment in your power, as I most earnestly wish to have some conversation with you, the sooner the better . . . pray do not mention this desire of mine to Ld Byron.

'I must trust to your usual kindness to me to forgive the Liberty I have taken . . .'

The result of this ill-starred intervention on Augusta's part, conceived with the best of intentions, was that Byron severed all intercourse with her for more than two years. He let Augusta know that she had forfeited his trust with a harshness that betrayed the underlying uneasiness of his own conscience: but he, Byron, was not to be thwarted in the pursuit of what he desired for himself; his independence to do what he willed was his prerogative, hurt whom he might in the process. Augusta was distraught, taking the blame for the rupture on herself. Towards Byron Augusta was completely unprotected; how vulnerable she was to his every action she was now to experience, and how ineffective time would be in assuaging the wound. A few days later, on 18th February, she wrote a pathetic letter to Hanson, asking for news of Byron:

'I am afraid from your not having written to me since our Interview that you have nothing of a favourable nature to communicate—I own I perfectly despair of my Brother ever altering his Tone to me—for when one has put oneself very much in the wrong, it is difficult to get right again. The only excuse I can make for troubling you again on this sad subject is the wretchedness it has inflicted on me, *time* seems rather to increase than to remove it, and to have lost his affection and esteem appears to me a still more severe affliction than his Death would have been.

'Pray be so kind to write me a line to tell me if you saw him and if he is gone back to Cambridge . . .'

Augusta appealed to Lord Carlisle, who with his customary kindness declared himself willing to try to help her, or rather

Byron, by speaking to Hanson, though he doubted if his being brought into the matter would be productive of any good; he might only be 'able to join his lamentations' with Hanson's in a common powerlessness to prevent Byron's rake's progress. For the latter had obtained his 'some hundreds' on his land-lady's security, and was experiencing the pleasures that London could offer a young man of eighteen with money in his pocket. At the beginning of March Augusta had the mortification of seeing him from a distance at the theatre. To his mother he expressed his determined desire to leave Cambridge and pass 'a couple of years' abroad, now that he had 'a few hundreds in ready Cash' by him. He intimated that, after spending a month in London, he might bring his horses and himself 'down to your residence in that *execrable* Kennel'. He hoped she had engaged another manservant, as his present servant must attend chiefly to his horses.

On receiving this impudent epistle Mrs Byron exploded in a letter to Hanson, written on 4th March:

'That Boy will be the death of me, and drive me mad! I will never consent to his going Abroad. Where can he get Hundreds? Has he got into the hands of Moneylenders? He has no feeling, no Heart. This I have long known; he has behaved as ill as possible for years back. This bitter Truth I can no longer conceal; it is wrung from me by *heart-rending agony* . . . God knows what is to be done with him—I much fear that he is already ruined; at *eighteen*!!!—Great God, I am distracted I can say no more.'

The depth of the tenderness of Augusta's feelings towards Byron was now the measure of her distress in realising how irretrievably separated she was from him. From being his closest confidant she was thrust out so completely that it was as if she did not exist—had never existed; he refused to see her; her letters were left unanswered. For news of him she had only rumour (and gossip was not reassuring—he had bought a carriage; he was seen in Brighton with a girl dressed to pass off as his brother; he was writing verse in the country; his debts were mounting) or the family solicitor Hanson. In February, 1807, she wrote to the latter, asking if he would be kind enough to call on her at Grosvenor Place. 'I cannot *forget* I have a Brother or cease to feel anxiety about him and I

59

know of no other method of obtaining any intelligence.' About the same time she received from Mrs Byron two copies of Byron's second book of verse, *Poems on Various Occasions* (the first, *Fugitive Pieces*, published a few months earlier, had been withdrawn) and a further copy was sent to her by Hanson. Writing to thank him for the book, which (Augusta informed him) she had not the courage to show Lord Carlisle, fearing his disapproval, she revealed how her break with Byron preyed on her mind and feelings: 'It is unfortunate for me that I can't feel that indifference for Byron which he does for me, at least so far as regards my own peace. I can't help deploring his wasting all his Time at Southwell in Idleness and ill humour with the whole world. But this is a subject I ought never to begin, as it makes me melancholy and wretched.' In the following month she wrote to Byron at Southwell, to inform him that old Joe Murray, the 'Wicked Lord's' servant, had been dismissed from the Duchess of Leed's service, and to seek his help in finding him a position. She received no reply, but Byron undertook to pay Murray a monthly retainer of five pounds.

If, of the two stars Augusta had set her course by, one had sunk, the other shone more brightly in the spring of 1807. A change in George Leigh's material affairs had finally overcome his father's objections to his marriage, and the wedding was arranged for the autumn. Before leaving London in July for Castle Howard, Augusta tried once more to bring about a reconciliation with Byron. On the 17th of the month she wrote to Hanson: 'If you are in Town and have heard of my Brother, will you tell me if you think there is the slightest hope of his forgiving me—or the least possibility of my doing *any* thing in the world to obtain his forgiveness. I would not torment you, but that I am sure you wish for a reconciliation between us and that I am *perfectly wretched* at his continuing angry, and you know there is not anything I would not do to regain his good opinion and affection, which I trust I don't *quite deserve* to have lost—for that idea would greatly augment my distress . . . I shall remain here till next week, and could there in the period be any chance of bringing about a reconciliation with my Brother I can't tell you how happy I should be . . . I did write him a line on his arrival [from Cambridge] to beg 10

The first Lord Byron c. 1644. Painting by William Dobson

Byron's mother. Painting by Thomas Stewardson

Minutes conversation with him but have had no answer . . .'

Apparently Hanson sent her a hopeful reply, for Augusta wrote to tell him how obliged she was for his kind letter 'and all the welcome Intelligence it contains. I am most grateful to you for your kindness on a subject which concerns my happiness so materially. God grant that your Predictions may be verified and that I may see my Brother . . .' But there is no record that a meeting took place; and on 17th August, 1807, when Augusta was married to Colonel George Leigh, it does not appear that Byron had relented even so far as to convey his good wishes for his sister's future happiness.

IV
Marriage
1807 – 1812

THE CHANGE in financial circumstances which allowed
George Leigh to marry Augusta in the summer of 1807 must
be attributed to his father's influential position as equerry to
the Prince of Wales. Charles Leigh, who had been com-
missioned as ensign in the 3rd Foot Guards in 1764, saw service
in the American War, and in 1776 was appointed to the
household of the Prince, at that time an unruly boy of fourteen.
Promoted to colonel in 1782, Leigh played a prominent part
in the capture of Valenciennes by the Duke of York in July,
1793, during the wars in the Low Countries against revolu-
tionary France. There was something like an ironic coincidence
in the episode, for the Leighs had a house in Valenciennes,
the very house in which his brother-in-law, 'Mad Jack'
Byron, had died three years earlier. In 1794 Major-General
Leigh (he had been promoted the year before) took up his
appointment as Governor of the Leeward Islands, where he
resided in Antigua for a sojourn of two years. He was raised
to a full general in 1803, and six years later was appointed
Colonel of The Buffs. At his death in 1815 he was Groom of
the Bedchamber to the Prince Regent and Lieutenant-
Governor of the Isle of Wight.

It was General Leigh's influence which secured for his son
the appointment as equerry to the Prince, and it was the
latter's generosity in presenting George Leigh with the house
which went with the stud at Six Mile Bottom that allowed him
at last to marry Augusta. The house was in itself no great
thing—a long, rambling building, without plan, which
suggested that sections had been added as the necessity arose;
but it was a home, and its proximity to Newmarket was a
strong inducement to George Leigh to move in with his wife
in the autumn of 1807. If Augusta was unhappy at her
estrangement from Byron, it was with a sense of the boundless

possibilities of happiness that she, a sanguine young woman of twenty-three, settled in at Six Mile Bottom in a house of her own and with a husband whom she had waited so long to marry.

By the spring of 1808 Byron's hostility towards Augusta had thawed—possibly they had met in London during the winter. In the previous November he had been in touch with his guardian, sending him a copy of his verses, *Hours of Idleness*, with a dedication: 'To the Right Honourable Frederick, Earl of Carlisle, Knight of the Garter, etc. etc. the second edition of these poems is inscribed, by his obliged ward and affectionate kinsman, the author'. Lord Carlisle wrote a courteous, even flattering, letter in reply, and presented Byron with a copy of his 'own few trifles'. Then, at Christmas, Byron came down from Trinity for good and set up his London headquarters at Dorant's Hotel. His activities at this time he described in a letter to John Cam Hobhouse, whose acquaintance he had made at Cambridge: 'I am buried in an abyss of Sensuality. I have renounced *hazard*, however, but I am given to Harlots, and live in a state of Concubinage. I am at the moment under a course of restoratives by Pearson's prescription, for a debility occasioned by too frequent connection . . . I have some thoughts of purchasing D'Egville's pupils; they would fill a glorious harem.' The appearance in February of Brougham's savagely venomous attack on *Hours of Idleness*, although Byron had heard that something unpleasant was brewing, threw him off his balance. However, it was but momentary; what filled his mind was anger and a desire for revenge—it 'was rage and resistance and redress—but not despondency or despair', as he afterwards told Shelley. His vengeance he sought in rhyme; the result was to be *English Bards and Scotch Reviewers*.

At the end of April, 1808, Byron wrote to Augusta at Six Mile Bottom (relations had warmed to its being 'My dear Augusta' again), with a request that Colonel Leigh would speak to the Prince of Wales on behalf of a friend of his named Wallace who had been ordered to join his regiment stationed in the East Indies, where he had already served nine years and was reluctant to return. He told Augusta that he had met his cousins Julia and George Byron, the children of 'Mad Jack's'

63

brother, George Anson Byron, the second son of 'Foulweather Jack'. He did not admire Julia, although she was pretty, since he had heard she was clever, 'a very great defect in a woman, who becomes conceited in course . . .' George, he thought, 'will prove the best of the family, and will one day be Lord B'. He did not care how soon. Augusta must have told him of her condition, for he went on: 'Pray name my nephew after his uncle; it must be a nephew (I *won't* have a *niece*), I will make him my heir; for I shall never marry, unless I am ruined, and then his *inheritance* would not be great. George will have the title and his *laurels*; my property (if there is any left in five years time) I can leave to whom I please, and your son shall be the legatee . . .'

Now that 'Baby' Byron was reconciled with her and seemed to be resuming the ties of affection that once bound them close, Augusta was finding pleasure in the simple routine of her life in Cambridgeshire. There was very little money; however, her own needs were small. George's tastes were not so simple; but in the summer and autumn he had to spend much time with the regiment, which was rumoured to be part of a cavalry contingent being trained by Lord Paget for service against the French in Spain. Augusta supervised her household, conducted her husband's correspondence as well as her own, and prepared for the birth of her child. Taking the carriage, she would drive along the beautiful beech-lined road through the down-like countryside, then, crossing the Devil's Dyke, follow the road that skirted the south of the Heath and entered the town of Newmarket. The Leighs were well known there. Augusta was the 'young colonel's' wife, the 'old colonel' being the General, who was remembered as the Prince of Wales' equerry at the time when he still raced on the Heath, before his quarrel with the Jockey Club. At the turn of the century 'Colonel' Leigh had been at the centre of a fracas which was still remembered in Newmarket. William Chifney, son of the Prince's veteran jockey Sam, one day heard the Colonel express sentiments which reflected on the probity of his father. A youth at the time, he went away and took private boxing lessons. Later, meeting the Colonel in the High Street, he set about him, knocked him down and would have seriously injured him if bystanders had not intervened to restrain him. For this offence he was sentenced to six month's imprisonment in Cambridge Gaol. On his release Colonel Leigh went up to him and shook him by the hand; both Leighs, father and son, bore no ill will to the Chifneys, nor in turn did they. On other days Augusta would drive over to the Gogmagog Hills to visit her half-brother, the Duke of Leeds, whose house was set in the beech-woods of Wandlebury Ring; from the front garden one looked over the low ground to the north, where the towers and spires of Cambridge showed through the golden haze. She may have thought of 'Baby' Byron, but he was no longer at the university; on the expiry of Lord Grey de Ruthyn's lease in the summer, he had set himself up in neglected Newstead and (although Augusta did not know it) was hard at work on his brilliantly malicious revenge.

On 4th November, 1808, at Lord Chichester's house in Stratton Street Augusta gave birth to a girl, Georgiana Augusta, who, when she was christened in the following January, had as her sponsors the Princess of Wales, the Countess of Carlisle and the Countess of Chichester. The event took place only a week after George Leigh, in command of the 10th Dragoons, had sailed from the Isle of Wight for Spain. In his absence Augusta stayed on with the Chichesters in London, nursing her child and anxious for news of George.

Reports from the Peninsula were grave. In December it was learned that Napoleon himself was in Spain with great reinforcements of troops and guns, that Madrid had been retaken by the French, and that the survival of the small British expeditionary force of 30,000 men under Sir John Moore hung in the balance. From the journal kept by Captain Gordon we catch a glimpse of Colonel Leigh on the disastrous mid-winter retreat over the mountains of northern Spain to Corunna. The British cavalry, magnificently led by Lord Paget (later Marquess of Anglesey, the hero of Waterloo, where he lost a leg, after which he was affectionately known as 'One-Leg'), covered the retreat of the dispirited infantry against the overwhelming French advance. The Tenth were in action outside Mayorga on Boxing Day. Lord Paget, seeing an opportunity to inflict a sharp defeat on a body of French cavalry, ordered Brigadier Slade to attack. He 'moved off at a trot', says Captain Gordon, 'but had not advanced far when he halted to have some alteration made to the length of his stirrups. An aide-de-camp was sent to enquire the cause of this delay, and the squadron was again put in motion; but the General's stirrups were not yet adjusted to his mind and he halted again before he had advanced a hundred yards. Lord Paget, whose patience was by this time quite exhausted, then ordered Colonel Leigh to take the head. The Tenth charged gallantly, routed the enemy, and took between forty and fifty prisoners, with little loss on their part.' Moore's bedraggled army reached Corunna on 11th January and dug itself in to await the transports, which arrived on the 14th. Two days later Soult advanced in force but failed to dislodge the defenders; Moore was about to deliver a counter-attack, when he fell mortally wounded. By the end of January the survivors were back in England, Colonel Leigh and most of the 10th Dragoons among them.

On 30th November Byron wrote from Newstead to congratulate Augusta on the birth of her child, reverting to the old affectionate form of address, 'My dearest Augusta'. 'I return you my best thanks for making me an uncle, and forgive the sex this time; but the next *must* be a nephew.' He told that his financial prospects were better than once he had feared. Then he went on: 'I am living here *alone*, which suits my inclination better than society of any kind. Mrs Byron I have shaken off for two years, and I shall not resume her yoke in future; I am afraid my disposition will suffer in your estimation; but I can never forgive that woman, or breathe in comfort under the same roof. I am a very unlucky fellow, for I think I had naturally not a bad heart; but it has been so bent, twisted, and trampled on, that it has now become as hard as a Highlander's heelpiece.'

Byron told her that he had seen Colonel Leigh in Brighton in July, 'where I should have been glad to see you; I only know your husband by sight, though I am acquainted with many of the Tenth. Indeed my relations are those whom I know least, and in most instances, I am not very anxious to improve the acquaintance. I hope you are quite recovered, I shall be in town in January to take my seat, and will call, if convenient; let me hear from you before . . .' This letter he followed with another in mid-December. 'When I stated in my last that my intercourse with the world had hardened my heart, I did not mean from any matrimonial disappointment, no, I have been guilty of many absurdities, but I hope in God I shall always escape that worst of evils, Marriage. I have no doubt there are exceptions, and of course include you amongst them . . .' Byron then gave Augusta an account of the solitary life he was leading. 'My Library is rather extensive, (and as perhaps you know) I am a mighty Scribbler; I flatter myself I have made some improvements in Newstead, and, as I am independent, I am happy, as far as any person unfortunate enough to be born into this world, can be said to be so . . .'

This is the last letter of the Byron-Augusta correspondence to have been preserved until those written after the former's return to England in the summer of 1811; and the events of early 1809 make it most unlikely that they wrote to each other during the interval. On 22nd January Byron came of age, the Hansons doing the manorial honours for staff and tenants at Newstead, while the young Lord lunched by himself on chops and bottled ale at Reddish's Hotel in St James's. Before leaving Newstead for London Byron had written to Lord Carlisle for advice on (or rather assistance in) the procedure for taking his seat in the House of Lords, and to R. C. Dallas (whose sister was married to George Anson Byron) about the possibility of placing his satire with a London publisher. The priggish Dallas called on Byron at his hotel on his birthday and found him in high spirits—'indeed, so high' (he wrote) 'as to seem to me more flippant on the subject of religion, and on some others, than he had ever appeared before.' As he left, Byron handed Dallas the manuscript of *English Bards and Scotch Reviewers*.

Thinking his guardian would introduce him personally into the Lords and thereby waive troublesome formalities, Byron in the earlier version of his satire made a kindly reference to Lord Carlisle, juxtaposed with a humble one to himself (the latter to disguise his authorship):

Nor e'en a hackney'd Muse will deign to smile
On minor Byron, nor mature Carlisle.

67

Unknown to Byron, Lord Carlisle, who had been in ill health for some years, was at that time suffering from a serious nervous complaint. In his reply to Byron's letter, he did not offer personally to introduce him to the House, but instead rather formally and coldly (Byron thought) told him how to go about taking his seat. The most unfortunate result of this possibly not intended but nevertheless graceless action was that Byron had to prove his legitimacy to the Lord Chancellor, something that was a rare occurrence for a young lord. Hanson was obliged to go to much trouble looking up records of the creation of the Byron barony and establishing the legitimacy of births. Byron, 'extremely nettled', wrote Dallas, 'determined to lash his relation with all the gall he could throw into satire'. He went to work with a will, adding and altering, until, in the second edition, he had poured forth his spleen in these searing Popean couplets:

Lords too are bards, such things at times befall,
And 'tis some praise in peers to write at all.
Yet, did or taste or reason sway the times,
Ah! who would take their titles with their rhymes?
Roscommon! Sheffield! with your spirits fled,
No future laurels deck a noble head;
No muse will cheer, with renovating smile,
The paralytic puling of Carlisle.
The puny schoolboy and his early lay
Men pardon, if his follies pass away;
But who forgives the senior's ceaseless verse,
Whose hairs grow hoary as his rhymes grow worse?
What heterogeneous honours deck the peer!
Lord, rhymester, petit-maître and pamphleteer!
So dull in youth, so drivelling in his age,
His scenes alone had damn'd our sinking stage;
But managers for once cried, 'Hold, enough!'
Nor drugg'd their audience with the tragic stuff.
Yet at their judgement let his lordship laugh,
And case his volumes in congenial calf;
Yes! doff that covering, where morocco shines,
And hang a calf-skin on those recreant lines.

When *English Bards and Scotch Reviewers* appeared in March,

Augusta was aghast at the effrontery of Byron's attack on a man who, according to his own lights, had from his boyhood shown him nothing but kindness. She felt, too, that Lord Carlisle's personal affection for her, and the hospitality that she had received from him since childhood, were being insultingly thrown back by a Byron in his face. 'The paralytic puling of Carlisle', when the man was ill with a nervous disorder! If Byron felt wounded by Carlisle's neglect to assist him more materially in taking his seat, he had taken a more than ample revenge. He had not paused to consider how Augusta's feelings would be hurt by this lampooning of his (and, most certainly, her) benefactor. To her it was a quite uncalled for, indefensible expression of rancorous and insensitive bad taste. She herself had unjustly suffered by the exclusion from Byron's sympathy; she was now to realise that in his sensitivity, self-centred misanthropy and pride, he had forged an instrument powerful to wound; that already with him 'genius must guide when wits admire the rhyme'. Byron, though he published anonymously, was well known to have been the author.

Augusta, back at Six Mile Bottom with her husband and child, felt deeply the embarrassment of Byron's vehemence, as if she personally had been guilty of an act of gratuitous ingratitude. Yet, fearing to offend him by openly expressing her dismay, she remained silent. News reached her that Byron had taken his seat in the Lords, and was in London trying to raise a loan for a trip abroad, in which he was to be accompanied by Hobhouse. There were rumours also of 'orgies' at Newstead, where he had brought together a farewell house-party of Cambridge friends, who amused themselves by dressing as monks, drinking claret from a skull, and frolicking with the 'Paphian girls'. It was one of these friends, Scrope Berdmore Davies, a fashionable wit and gambler, who, after a successful night at the gaming-tables, furnished Byron with the loan of £4,800, which enabled him and Hobhouse to leave Falmouth on 1st July on the packet bound for Portugal. Childe Harold set out on his grand tour without taking leave of his mother or of Augusta,

> A sister whom he loved, but saw her not
> Before his weary pilgrimage begun . . .

She heard of his movements from time to time: arriving in Lisbon, the friends went overland to Cadiz and then, taking ship from Gibraltar, sailed to Valetta, where they paused long enough for Byron to fall in love with the lively Mrs Spencer Smith. The travellers went on through Albania and Greece, where Byron left his heart with the Maid of Athens, before sailing on the frigate *Salsette* for the Hellespont (which he swam, in imitation of Leander) and Constantinople. From the East Hobhouse returned to England, and Byron to Athens; there he put up in the Capuchin convent at the foot of the Acropolis. He afterwards explained that his reason for not writing to Augusta was his being told in Athens of her anger at his unmannerly treatment of his former guardian. By 1810 he had come to regret the intemperance of his satire, but he felt no compunction for having broken with Lord Carlisle. Writing to his mother from Constantinople on 28th June of that year, he declared: 'Though I was happy to obtain my seat without the assistance of Lord Carlisle, I had no measures to keep with a man who declined interfering as my relation on that occasion, and I have done with him, though I regret distressing Mrs Leigh, poor thing!—I hope she is happy!'

Augusta, indeed, was by this time not so sanguine of the happiness of the married state. With the Leighs, financial affairs had become tiresomely embarrassing. Although they had between them an income of some thirteen hundred pounds a year, George's way of life required a sum in excess of the seven hundred pounds which he retained for his private use. And in 1810 there occurred some mysterious event, which Augusta described as 'one of the most perplexing situations that I think anybody could be in', when Frederick Howard showed his 'kindness and friendship' by coming to George Leigh's rescue. It would be natural to see in this a reference to betting losses. His friends were of the racing world, and he followed the form so closely that he found it necessary to visit one race-meeting after another; he was seldom at home, except for the meetings at Newmarket. The hard-living, hard-drinking set to which he belonged—with men like Lord Darlington and Sir Harry Featherstonhaugh Fenbroom— were notorious for the high pace at which they lived; they had the means to support this extravagance, which, of course,

George lacked. He was not ill-natured (Augusta was still devoted to him, and stood beside him in adversity) yet he was weak, indolent, improvident, feckless, and egotistically exigent. Some years later Byron was to write to Augusta of her being 'so admirably yoked—and necessary as a house-keeper—and a letter writer—& a place-hunter to that very helpless gentleman your Cousin'. And elsewhere he remarked: 'She married a fool, but she *would* have him. They agreed, and agree very well and I never heard a complaint but many vindications of him.' Augusta now found that if important decisions had to be taken, it was she who had to take them; if any correspondence had to be conducted, it was she who wrote the letters—even including her husband's turf corre-spondence. With George so often away, she was often lonely. And in the summer of 1810 she discovered that she was again pregnant.

Her second daughter was born on 20th February, 1811, at Six Mile Bottom and was christened Augusta Charlotte at Gogmagog Hills, the Duchess of Leeds, Lady Gertrude Stanley and the Honourable Frederick Howard standing sponsors. Little Augusta was afterwards found to be mentally abnormal, and had to be looked after away from home at the cost of £200 a year, a heavy burden on the family's already straitened circumstances.

*

On 4th July, 1811, Byron was back in London and staying at Reddish's Hotel in St James's Street. Dallas called on him and was given *Hints from Horace* to take home. Returning the next morning, rather disappointed that travels in such exotic climes had not produced something more unusual, he concealed his regret and asked if Byron had not written other poems, more revealing of his tour of the archipelago, that he might see. On this request, Byron took from his trunk a bundle of manuscripts, which included *Childe Harold's Pil-grimage*, and gave them as an outright present to Dallas: 'They are not worth troubling you with, but you shall have them all with you if you like.' Having read *Childe Harold* overnight, Dallas was enthusiastic in his praise and eager to find a publisher. Finally he offered the poems to John Murray.

While these matters were in train, Byron was enraged by a scurrilous attack on his family in an article by an old enemy from his Cambridge days, Hewson Clarke, who, nettled by Byron's reflections on his lowly birth in the postscript to the second edition of *English Bards*, lashed out with little regard for truth in the March issue of *The Scourge*: 'It may be reasonably asked whether to be a denizen of Berwick-upon-Tweed be more disgraceful than to be the illegitimate descendant of a murderer; whether to labour in an honourable profession . . . be less worthy of praise than to waste the property of others in vulgar debauchery; whether to be the offspring of parents whose only crime is their want of title, be not as honourable as to be the son of a profligate father, and a mother whose days and nights are spent in the delirium of drunkenness . . .' One could hardly go much lower; and Byron sought the advice of the Attorney-General, Sir Vicary Gibbs, as to whether to take legal action for libel. His opinion was against starting legal proceedings, on the grounds that considerable time had elapsed since publication and that Byron's postscript had provoked the reply.

But these events were overshadowed by the news from Nottinghamshire that his mother was seriously ill, which was quickly followed by another message that she had died on 1st August. Receiving an advance of £40 from Hanson, Byron immediately went down to Newstead. Soon after his arrival he heard of the horrible death by drowning in the River Cam of Charles Skinner Matthews one of the most brilliant of his Cambridge friends. On 7th August he wrote to Scrope Davies: 'Some curse hangs over me and mine. My mother lies a corpse in this house; one of my best friends is drowned in a ditch. What can I say, or think, or do? . . . Come to me, Scrope, I am almost desolate—left almost alone in the world . . .' (About the same time he learnt of the death of Edelston, the Cambridge chorister, who had died while he was still abroad). A few days later he drew up his will, leaving the bulk of his estate to his cousin George Byron and giving instructions that his body should be buried 'without any ceremony or burial-service whatever' in the vault in the grounds of Newstead which contained the remains of his 'faithful dog' Boatswain. He added to these clauses a further one, stating that if his successors 'from bigotry, or otherwise, might think proper to remove the carcass', the estate should go to Augusta and her heirs.

Byron wrote on 21st August a reply to Augusta's letter of condolence, asking her to forgive his dilatoriness. 'I am losing my relatives and you are adding to the number of yours; but which is best, God knows . . . I hear you have been increasing his Majesty's Subjects, which in these times of War and tribulation is really patriotic. Notwithstanding Malthus tells us that, were it not for Battle, Murder and Sudden death, we should be overstocked, I think that latterly we have had a redundance of those national benefits, and therefore I give you all credit for your matronly behaviour.

'I believe you know that for upwards of two years I have been rambling round the Archipelago.' He went on to say that for all the good his return had brought, he might have stayed abroad, and that when he had 'repaired [his] *irreparable* affairs' he would go abroad again, 'for I am heartily sick of your climate and everything it *rains* upon, always save and except *yourself* as in *duty bound* . . .

'You say that you have much to communicate to me, let us have it by all means, as I am utterly at a loss to guess; whatever it may be it will be met with due attention.' He added as an afterthought that he had decided to get married, if he could 'find anything inclined to barter money for rank', after which he would return to his friends the Turks.

Augusta had been in London, where she had gone for specialist advice on Georgiana's health, and there she had met Scrope Davies, who told her that the child was just the kind that Byron would delight in. Replying to Byron's letter on 27th August, she retailed him this remark and then went on:

'Oh! that I could immediately set out to Newstead and show them [the children] to you. I can't tell you *half* the happiness it would give me to see it and *you*; but, my dearest B., it is a long journey . . . Mr Davies writes me word you promise to make him a visit bye and bye; *pray do*, you can so easily come here. I have set my heart upon it. Consider how very long it is since I've seen you.

'I have indeed *much* to tell you; but it is more easily *said* than *written*. Probably you have heard of many *changes* in our

73

situation since you left England; in a *pecuniary* point of view it is materially altered for ye worse . . .

'I have not time to write half I have to say, for my letter must go; but I prefer writing in a hurry to not writing at all. You can't think how much I feel for your griefs and losses, or how much and constantly I have thought of you lately . . . Your letter (some parts of it at least) made me laugh. I am so very glad to hear you have sufficiently overcome your prejudices against the *fair sex* to have determined upon marrying; but I shall be most anxious that my future *Belle Soeur* should have more attractions than merely money, though to be sure *that* is somewhat necessary. I have not another moment, dearest B., so forgive me if I write again very soon . . .' A postscript followed: 'Do write if you can'.

Byron replied immediately, saying that he knew nothing of the 'embarrassments' or the 'changes' Augusta mentioned— 'So you have much to tell, and all will be novelty.

'I don't know what Scrope Davies meant by telling you I liked Children, I abominate them so much that I have always had the greatest respect for the character of Herod. But, as my house here is large enough for us all, we should go on very well, and I need not tell you that I long to see *you* . . . Well, I must marry to repair the ravages of myself and prodigal ancestry, but if I am ever so unfortunate as to be presented with an heir, instead of a Rattle he shall be provided with a Gag . . . As you won't come, you will write; I long to hear all those unutterable things, being utterly unable to guess at any of them, unless they concern *your* relative the Thane of Carlisle,— though I had great hopes we had done with him . . . I will now take leave of you in the Jargon of 1794. "Health & *Fraternity*".'

The next day he wrote again, setting down his thoughts on paper before he went to bed. He had just heard of the Prince of Wales' quarrel with Colonel Leigh and could not 'help regretting on your account that so long an intimacy should be dissolved at the very moment when your husband might have derived some advantage from his R.H's friendship'. However, he assured her, she had a brother in him and a home at Newstead.

'I am led into this train of thinking by a part of your letter which hints at pecuniary losses. I know how delicate

74

one ought to be on such subjects, but you are probably the only living being on Earth *now* interested in my welfare, certainly the only relative, and I should be very ungrateful if I did not feel the obligation. You must excuse my being a little cynical, knowing how my *temper* was tried in my Non-age; the manner in which I was brought up must necessarily have broken a meek Spirit, or rendered a fiery one ungovernable; the effect it has had on mine I need not state . . .' Experience and travel had brought him now to laugh at things which before would have made him angry. 'But I am wandering—in short I only want to assure you that I love you, and you must not think I am indifferent, because I don't shew my affection in the usual way.' He concluded by asking if it was not possible to pay him a visit before Christmas.

Byron had been starved of love, and now Augusta's initiative in resuming their former relation, and her own present predicament, called forth that spontaneous affection, generosity and sensitivity to others' feelings that were so characteristic of him and made him to all his intimates so genuinely lovable—qualities which reflected the 'feminine sensibility' that his friends remarked in him.

Augusta replied from '6 Mile Bottom' on Saturday, 2nd September: 'My dearest Brother,—I hope you don't dislike receiving letters so much as writing them, for you would in that case pronounce me a great torment. But as I prepared you in my last for its being followed very soon by another, I hope you will have reconciled your mind to the impending toil. I really wrote in such a hurry that I did not say half I wished; but I did not like to delay telling you how happy you made me by writing. I have been dwelling constantly upon the idea of going to Newstead ever since I had your wish to see me there. At last a *bright thought* struck me.

'We intend, I believe, to go to Yorkshire in the autumn. Now, if I could contrive to pay you a visit *en passant*, it would be delightful, and give me the greatest pleasure. But I fear you would be obliged to make up your mind to receive my *Brats* too. As for my husband, he prefers the *outside of the Mail* to the *inside of a Post-Chaise*, particularly when partly occupied by Nurse and Children, so that we always travel *independent* of each other.

75

She continued with news of George Byron, whom she had seen in London, and of Frederick Howard's 'very pretty, very young' wife—he married a Miss Lambton. Then she went on: 'Now, my dearest Byron, pray let me hear from you. I shall be daily expecting to hear of a *Lady Byron*, since you have confided to me your determination of marrying, in which I really hope you are serious, being convinced such an event would contribute greatly to your happiness, PROVIDED her Ladyship was the sort of person that would suit you; and you won't be angry with me for saying that it is not EVERY *one* who would; therefore don't be too *precipitate*. You will *wish me hanged*, I fear, for boring you so unmercifully, so God bless you, my dearest Bro.; and, when you have time, do write. Are you going to amuse us with any more *Satires?* Oh, *English Bards!* I shall make you laugh (when we meet) about it.

'Every your most affecte Sis. and Friend
'A.L.'

With unerring insight Augusta had struck just the chords to which Byron would respond. 'Oh, *English Bards!*' and things to tell him to make him laugh. Byron always wanted someone with whom he could 'retrace the laughing part of life'. (After his death Hobhouse recorded that what he remembered most clearly of his friend was his laughter.) Byron straightway replied to Augusta's letter, telling her that she owed this third epistle to 'Silence and Solitude'. 'As to Lady B., when I discover one rich enough to suit me and foolish enough to love me, I will give her leave to make me miserable if she can. Money is the magnet; as to Women, one is as well as another, the older the better, we have then a chance of getting her to Heaven. So, your Spouse does not like brats better than myself; now those who beget them have no right to find fault, but *I* may rail with great propriety.

'My "Satire!"—I am glad it made you laugh for Somebody told me in Greece that you was angry, and I was sorry, as you were the only person whom I did *not* want to *make angry*. But how you will make *me laugh* I don't known, for it is a vastly *serious* subject to me I assure you; therefore take care, or I shall hitch *you* into the next Edition to make up our family party . . .' He continued in a playful, amused strain:

76

'If we meet in October we will travel in my *Vis.* and can have a cage for the children and a cart for the Nurse. Or perhaps we can forward them by Canal. Do let us know all about it, your "bright thought" is a little clouded, like the Moon in this preposterous climate. Good even, Child.'

Byron visited Cambridge in October, but Augusta was not at Six Mile Bottom; she had written in the first week of September to say that she doubted if she would be able to see him and Newstead before Christmas. Cambridge was desolate with memories for Byron, in spite of the presence of Scrope Davies, who was a fellow of King's, and Francis Hodgson, the translator of Juvenal, also at King's. (The latter was something of a gay dog as a young man: he reformed, however, and later became a clergyman and Provost of Eton.) Restless, Byron returned to London to await the publication of *Childe Harold*. His interest in politics revived and on 27th February, 1812, he delivered his maiden speech in the House of Lords, when he spoke feelingly and well against the bill to impose the death-penalty for frame-breaking. On the 10th March *Childe Harold* was on sale to the public; within three days of official publication the original edition of five hundred copies was exhausted. By the middle of the month Byron was surprised to find himself famous. Augusta receded into the background, with her financial worries, her helpless husband and her small children. On 3rd June she gave birth to her third child, a son, George Henry John, whose name she neatly entered in her bible, with the fact of his christening at Six Mile Bottom and the names of his sponsors, the Duke of Leeds and Sir H. Featherstonhaugh Fenbroom.

V
With Byron
1813 - 1814

IN THESE early days of the regency the political power of
the Whig aristocracy, which had been paramount throughout
much of the eighteenth century, was in eclipse; but nowhere
did the splendour of this society shine more brilliantly than in
the drawing-rooms of the leading Whig families, such as the
Hollands, Devonshires, Jerseys and Melbournes. Byron had
been a welcome visitor to Holland House before the *éclat* that
followed on the phenomenal overnight success of *Childe Harold*
in March, 1812. Thereafter he was the lion of the season,
his name was on every lip, and the street in front of his
lodgings was cluttered with carriages bearing him invitations
to dinner, the theatre or balls. One night at Lady Westmore-
land's his hostess brought up Lady Caroline Lamb to introduce
to Byron, but this eccentric young woman first looked him
fairly in the face and then provocatively turned on her heel.
Nothing could have intrigued him more. Not long after Lady
Caroline was sitting with Lady Holland at Holland House
when Byron's name was announced. On Lady Holland's
offering to present him, Byron turned to Caroline and enquired,
'That offer was made to you before; may I ask why you
rejected it?' This was the beginning of that vertiginous affair
which was to go far beyond the liberal limits imposed by
regency convention.

At first there is no doubt that Byron was genuinely attracted
and attached to this 'wild, delicate, odd, delightful person';
but there was another side to his relation with Caroline Lamb.
He had had previously little to do with women of his own
station and he was flattered by Caroline's flaunted infatuation;
also his vanity was not a little piqued by Lady Bessborough's,
her mother's, remark that she was certain that he was not
loved and that Caroline was only leading him on. But by
September Byron was weary of Caroline's reckless extrava-

gances, so that when her family finally removed her out of harm's way to Ireland, he could write to Lady Melbourne, Caroline's mother-in-law: '. . . I wish this to end, and it shall not be renewed on my part . . . I am tired of being a fool, and when I look back on the waste of time . . . I am—what I ought to have been long ago. It is true from early habit, one must make love mechanically, as one swims. I was once very fond of both, but now as I never swim, unless I tumble into the water, I don't make love till almost obliged . . . I will say no more on this topic . . .' Unfortunately he reckoned without Caroline Lamb; he was to say a great deal more.

On the publication of *Childe Harold*, Byron had sent a copy to Augusta with an affectionate inscription on the flyleaf: 'To Augusta, my dearest sister, and my best friend, who has ever loved me better than I deserved, this volume is presented by her *father*'s son, and most affectionate brother, B.' Augusta, engrossed in the care of her three small children and the running of the house, distracted by the lack of money and the unlikelihood of her husband's ever providing an assured income, heard of Byron's triumphal progress only by report. To her way of thinking his affair with Caroline Lamb could only be damaging; what he must do, and quickly, was to find the right girl, marry her and settle down. The idea had also occurred to Byron. Using as intermediary Lady Melbourne, with whom he was now in almost daily contact, Byron had sent a curiously ambivalent proposal to Annabella Milbanke, the only daughter of Sir Ralph Milbanke, Lady Melbourne's brother. Annabella, whom he hardly knew, having only met her in London drawing-rooms, where her serious, studious demeanour had attracted him by its very inappropriateness in those giddy circles, had had the resolution to refuse him. He received the refusal lightly: '. . . I am more proud of her *rejection* than I can ever be of *another's acceptance* . . . the *hope* of obtaining *her* . . . was more pleasing than the possession of St. Ursula and the 11,000 virgins (being a greater number than have ever *since* existed at the *same time* in that capacity) could possibly have been . . .' He sought relaxation elsewhere, going away to the country with Lady Oxford; there, living 'like the gods of Lucretius', he put out of mind with present pleasures the impertinent impetuosities of Caroline Lamb, the rejection by the 'Princess of Parallelograms' (as he called the blue-stocking Annabella Milbanke) and his own desperate financial affairs.

In August Newstead had been put up for auction, but it was withdrawn at 113,500 guineas. The following day an offer of £140,000 was made by a lawyer named Thomas Claughton, and this was accepted, with the proviso that £25,000 be paid as deposit, to be forfeited if the deal was not carried through by the purchaser. Hearing of the sale, Byron's creditors began to press for payment; but it was soon clear that Claughton had regretted his bargain and would be dilatory in completing. Byron, knowing well the plight of Augusta's husband, was doubly distressed that he was unable to raise money to help in that quarter.

In March 1813, he wrote to her from 4 Bennet Street, St James's, regretting his inability to be of immediate assistance: 'My dearest Augusta,—I did not answer your letter, because I could not answer as I wished, but expected that every week would bring me some tidings that might enable me to reply better than by apologies. But Claughton has not, will not, and I think, cannot pay his money, and though, luckily, it was stipulated that he never should have possession till the whole was paid, the estate is still on my hands, and your brother consequently no less embarrassed than ever. This is the truth; and is all the excuse I can offer for inability, but not unwillingness, to serve you.'

He told Augusta of his intention to go abroad in the summer, but hoped to see her before his departure. He continued: 'You have perhaps heard that I have been fooling away my time with different "regnantes", but what better can be expected from me? I have but one *relative*, and her I never see. I have no connections to domesticate with, and for marriage I have neither the talent nor the inclination.' His parliamentary plans had come to nothing, although he had spoken twice in the last session; he did not care 'to strut another hour' on that particular stage. 'I am thus wasting the best part of life, daily repenting and never amending.' He informed her casually that he was going off with the Oxfords to Herefordshire. 'I see that you put on a *demure* look at the name, which is very becoming and matronly in you; but you won't be sorry to hear that I am quite out of a most serious scrape with another singular personage which threatened me last year, and trouble enough I had to steer clear of it, I assure you . . . I am a fool, and deserve all the ills I have met, or may meet with . . .'

The spring of 1813 was a time of constant anxiety for Augusta at Six Mile Bottom. There were periods when there was insufficient money to pay the servants or to meet the household bills; the children were ill; and Colonel Leigh was as hopelessly improvident as ever, borrowing from his friends to pay his gambling debts. Byron, in his desire to raise funds to come to her aid, and for himself to get abroad, away from the importunities of Caroline Lamb, instructed Hanson to sell all the furniture, pictures and plate which were not included in the sale of Newstead to Claughton. A chancery action to secure the balance of the deposit had meanwhile been brought against this reluctant purchaser.

In December of the preceding year, Caroline had burned Byron in effigy, with 'his book, ring and chain' at Brocket Hall, the Melbourne's country house, where village children, decked for the occasion in white, danced around the fire, while an address, written by Caroline, was spoken by a page:

> Is this Guy Faux you burn in effigy?
> Why bring the traitor here? What is Guy Faux to me?
> Guy Faux betrayed his country, and his laws.
> England revenged the wrong, his was a public cause,
> But I have private cause to raise this flame.
> Burn also these, and be their fate the same . . .
> [*Puts the basket in the fire under the figure*]

By forging Byron's signature she obtained from John Murray, the publisher, a portrait of her former lover. She demanded an interview with Byron, which he was for long unrelenting in refusing her. In June he wrote in one of his many letters of protestation at her antics to his confidante, Lady Melbourne, that 'your plague and mine has, according to her own account, been in "excellent fooling" '. Partly to avoid her machinations, Byron remained much of the spring in the country, staying with the Oxfords or the Jerseys, and only coming to London to try to stir Hanson into action or to see to the publication of

The Giaour, which Murray brought out in early June. At the end of May Byron wrote to Augusta, inviting her to meet him in London later in the month, when the Oxfords would have sailed for Sicily. He was already tiring of the autumnal charms of Lady Oxford. However, when they did leave and Augusta's arrival on 26th June prevented him seeing her off, he wrote to Lady Melbourne that he 'felt more Carolinish about her' than he had expected.

Augusta had not seen 'Baby' Byron since he had left for his grand tour in 1809, and indeed very little of him since her 'abominable' (his word for it) marriage in 1807. He now wrote her two short notes to the Harrowbys' in Berkeley Square, where she was to stay, the first asking her to get in touch with him when she arrived. The second in reply to her notice of her arrival he wrote before going to bed and sent around to Berkeley Square by his servant, Fletcher, the following morning, Sunday, 27th June: 'My dearest Augusta,—And if you heard *whom* I had put off besides my journey—you would think me grown strangely fraternal. However, I won't overwhelm you with my *own praises*. Between one and two be it—I shall, of course, prefer seeing you all to myself without the encumbrance of third persons, even of *your* (for I won't own the relationship) fair cousin [Lady Gertrude Howard, now married to William Sloane Stanley] of *eleven page* memory, who by the by, makes one of the finest busts I have seen in the Exhibition, or out of it. Good night! . . . P.S. Your writing is grown like my Attorney's, and gave me quite a qualm, till I found the remedy in your signature.' (Augusta wrote a bold, even, fluidly cursive hand; much more legible than Byron's own—'a washerwoman's laboured scrawl' in the courtesan Harriet Wilson's opinion, though there was nothing laboured about it; rather it revealed the lightning rapidity of composition.)

Augusta at twenty-nine (as we see in the sketch by George Hayter, painted in 1812) bore a remarkable family resemblance to Byron: she had the same large eyes, fine nose and expressive mouth; her dark brown hair, worn high, fell in delicate curls at the temples; her figure was gracefully curved, soft, even voluptuous. Shy and reserved in company, she had the old way when alone with Byron (which delighted him) of mimicry

82

and gentle mockery, solving all strain in irrepressible laughter. Like her half-brother, she would pout if momentarily put out, and she had the same difficulty in pronouncing her r's. But, more than all else, he found in her the most complete, spontaneous and instinctive sympathy; they were both Byrons, they spoke the same language; through their veins the same blood, which responded to similar impulses, feelings and emotions, flowed. For years each had frustratedly sought the other's presence; now for the first time they were together and alone. Within a short while Byron was writing to Tom Moore: 'My sister is in town, which is a great comfort,—for never having been much together, we are naturally more attached to each other.' Augusta, escaped from the harassing presence of her indolent husband and her demanding children, was charmed with the company of this new 'Baby' Byron, famous, self-assured in society, grown slim and elegant, at once so comic and altogether delightful. She felt the exciting paradox of his being a stranger whom she had known all her life.

That Sunday evening Byron called for Augusta to escort her to Lady Davy's where they were to meet the redoubtable Madame de Staël. For both of them it was a new sensation, and a most pleasurable one, to be together before third persons. On July 1st Byron wrote to Lady Melbourne asking if she could let him have a 'she voucher' for a ticket to the masque at Almack's on the following day. 'It is for my sister, who I hope will go with me. I wish she were not married for (now I have no home to keep) she would have been so good a housekeeper. Poor soul! she likes her husband. I think her thanking you for your abetment of her abominable marriage (*seven years* after the event!!) is the only instance of similar gratitude on record. However, now she is married, I trust she will remain so.' Byron received Augusta's visits in the afternoons at Bennet Street and returned them at the Harrowbys', and in the evening he accompanied her with growing pleasure to the theatre, assemblies and routs. At a reception at Lady Glenbervie's Miss Annabella Milbanke observed the couple sitting together on the sofa and noted Byron's affectionate manner towards his sister, which characteristically she put down to Augusta's ability to educe his gentler qualities. Everywhere they were seen together.

However, Augusta was not present at Lady Heathcote's small waltzing party on the night of 5th-6th July, when Caroline Lamb achieved her most resounding effect so far in drawing attention to herself. Byron retailed the scandal to her next day. He had seen Caroline before supper and had spoken to her. '. . . one of the few things I said was a request to know her will and pleasure, if there was anything I could say, do, or not do to give her the least gratification.' At this she turned her back on him, without replying. As he was taking Lady Rancliffe in to supper, he ran into Caroline, who took his hand as they passed and pressed it against some sharp object, saying, 'I mean to use this'. 'Against me, I presume?' Byron enquired and made light of the episode, '. . . though, of course, had I guessed her to be serious, or had I been conscious of offending I should have done everything to pacify or prevent her.' At four in the morning Lady Ossulstone came up to him 'looking angry (and, at that moment, ugly)' with some confused message from Lady Melbourne of a scene with Caroline, adding her own observation that he 'must have behaved very ill'. He left the party at five, 'totally ignorant of all that passed. Nor do I know where this cursed scarification took place, nor when—I mean the room—and the hour.'

Many years later (in 1824) Caroline described the famous scene in a letter to Medwin. She might have then glossed over the details, but never could she forget the ignominy of it. 'He [Byron] made me swear that I was never to waltz. Lady Heathcote said: "Come, Lady Caroline, you must begin." I bitterly answered, "Oh, yes! I am in a merry humour." I did so, but whispered to Lord Byron: "I conclude that I may waltz *now*?" He answered sarcastically, "With everybody in turn—you always did it better than anyone. I shall have pleasure in seeing you." I did so; you may judge with what feelings! After this, feeling ill, I went into a small inner room where supper was prepared. Lord Byron and Lady Rancliffe entered. Seeing me, Lord Byron said, "I have been admiring your dexterity." I clasped a knife not intending anything. "Do, my dear", he said; "but if you mean to act a Roman's part, mind which way you strike with your knife—be it at your own heart, not mine—you have struck there already." "Byron!" I said, and ran away with the knife. I did not stab myself. It is false, Lady Rancliffe and Lady Tankerville screamed and said I would do so. People pulled to get it from me. I was terrified. My hand got cut, and the blood came over my gown. I know not what happened after—but this is the very truth. . . . I never held my head up after—never could . . .'

Augusta spent about three weeks in London, seeing something of her own friends, particularly Lady Gertrude Stanley and the Hon. Mrs George Villiers (as Theresa Parker, Augusta had known her since childhood); but mostly she was with Byron at home or on shopping expeditions—he was setting himself up for his proposed eastern trip with an extensive wardrobe and costly presents for foreign potentates and dignitaries—or at the customary evening parties. Some money had been squeezed out of Claughton and Byron was happy to be able to relieve his sister from the most pressing of her difficulties. He had written to John Wilson Croker, Secretary to the Admiralty, on 13th July, sounding him as to his prospects of securing a passage on H.M.S. *Boyne*, which was about to leave in command of Captain Carlton to reinforce the Mediterranean squadron under Sir Edward Pellew. But so in two minds about the future was Byron that on 13th July, the same day as he wrote to Croker, he was making enquiries of Tom Moore of the suitability of Lady Adelaide Forbes as a wife: 'I am amazingly inclined—remember I say but *inclined*—to be seriously enamoured with Lady A.F . . . you know her; is she *clever*, or sensible, or good-tempered? either *would* do . . . I scratch out the *will* . . .' Then, soon after Augusta had returned home, he followed her to Six Mile Bottom and spent a few days with her, travelling back to London by night. From 9th July until the 30th, there is only one letter from Byron to his congenial confidante, Lady Melbourne; this was written on the 18th in answer to Annabella Milbanke's report, which she did not credit, that he had dealt unfairly with Claughton, 'who from the imprudent eagerness of youth' had bid more than Newstead was worth. He told Lady Melbourne to answer as she saw fit; 'I am not very fond of defending myself. I shall, however, have an immediate explanation with the interesting *youth* (a lawyer of forty-five years) . . .'

To Lady Melbourne, who had chaffed Byron about his refusal to tell her anything of his doings, he wrote on 30th

July: 'I don't tell you anything! My God, everybody rates me about my confidences with you. Augusta, for example, writes to-day, and the last thing she says is "This must not go to Ly Me", and, to punish you, *it shan't.*'

About the beginning of August Byron paid another visit to Augusta in Cambridgeshire, and brought her back to London with him to stay with the Hon. Mrs Villiers in Knightsbridge. He had overcome her natural hesitation and she now declared her resolution to go abroad with him. On 5th August, Lady Melbourne was alarmed to receive a letter from Byron, announcing blandly: 'My sister, who is going abroad with me, is now in town, where she returned with me from Newmarket. Under the existing circumstances of her lord's embarrassments, she could not well do otherwise, and she appears to have still less reluctance at leaving this country even than myself.'

It is impossible for us to know when Byron's relations with Augusta changed from an affectionate attachment to the passionate liaison which altered so radically the direction of both their lives and brought such irretrievable ruin on all who were concerned. But by 22nd August Byron could refer cryptically to this new passion to Moore: '. . . the fact is, I am at this moment in a far more serious, and entirely new, scrape than any of the last twelve months,—and that is saying a good deal. It is unlucky we can neither live with nor without these women.'

Try as he might, Byron at first could not bring himself to divulge his secret to Lady Melbourne: part of his mind looked for the relief of having such a reliable, tried and experienced woman in his confidence, but another part baulked at the prospect of her disapproval. On 8th August he wrote that he had been 'occupied to weariness with various somethings and nothings'—he had, in fact, been acting for Scrope Davies in an affair of honour with Lord Foley and had arranged an amicable settlement. Three days later, he was still stalling: 'I ought to have called on you, and I ought all kinds of *oughts*, for omitting which I can only plead many excuses which will not amount to one apology. As this is the case, I shall omit them altogether, having already written, and destroyed, two in-effectual notes about that [he does not say what] and other subjects.' Caroline, he reports, has been mercifully quiet of

86

late. 'The few things I wished to have said to you did not at all concern her or hers . . . I should have been glad of your advice how to untie two or three "gordian knots" tied around me. I shall cut them without consulting anyone, though some are rather closely twisted round my *heart* (if you will allow me to *wear* one) . . . Perhaps I shall not see you again; if not, forgive my follies, and like me as much as you can . . .' He finished with a postscript that the *Boyne* proposal was off, since the passage was only for himself and one servant. He had, since he last saw her, 'found fifty better reasons than ever for migrating'.

He began his next letter, written on 18th August, with an admission of his folly: 'I *am* "a very weak person", and can only answer your letter. I have already written and torn up *three* to you, and probably may finish in the same way with ye present.' The plague, which was raging in the Levant, might make the trip impossible for the immediate future. He was on the verge of revealing his secret in exchange for some intriguing information from Lady Melbourne. 'Tell me', he wrote, 'and in return I will tell—no I won't . . .' He had received 'some sermons and fruit' from Caroline. But these trifles were all beside the point. 'I have scribbled on without saying a single thing I wished to say . . .' Still he could not bring himself to confess it. With Augusta back at Six Mile Bottom, he was a prey to his eternal vacillation. On 20th August, he resumed his compulsive correspondence with Lady Melbourne: 'When I don't write to you, or see you for some time, you may be very certain I am about no good—and *vice versa* . . . Make my best respects, and don't be angry with me—which you will, however; first, for some things I have said, and then for others I have not said . . .'

Lady Melbourne must have been sadly puzzled by all these cryptic half-hints of serious revelations; if he had nothing important to discover, why these proffered allusions and constant retreats? Augusta, he informed her, wished to go to Sicily, 'or elsewhere', and he also desired to get abroad; she, however, wanted to take one of her children, and the plague made this dangerous. But Lady Oxford has sickened him of all children; 'besides, it is so superfluous to carry such things with people—if they want them, can't they get them on the spot?' This last remark, so crudely linking Lady Oxford with Augusta, was enough to shock even so worldly-wise a woman as Lady Melbourne. She bluntly pointed out to Byron that a continuance of such a relationship with Augusta, interpret it as one might (and there may have been an element of jealousy in her warning), would forever ostracise him from English society. On 31st August he replied: 'My dear LY ME,—Your kind letter is unanswerable; no one but yourself would have taken the trouble; no one but me would have been in the situation to require it. I am still in town so that it has as yet not had all the effect you wish . . .'

It is not difficult to understand the new intensity of Augusta's feelings for Byron. The maternal (for it was more than sisterly) part had always existed. The natural companionship of John Byron's children had been arbitrarily thwarted. Her own marriage had been a painful disappointment, and the happiness she had sought in husband, children and home had been denied her. Her shyness with strangers hid a nature that was affectionate, responsive, gay; her liveliness of mind was added to by a gift for mimicry and irony. A buoyant and naturally sanguine disposition wanted only sympathetic circumstances in which to blossom into irradiating warmth and friendliness, and a gaiety that was infectious. She was no feather-brained fool, but a sensitive, intelligent and well-disposed woman. Byron realised (and regretted) that there was no woman who could understand him like Augusta. The Byronic pose was quickly dropped in her presence; it could not stand up to mockery. (The only one of his acquaintances who could pierce this Wertherism—Byron did not exhibit it to his friends like Hobhouse—was Scrope Davies, who one day when Byron exclaimed, 'I shall go mad!' murmured with his irresistible stammer, 'Much more like silliness than madness.') Augusta could unfailingly intuit the response that would rescue him from his melancholia or exaggeration; she knew that beneath the panache of this fashionable young man of the world were the scars from his congenital lameness and from a lamentable childhood with his vulgar, unbalanced mother. She was fascinated by Byron's beauty and by the brilliance of his talk, but not over-awed; nor was she put out by his petulance, vanity and flashes of extraordinary childishness. She moved easily with him from mood to mood, the passage from one to the other marked usually by a droll witticism and laughter.

The culmination of this unrestrained intimacy was their going to bed together. To Lady Melbourne Byron took the blame for this step on himself. Their feelings for each other were such that in the logic of the moment it seemed perfectly natural and appropriate; regrets came only after the event. Lady Melbourne's remonstrations were answered by Byron in a letter in January 1814: 'I do not see how you could well have said less, and that I am not angry may be proved by saying a word more on ye subject.' He had presumably confessed to her in person at Melbourne House. 'You are quite mistaken, however, as to *her*, and it must be from some misrepresentation of mine that you throw the blame so completely on the side least deserving and least able to bear it. I dare say I made the best of my own story, as one always does from natural selfishness without intending it, but it was not her fault, but my own *folly* (give it what name may suit it better) and her weakness, for the intentions of both were very different, and for some time adhered to, and when not, it was entirely my own—in short, I know no name for my conduct. Pray do not speak so harshly of her to me—the cause of it all . . .' In April he was still trying to overcome Lady Melbourne's incredulity as to Augusta's innocence: '. . . it must be some selfish stupidity of mine in telling you my own story, but really and truly,—as I hope mercy and happiness for her— by that God who made me for my own misery, and not much for the good of others, *she* was not to blame one thousandth part in comparison. She was not aware of her own peril until too late, and I can only account for her subsequent "abandon" by an observation which I think is not unjust, that women are much more *attached* than men if they are treated with anything like fairness or tenderness.'

Byron loved Augusta in a way that he loved no other woman, as the sequel was to prove. Yet he betrayed her to Lady Melbourne, later to Annabella, when she was his wife; and almost certainly to Caroline Lamb—the last person to trust with a confidence so damaging to both Augusta and himself. Augusta was, in one sense at least, a victim of elements in Byron's character of which she was at this time unaware— but she was nevertheless a willing victim. At twenty-five

Byron already felt he had outlived life. He had been awakened sexually at the age of nine by May Gray, his Scottish nurse, who had taught him to read the Bible. Hobhouse, much later, learned from Hanson how 'a free Scottish girl used to come to bed and play tricks with his person, Hanson found out and asked Lord B.—who owned the fact—the girl was sent off—' Byron himself refers to the precocity of his feelings for Mary Duff in the entry in the *Journal* for 26th November, 1813: 'How very odd that I should have been so utterly, devotedly fond of that girl, at an age when I could neither feel passion, nor know the meaning of the word. And the effect! . . . How the deuce did all this occur so early? where could it originate? I certainly had no sexual ideas for years afterwards; and yet my misery, my love for that girl were so violent, that I sometimes doubt if I have ever been really attached since . . .' As a young man he already felt he had 'anticipated life'. Byron might well be said to have shared something of Blake's experience of having 'grown old in love from seven to seven times seven', only he had crowded these passions into a much shorter compass of time. Moreover, with him the feelings for those whom he loved, both men and women, were, as he rightly described them 'passions'. The sexual element in even his most ideal love or 'pure passion' was always present. Byron himself saw this mixture of sentiment and sensuality in the 'antithetical mind' of Robert Burns: 'It seems strange; a true voluptuary will never abandon his mind to the grossness of reality. It is by exalting the earthly, the material, the *physique* of our pleasures, by veiling these ideas, by forgetting them altogether, or, at least, never naming them hardly to one's self, that we alone can prevent them from disgusting.'

Byron had the courage—and this, among his splendid talents, is one of the marks of his genius—to act out his feelings, to carry them to their logical conclusion in action. If a social or religious convention barred the way to the natural expression of a natural feeling, he then stigmatised this code or dogma as cant, as hypocrisy. His Calvinistic upbringing, however, especially in the notion of predestination, had deeply impressed itself on his mind; and, try as he would, he was not able to eradicate the idea that he was a foredoomed man, one of the fallen angels, fatalistically bound to his worst self, marked with the brand of Cain. The history of the Byrons justified the most melancholy view of his own future; his experience confirmed the reality of human depravity. His intellect showed him clearly the possible consequences of his actions, but his pride would not allow him to profit by pusillanimity—or by prudence. As Sir Walter Scott remarked, Byron's religious feelings were disposed towards Catholicism; but he would have been (*per impossibile*) a Catholic without belief in the doctrine of grace. However clearsightedly he observed himself and others, his certainty that his behaviour was predestined did not save him from the remorse which accompanied his acts. Remorse he felt deeply, but not guilt. Goethe considered Byron childish as a thinker, yet the German was fascinated by the force within Byron that drove him to a course of continual revolt that must in the end be self-destructive. And Byron himself clearly recognised this and accepted it.

During the late summer and early autumn of 1813, while Byron in London was bringing out the much added-to new editions of *The Gaiour*, a prey to moral indecision between his desire for Augusta and his longing to get abroad, he received a long letter from Annabella Milbanke, who had persuaded herself (she could persuade herself almost anything) that she might write to her rejected suitor in terms of disinterested friendship. She told him how earlier she had studied his character. 'I felt for you, and I often felt with you.' She confessed of herself: 'It is my nature to feel long, deeply and secretly, and the strongest affections of my heart are without hope.' Characteristically she offered him some good advice: 'No longer suffer yourself to be the slave of the moment, nor trust your noble impulses to the chances of Life. Have an object that will permanently occupy your feelings & exercise your reason. Do good . . . to benefit man you must love him, and you must bear with his infirmities . . .' Fearing that Lady Melbourne might 'look for design' in her writing to him, she asked Byron not to mention the fact to her. 'The slave of the moment' replied to this far from ingenuous letter, admitting to Annabella that he had preferred her to all others—'it was then the fact; it is so still . . .' On the score of friendship, he said that he must be candid: 'It is a feeling towards you with which I cannot trust myself. I doubt whether I could help loving you . . .'

Augusta in Cambridgeshire had no such distractions. Her present money troubles relieved by Byron's generosity, she could turn over more leisurely in her mind the profound, the alarming change that had come about in her relations with Byron. There were moments when she was filled with a sense of untrammelled happiness, when she recalled his kindness, his affectionate sympathy for her concerns and worries, and the delightful freedom of his company. In his presence the insecurity of her childhood and adolescence was forgotten; the world existed only as the moment, and the moment held the certainty of this sharing in the spontaneous pleasure of their common awareness. The lightest thought, the most fleeting feeling, the deeper emotions, flowed so naturally between them as to seem but an extension of the consciousness of one into the other. In remembering these moments Augusta must have felt an exhilaration of spirit that had no place for misgiving and little or no remorse for an act which was simply the seal to the pleasure they found in each other. Yet no doubt there were other times when she could scarcely bring herself to believe in the actuality of what had taken place. To a mind like Augusta's it was not so much the fact of incest that was troubling; it was rather the loss of the innocence of the earlier relation of brother and sister, to be replaced by something profoundly unpredictable, capable of drastically changing the world to which she was accustomed into something she knew not what. The delightful daydream of going abroad with Byron, the prospect of the pleasure to be had in being with him continually, the release from her present painful domestic circumstances—the thought of these desired objects faded before the reality which she was too clear-headed and practical to deny.

Augusta's letters to Byron at the end of August and the beginning of September reflected the retreat in her thinking from her earlier acceptance of Byron's proposal to travel together. On 6th September Byron wrote again to Miss Milbanke, giving his hedonistic view that 'the great object of life is sensation—to feel that we exist, even though in pain. It is this 'craving void' which drives us to gaming—to battle—to travel . . .' Nothing could be more apt to describe his own thoughts and feelings at that moment. Hearing from Augusta that she had decided that she could not go with him, that her place was with her husband and family, Byron on the 8th suddenly decided to set out for Six Mile Bottom. He wrote that day to Lady Melbourne:

'My dear LY ME,—I leave here tomorrow for a few days, come what may; and as I am sure that you would get the better of my resolution, I shall not venture to encounter you. If nothing very particular occurs, you will allow me to write as usual; if there does, you will probably hear *of*, but not *from* me (of course) again.

'Adieu! Whatever I am, and wherever I may be, believe me most truly your obliged

and faithful B.'

Lady Melbourne, more deeply worried than ever, replied immediately, sending her letter around to Bennet Street by servant the same evening, asking Byron to call on her, if possible, and to write to her 'at all events'; but he had gone out before the letter arrived. Byron answered next day, assuring her that he would write, 'till the moment arrives (if it does arrive) when I feel that you ought not to acknowledge me as a correspondent—in that case, a sense of what is due to yourself, and a very grateful remembrance of all you have done to save one not worth preserving, will, of course, close our correspondence and acquaintance at once—the sincerest and only proof I could then afford of the value I set upon your friendship.'

Byron, determined to fill the 'craving void' by seeing Augusta again, and in the hope of changing her decision, left London for Newmarket in the second week in September. But Augusta, although delighted to have Byron with her, was firm in her refusal. This unexpected attitude in one whom he had thought pliant (or compliant) put him in no good humour with her or himself; and the stay was not a happy one. Augusta's chief reason for declining was one of loyalty to her husband; she could not bring herself to leave George Leigh to bear his difficulties alone—or to leave him with the care of the children. Byron, not used to having his wishes thwarted, was

93

piqued and took himself off to Cambridge on the 12th. There he 'swallowed' with Scrope Davies six bottles of burgundy and claret in the course of three hours. He was in an overwrought and undecided state, and after spending a day with his friend drove back to London, which he reached at three in the morning. From there he wrote to Augusta on the same day, 15th September, in a very different tone from his usual affectionate style: 'Tonight I shall leave . . . again, perhaps for Aston or Newstead. I have not yet determined, nor does it much matter. As you perhaps care more on the subject than I do, I shall tell you when I know myself.

'When my departure is arranged, and I can get this long-evaded passage, you will be able to tell me whether I am to expect a visit or not, and I can come to or meet you as you think best.' 'My dearest' had diminished to 'my dear Augusta'.

He was feeling too feverish and restless to remain in London, but before leaving Aston, near Rotherham, where he now accepted a long-standing invitation to visit his old friend Wedderburn Webster, he wrote to Murray asking him to look out for a ship sailing for the Mediterranean, which would take passengers—himself and a friend and his three servants. This suggests that he still had in mind that Augusta might eventually accompany him. It was on Augusta's account that Byron, in an attempt to exorcise her hold over him—'to vanquish my demon'—set out for Aston Hall, in the hope of relieving the perplexity of his mind and feelings by 'transferring' his 'regards to another'. He had heard that Lady Frances, Wedderburn's wife, was 'a pretty, pleasant woman', though in somewhat delicate health. And there were to be other female members of the Aston house-party.

The turmoil in Byron's mind during these early months of his passion for Augusta was to some extent assuaged by the composition in the late hours of the night of the additions to *The Giaour*. In this poem there appeared the revealing verses:

> The keenest pangs the wretched find
> Are rapture to the dreary void,
> The hapless desert of the mind,
> The waste of feeling unemploy'd . . .

The confessions to Lady Melbourne of his entire responsibility for the turn the liaison with Augusta had taken are perhaps reflected in the well-known lines:

> Yes, Love indeed is light from heaven;
>   A spark of that immortal fire
> With angels shared, by Alla given,
>   To lift from earth our low desire . . .
> I grant *my* love imperfect, all
> That mortals by the name miscall;
> Then deem it evil, what thou wilt;
> But say, oh say, *hers* was not guilt!

He wrote of these additions in a letter to Lady Melbourne on 28th September: '. . . you, who know how my thoughts were occupied when these last were written, will perhaps perceive in parts a coincidence in my own state of mind with that of my hero; if so, you will give me the credit for the feeling, though on the other hand I lose in your esteem.' The 'scorching' days of July, when 'the lava of his imagination' might have burnt up his sanity, returned in the autumn with a fervid intensity which found its sole relief in verse.

95

VI

The Summer of the Sovereigns

1814

IN THE early autumn of 1813 Augusta found herself again
to be pregnant. The possibility of Byron's paternity of her
child was covered, at least outwardly, by the fact that she had
slept with her husband about the assumed time of its conception. Her feelings towards Byron were for the moment confused,
and she was grateful to be with her husband and family at
Six Mile Bottom. At the end of September she received a
letter from Lady Frances Wedderburn Webster inviting her
to join the house-party at Aston Hall after the Doncaster
races, where Byron would be returning from a short sojourn
in London. Augusta was feeling far from well, and she did
not relish the thought of being in Byron's company in the
presence of the heterogeneous collection of guests gathered
together by 'Bold' Webster, a silly, cantankerous fellow for
whom she had little regard; so she replied to Lady Frances,
pleading sickness as an excuse for her refusal. She wrote at the
same time to Byron, but he was put out by her declining
Lady Frances' invitation and in his pique did not reply to
her letter. Not hearing from him for a week, she wrote again,
asking if she had offended him. Byron answered in a short
note on 10th October: 'I have only time to say that I am not
in the least angry, and that my silence has merely arisen from
several circumstances which I cannot now detail. I trust you
are better, and will contrive best, Ever, my dearest, Yours, B.'

This cryptic reference to 'several circumstances' is explained
by his absorption in the seduction of his host's wife, Lady
Frances, of which he furnished a detailed day-to-day account
in the marvellously ironic correspondence with Lady Melbourne. The latter was only too eager for Byron to transfer
his regards from Augusta to anyone else who was willing to
reciprocate them, and now gave him encouragement, she
like some more benign Marquise de Merteuil to an amused

though ultimately tender-hearted Vicomte de Valmont. Augusta was sadly perplexed when nearly a month passed without her hearing from Byron. Then on 8th November he wrote: 'I have only time to say that I shall write tomorrow, and that my present and long silence has been occasioned by a thousand things (with which you are not concerned). It is not Ly C[aroline] nor O[xford]; and perhaps you may guess, and, if you do, do not tell. You do not know what your being here with me might have prevented. You shall hear from me tomorrow; in the meantime don't be alarmed. *I* am in no *immediate* peril . . .' Jealousy of other women in Byron's life was not an element in Augusta's make-up, but she would hardly have been human had she not been a little hurt by the inadequate reasons for his not writing to her—and it was so typical of 'Baby' Byron to blame her for his own weaknesses. She would indeed have been hurt if she had known what confidences had been shared with Lady Melbourne, and that comparing his progress in seducing Lady Frances with his relation to herself he had crudely remarked, 'I remember my last case was the reverse, as Major O'Flaherty recommends, "we fought first and explained afterwards".'

Byron left Aston Hall on 19th October and returned to London. On his previous short visit he had drawn up a new will, revoking that of 1811; by this he left half his property to his cousin and heir George Byron and half to Augusta. Both Lady Frances and Augusta were occupying his mind when he set himself to the composition of *The Bride of Abydos*. In a letter of 4th November he explained his seclusion to Lady Melbourne: 'For the last three days I have been quite shut up; my mind has been from *late* and *later* events in such a state of fermentation, that as usual I have been obliged to empty it in rhyme, and am in the very heart of another Eastern tale—something of the *Giaour* cast—but not so sombre, though rather more villainous. This is my usual resource; if it were not for some such occupation to dispel reflection during *inaction*, I verily believe I should very often go mad . . .' ('All convulsions end with me in rhyme', as he told Tom Moore.) 'I have written this . . . to wring my thoughts from reality, and take refuge in "imaginings", however "horrible" . . .' It was about this time that he spoke openly on the theme

97

of incest at Holland House, remarking that it was not universally regarded as sinful. As the poem was originally written, Selim and Zuleika were brother and sister, but he thought better of this and altered the first draft. Writing to Professor Clarke of Cambridge, he explained: '. . . I felt compelled to make my hero and heroine relations, as you well know that none else could there obtain that degree of intercourse leading to genuine affection; I had nearly made them rather too much akin to each other; and though the wild passions of the East, and some great examples in Alfieri, Ford and Schiller (to stop short of antiquity), might have pleaded in favour of a copyist, yet time and the north . . . induced me to alter their consanguinity and confine them to cousinship.'

More unsettled than ever, Byron began a journal on 14th November, which he opened with a record of his own disillusionment: 'At five-and-twenty, when the better part of life is over, one should be *something*;—and what am I? nothing but five-and-twenty—and the odd months. What have I seen? the same man all over the world,—ay, and woman too . . .' He referred to *The Bride of Abydos*: 'I believe the composition of it kept me alive—for it was written to drive my thoughts from the recollection of—

"Dear sacred name, rest ever unreveal'd."

At least, even here, my hand would tremble to write it.'

Annabella Milbanke was still his correspondent, but although he replied (often at length) to her letters, she occupied little space in his thoughts, which were centred on Lady Frances, with whom he was in touch, and Augusta. On 25th November he wrote to Lady Melbourne, hinting of the possibility of a duel with 'Bold' Webster. If he were killed, he wrote, 'C[aroline] would go wild with *grief* that *it did not happen about her.* Ly O[xford] would say I deserved it for not coming to Cagliari—and—poor—[Augusta] she would be really uncomfortable. Do you know I am much afraid that that perverse passion was my deepest after all . . .' Some days before the publication of *The Bride of Abydos*, on 2nd December, Byron had Murray send an advance copy to Augusta. They were corresponding frequently: on 24th November Byron noted in his journal: 'I am tremendously in arrear with my

letters—except to —, and to her my thoughts overpower me.'
On 29th November Augusta posted to Byron a curl of her hair
tied with white silk and enclosed in a sheet of paper on which
she wrote her signature—'Augusta'. With the lock of hair
was the message:

> Partager tous vos sentimens
> ne voir que par vos yeux
> n'agir que par vos conseils, ne
> vivre que pour vous, voila mes
> vouex, mes projets, & le seul
> destin qui peut me rendre
> heureuse.

On the outside of the packet Byron wrote the words—and his
scrawl contrasts strikingly with Augusta's neat, firm handwriting:

> La Chevelure of
> the *one* whom I
> most loved +

How autobiographical he regarded *The Bride of Abydos* is
revealed by some remarks in a letter to Lady Melbourne on
25th November. He told her that some friends had liked it;
'the public is another question, but it will for some *reasons*
interest you more than anybody. Those I leave you to discover . . .
you know me better than most people, and are the only
person who can trace, and I want to see whether you think
my *writings* are *me* or not . . .' And to underline the point,
he added a postscript: 'When I speak of this *tale* and the
author, I merely mean *feelings* . . . This no one but *you* can tell.'
Lady Frances had by the beginning of December faded from
his mind, which was now wholly taken up by thoughts of
Augusta. Try as he might, he could not overcome the desire
for her presence; his letters to Lady Melbourne tailed off; he
knew too well what she thought, and he lacked the resolution
to heed her warnings. He reported his malaise in his journal:
'I take up books, and fling them down again. I began a
comedy, and burnt it because the scene ran into *reality*;—a
novel for the same reason. In rhyme I can keep away from

99

facts; but the thought always runs through, through . . . yes, yes, through.'

In his letters to Augusta at this period Byron communicated something of his distress of mind and his indecision. Her feelings also had swung right round; she was now drawn instinctively, compulsively towards Byron. In the second week in December he had declared his intention to visit her, but characteristically procrastinated. In his journal he wrote: 'I am too lazy to shoot myself—and it would annoy Augusta . . .' Finally on 15th December Augusta could tolerate the strain no longer, and she arrived in London. In his journal the entries for 14th, 15th, 16th December were simply two sentences: 'Much done, but nothing to record. It is quite enough to set down my thoughts—my actions will rarely bear introspection.' After the entry for the 18th he put down his journal, and he did not take it up again for nearly a month. To relieve the pressure on his mind he began *The Corsair*, which was even more self-revealing and passionate than the earlier poems. He took for his motto Tasso's words from *Jerusalem Delivered*: '*I suoi pensieri in lui dormir non ponno*'—'Within him his thoughts cannot sleep'. Writing late into the night, after seeing Augusta home, he poured out those impassioned verses, in this way coming to grips with thoughts and feelings which were otherwise unmanageable. There was a truth here not even attained in his correspondence with Lady Melbourne. On 22nd December, taking the unfinished manuscript with him, he accompanied Augusta back to Six Mile Bottom. They had entered on a new stage in their relationship; Byron had reluctantly to admit that he was unable to live without her.

He returned to London on 27th December with the first draft completed, written at a rate of almost two hundred lines a day. To Dante's quotation, with which he prefixed the second canto, '*Conoscete i dubbiosi desiri?*', he had answered:

> There is a war, a chaos of the mind,
> When all its elements convulsed, combined,
> Lie dark and jarring with perturbed force . . .

and he had found a solution in the imagined actions of his hero Conrad in the beloved Greek Archipelago—there where

O'er the glad waters of the dark blue sea,
Our thoughts as boundless, and our souls as free . . .

And to the present problem of his relation with Augusta he
had likewise found a solution—in its complete acceptance.

While he was staying with Augusta it had been decided
that they should visit Newstead together, which Augusta had
still not seen; but only after Byron had prepared *The Corsair*
for the publishers. Besides Annabella Milbanke and Lady
Frances Webster, Byron had now another correspondent, his
old childhood flame Mary Chaworth-Musters, who wrote to
him of her unhappy marriage and her desire for them to
meet. Byron informed Augusta of having received another of
her *larmoyante* letters: '*all friendship*—and really very simple
and pathetic—*bad usage*—*paleness*—*ill health*—*old friendship*—
once—*good motive*—virtue—and so forth . . .' Byron used Mary
Chaworth as a pretext to veil from Lady Melbourne where his
feelings truly lay, when he took up again his correspondence
with her on 8th January—'I have had too much in my head
to write'—but this sophisticated old lady early saw through
his subterfuge. In a long letter to her on the 11th he explained
why he did not wish to see Mary: 'The kind of feeling which
has lately absorbed me has a mixture of the terrible, which
renders all other, even passion (pour les autres) insipid to a
degree; in short, one of its effects has been like the habit of
Mithridates, who by using himself gradually to poison of the
strongest kind, at last rendered all others ineffectual when he
sought them as a remedy for all evils, and a release from
existence.' At the close of the letter he anticipated Lady
Melbourne's wishing to withdraw from their correspondence
—'We shall perhaps not correspond much longer . . .' Two
days later he wrote again, to justify Augusta, on whom Lady
Melbourne looked as the prime mover in the matter—'Pray
do not speak harshly of her to me—the cause of all.'

In mid-January Augusta arrived in London, and on the
17th the couple set out for Newstead in his enormous coach
('like a 74'), although heavy snows had almost blocked the
Great North Road. Once in front of the cheerful fires in the
Abbey, sequestered from all the world by the fall of snow
which weighed down the trees of the park and rendered the

roads impassable save occasionally for the mails, which were carried on horseback from Nottingham, Byron and Augusta settled in for a delightful three weeks together on what was, to all intents, their honeymoon. On 29th January, at the end of a long letter, as if as an afterthought, he informed Lady Melbourne from his present comfortable position that Augusta was there, 'which renders it much more pleasant, as we never yawn or disagree; and laugh much more than is suitable to so solid a mansion; and the family shyness makes us more amusing companions to each other than we could be to any one else.' In his contentment he only put pen to paper to write letters; to Hanson he explained: 'Our coals are excellent, our fire-places large, my cellar full, and my head empty; and I have not yet recovered my joy at leaving London.' In fact, both of them had seldom experienced such a period of un-interrupted happiness; let Lady Melbourne chafe and warn of dangers or George Leigh complain of worries and un-justified neglect; here, alone and safe from outside disturbance while the snow still lay thick on woods and lakes, they were aware only of the fascination and the pleasure of each other's undivided company. On 1st February Byron wrote to Hanson: 'Mrs. L. is with me, and being in the family way renders it doubly necessary to remain till the roads are quite safe.' It was not until the 6th that they left the Abbey, by which time Byron had heard from Murray of the phenomenal success of *The Corsair*—on the day of publication ('a thing perfectly unprecedented') ten thousand copies had been sold. By the end of the month Murray had disposed of twenty-five thousand copies.

When Augusta had returned to Six Mile Bottom, Byron, back in London, experienced the full blast of Tory disapproval at the 'Lines to a Lady Weeping' which had been published in the volume of *The Corsair*. The verses attacking the volte-face of the Prince Regent had appeared anonymously some time earlier; now that it was known that Byron was the author, *The Courier* and the *Morning Post* kept up their political attacks on him daily for over a fortnight. Byron refused to allow Murray to withdraw the lines—'I have that within me, that bounds against opposition.' His mind was, as so often, in a turmoil, not (as his friends thought) by reason of the attacks of the press. On the 11th he wrote to Lady Melbourne: 'But all these externals are nothing to *that within*, on a subject to which I have not alluded.' It was Augusta who was troubling him; he realised now more surely than he would admit to any of his correspondents that the 'perverse passion' was the strongest with him; that he felt he could not live without Augusta. But how was it possible to live with her? His friends found him 'much out of spirits', yet only Lady Melbourne knew his secret; although Caroline Lamb suspected something was in the air, she was unable to discover in what direction his feelings turned. On 18th February he took up his journal again, to comment on his low mood: 'I wonder if I am or not [out of spirits]? I have certainly enough of "that perilous stuff which weighs upon the heart", and it is better they should believe it to be the result of these attacks than of the real cause; but—ay, ay, always *but*, so the end of the chapter.'

In reply to Lady Melbourne's suggestion that Augusta had forbidden him to visit Melbourne House, Byron wrote on 21st February: 'I am not "forbidden" by [her], though it is very odd that like everyone she seemed more assured (and not very well pleased) of your influence than any other; but I suppose, being pretty certain of her own power—always said, "Do as you please, and go where you like"—and I really know no reason for my not having been where I ought, unless it was to punish myself—or—I really do not know why exactly. You will easily suppose that, twined as she is round my heart in every possible manner, dearest and deepest in my hope and my memory, still I am not easy . . . In short I cannot write about it. Still I have not lost all self-command. For instance I could at this moment be where I have been, where I would rather be than anywhere else, and yet from some motive or other—but certainly not indifference—I am here and here I will remain; but it cost me some struggles. It is the misery of my situation, to see it as you see it, and to *feel* it as I feel it, on *her* account . . . But I will drop ye subject.'

Throughout February and March he sought some relief from despair in the social life which London offered, but often he refused invitations and spent the evenings alone. He foresaw only too clearly that his continued relation with Augusta would bring down ruin on her whom he loved most. He must find himself a wife—marriage was the only solution; for he understood with that realism which never left him that he could not live without feminine company: 'There is something to me very softening in the presence of a woman, some strange influence . . . which I cannot account for, having no high opinion of the sex . . .' He thought for a moment of Lady Charlotte Leveson-Gower, Lady Stafford's daughter, who had something of the 'shyness of the antelope' about her; but she was a relation of the Carlisles, and although Augusta had tried to persuade him to make up his quarrel with Lord Carlisle, he could not bring himself to do so. And yet, he reflected: 'I have refused *every* body else, but I can't deny her any thing . . .' Everyone for the last two years had been trying 'to accommodate this *couplet* quarrel, to no purpose. I shall laugh if Augusta succeeds.'

Augusta was expecting her confinement in April. In her difficulties with her husband and family, she carried about with her the tenderest memories of her Newstead visit and her devotion and love for Byron. As her time approached, she longed to see him again; and finding George Leigh had proposed a visit to Yorkshire at the beginning of April, she wrote to Byron inviting him to Six Mile Bottom. He had just moved into his new quarters at the Albany on 28th March, but leaving his furnishing incomplete, he drove to Newmarket on 2nd April. Augusta was delighted; and Byron had not the heart or mind to drag himself away to meet Hobhouse in Cambridge on the 5th, as he had planned; instead he returned directly to the Albany on 7th April. On 15th April, 1814, Augusta gave birth to a daughter, Elizabeth Medora (named after one of the heroines of *The Corsair*), who was christened at Six Mile Bottom on 20th May, when the Duchess of Rutland, Mrs Wilmot and Byron stood as sponsors.

Annabella Milbanke wrote to Byron about this time tentatively proposing that he visit her family at Seaham on the Durham coast; but, before replying, Byron asked for the approval of '*la tante*', as he called Lady Melbourne, whose permission (he thought) might well be withheld. It was not. However, on 24th April she wrote to him, in learning of the

104

birth of Augusta's child, asking whether his passion and the dangers attendant on it were worth while. Byron replied: 'Oh! but it is "worth while", I can't tell you why, and it is *not* an "*Ape*", and if it is, that must be my fault; however, I will positively reform. You must however allow that it is utterly impossible I can ever be half so well liked elsewhere, and I have been all my life trying to make someone love me, and never got the sort that I preferred before. But positively she and I will grow good and all that, and so we are *now* and shall be these three weeks and more too.' This reference to the mediaeval belief that the child of incest would be an ape cannot be regarded equivocally as proof that Byron admitted his paternity; there was also a belief at that time that any strong influence on the mother before birth would affect the child. It may have been this influence which Byron confessed to—'that must be my fault.'

Byron was quite irresolute whether to accept Annabella's invitation. In his correspondence henceforth with Lady Melbourne he would refer to Annabella as 'your A' and to Augusta as 'my A'. On 30th April he repelled strongly Lady Melbourne's attack on 'my A': 'As for *your* A', I don't know what to make of her. I enclose her last but one, and *my* A's last but one, from which you may form your own conclusions on both. I think you will allow mine to be a very extraordinary person in point of *talent*, but I won't say more . . .' But he could not let the matter rest: 'As for my A, my feelings towards her are a mixture of good and diabolical. I hardly know one passion which has not some share in them, but I won't run into the subject.' He concluded the letter with a confession of his undiscriminating dependence on women—'my heart always alights on the nearest *perch* . . .'

The following day he alluded again to Augusta's qualities: '*She* surely is very clever, and not only so but in some things of good judgement: her expressions about A[nnabell]a are exactly your *own*, and these most certainly without being aware of the coincidence—and excepting our one *tremendous* fault, I know her to be in point of temper and goodness of heart almost unequalled; now grant me this, that she is in truth a very *loveable* woman and I will try and not love her any longer. If you don't believe me, ask those who know her *better* . . . It is

indeed a very *triste* and extraordinary business, and what is
to become of us I know not, and I won't think just now . . .
Did you observe that she says, "*if* la tante approved she
should"? She is little aware how much "la tante" has to
*dis*approve . . .' In a second P.S. he added: 'It, indeed, puzzles
me to account for [Augusta]: it is true she married a fool,
but she *would* have him . . . As for me, brought up as I was,
and sent into the world as I was, both physically and morally,
nothing better could be expected, and it is odd that I always
had a foreboding and I remember when a child reading the
Roman history about a *marriage* I will tell you of when we
meet, asking ma mère why I should not marry X [his symbol
for Augusta].'

On 4th May Byron wrote to Moore enclosing some verses
to be set to music—'which cost me something more than
trouble'. In these impassioned lines he pours out, with un-
believable boldness and defiance, the tortured profundity of
his love for Augusta:

I speak not, I trace not, I breathe not thy name,
There is grief in the sound, there is guilt in the fame:
But the fear which now burns on my cheek may impart
The deep thoughts that dwell in that silence of heart.
Too brief for our passion, too long for our peace,
Were those hours—can their joy or their bitterness cease?
We repent, we abjure, we will break from our chain,—
We will part, we will fly to—unite it again!
Oh! thine be the gladness, and mine be the guilt!
Forgive me, adored one!—forsake, if thou wilt;—
But the heart which is thine shall expire undebased,
And *man* shall not break it—whatever *thou* mayst.
And stern to the haughty, but humble to thee,
This soul, in its bitterest blackness, shall be;
And our days seen as swift, and our moments more sweet,
With thee by my side, than with worlds at our feet,
One sigh of thy sorrow, one look of thy love,
Shall turn me or fix, shall reward or reprove;
And the heartless may wonder at all I resign—
Thy lip shall reply, not to them, but to *mine*.

It was at this time, in early May, that, Claughton having

belatedly paid part of the principal for Newstead, Byron sent Augusta £3000, ostensibly as a loan to pay off some of the Colonel's debts, but in reality as a gift to her. 'I have money at Hoare's, and more coming in soon, so don't mind me. You can't be off this sum now, and I heartily hope that it may be useful and adequate to the occasion. Now, don't "affront" me by any more scruples.' And on the 14th, his mind full of Augusta, Byron began *Lara*, the sequel to *The Corsair*, a poem in which Conrad (now Lara) returns to his feudal home for the first time since boyhood, accompanied by the beautiful Gulnare in the disguise of the page Kaled. The opening lines, which he later suppressed, betrayed the bent of his thoughts:

When she is gone—the loved, the lost—the one
Whose smile had gladdened though perchance undone—
Whose name too deeply cherished to impart
Dies on the lip but trembles in the heart—
Where sudden mention can almost convulse
And lightens through the ungovernable pulse . . .
Let none complain how faithless and how brief
The brain's remembrance, or the bosom's grief—
Or e'er they thus forbid us to forget,
Let Mercy strip the memory of regret,—
Yet selfish still, we would not be forgot—
What lip dare say, "my Love, remember not,"—
Oh best and dearest, thou whose thrilling name
My heart adores too deeply to proclaim . . .

Following the peace of Paris and Napoleon's exile to Elba, Byron, whose earlier sympathies were undisguisedly favourable to the deposed Emperor, joined in the festivities and revelry which occupied war-weary London in this 'summer of the sovereigns'. Later he wrote to Murray: 'I wrote while undressing after coming home from balls and masquerades, in the year of revelry 1814.' He had made a half-hearted attempt to interest himself again in Lady Adelaide Forbes, using Tom Moore as an intermediary. Lady Caroline Lamb had reappeared on the London scene, and he was soon wearily informing Lady Melbourne of Caroline's complaints of his 'barbarous usage' of her and of his 'immediate marriage' (as arranged by Lady Caroline) to Lady Adelaide. But it may have been that Caroline knew more than he suspected; for she wrote him a note early in June: 'I go to the 'squerade—shall you—tell your sister to try & not dislike me. I am very unworthy of her I know it & feel it but as I may not love you nor see you, let her not judge me harshly—let her not pass me by as Lady Gertrude Stanley does, & Lady Rancliffe. Tell her I feel my faults my crime sooner—but try & make her forgive me, if you can, for I love that Augusta with my heart because she is yours and is dear to you.' Hobhouse, too, a few weeks earlier had, after seeing Byron, written in his diary: 'Today I discover a frightful sign of what I yet know not'; and three days later, walking home with Douglas Kinnaird (another of Byron's intimate friends) after a performance of the actor Kean's, they 'made mutual confessions of frightful suspicions'. Tongues were thus already beginning to wag—and among them Byron's own.

About this period (or a little later) in spite of his protestations to Lady Melbourne of his continuing refusal to see Caroline, which this wise old woman mistrusted (he had assured her of their 'mutual decorum'—'villainous mutualities' she substituted), Caroline had worked on the tender side of his ambivalent nature. It seems that there was a meeting at the Albany, where Caroline kept intruding at all hours. Her own account, given later to Medwin, may have had a basis of truth—she also two years afterwards gave a more detailed description of the event to Annabella. To Medwin she wrote: 'As he pressed his lips on mine (it was at the Albany) he said, "Poor Caro, if everyone hates me, you, I see will never change" . . . & I said, "Yes, I *am* changed, & shall come near you no more."—For then he showed me letters, & told me things I cannot repeat, & all my attachment went. This was our last parting scene.' But Caroline was not one to forget Byron or to cease to pester him, and her persistence nearly caused him to take the very action that Lady Melbourne had so long feared.

On 10th June Byron wrote to his loyal confidante about his relations with Augusta and Caroline: "All you say is exceeding true; but who ever said, or supposed that you were not shocked, and all that? You *have* done everything in your power; and more than any other person breathing would

108

have done for *me*, to make me act rationally . . . I am as mad as C. on a different topic, and in a different way; for I never break out in scenes, but am not a whit more in my senses. I will, however, not persuade *her* into any *fugitive* piece of absurdity, but more I cannot promise. I love no one else . . .'
On the 26th his fury with Caroline's indiscretions burst out afresh: 'She may hunt me down—it is the power of any mad or bad woman to do so by any man . . . torment me she may; how am I to bar myself from her! I am already almost a prisoner; she has no shame, no feeling, no one estimable or redeemable quality.

'These are strong words, but I know what I am writing; they will avail nothing but to convince you of my determination. My first object in such a dilemma would be to take [Augusta] with me; that might fail, so much the better, but even if it did—I would lose a hundred souls rather than be bound to C . . .'

Two days after the splendid masquerade given by Watier's Club on 1st July in honour of the Duke of Wellington, which Byron attended in the habit of a monk, he left London for Six Mile Bottom and Cambridge. He had not seen Augusta since a week before the birth of Medora, and he spent a happy three days in her company before he left to meet Scrope Davies, Hobhouse and Kinnaird in Cambridge. From there he returned to London, determined to bring the Newstead business to a conclusion with the defaulting Claughton. While at Newmarket he had obtained Augusta's consent to accompany him, with her children, to the sea at Hastings, and on his return to London he settled to take Hastings House, which was recommended by a friend on the ground of its 'retirement and picturesqueness', for a month from 13th July. Augusta then came to London with the children and put up at an hotel in Albemarle Street, but delays over the settlement with Claughton kept them in town until the 20th. On the day before they left Annabella Milbanke persuaded her father to write, inviting Byron to Seaham.

The sea acted as a tonic on Byron's fevered spirits; besides Augusta and the children he had the congenial company of Hodgson, his Cambridge friend, and his cousin George Anson Byron. The summer days passed pleasantly, as Byron reported to Moore: 'I have been swimming and eating turbot, and smuggling neat brandies and silk handkerchiefs,—and listening to my friend Hodgson's raptures about a pretty wife-elect of his,—and walking on cliffs, and tumbling down hills and making the most of the *dolce far-niente* for the last fortnight.' For Augusta it was as if they had set up house together, but she was aware that this shared happiness could not last. They both realised that there was but one conclusion—that Byron should find a wife; and Augusta set out to sound her favourite candidate, Lady Charlotte Leveson-Gower, whom she considered a more suitable companion for him than the austere blue-stocking Annabella. While they were at Hastings, Byron's correspondence with Lady Melbourne entirely ceased; she would not have approved his being together with Augusta. Later he told her how Augusta had persuaded him to marry, 'because it was the only chance of redemption for *two* persons'. But as the summer days drifted away and nothing had been decided, Byron became increasingly restive and moody. 'I am in some respects', he confided to Moore, 'happy, but not in the manner that can or ought to last,—but enough of that.' In a violent fit of anger he flung an ink-pot from his window, to discover the following morning that he had begrimed the petticoat of a statue of Euterpe in the garden. It was time to return to London, where he arrived with Augusta and the children on 11th August.

Four days later he despatched a letter and four brace of grouse as a peace-offering to Lady Melbourne. On the 20th he finally settled with Claughton for an indemnity of £25,000, and the Abbey returned to his possession. The following day he set off for Newstead, accompanied by Augusta and her family. Annabella was still writing him long, wearisome letters to which he dutifully replied. Once settled in the Abbey with Augusta he was contented enough with idleness—reading, fishing and swimming in the lake, they savoured together the simple pleasures of an idyllic summer. As for future plans, these were, Augusta reported, in a 'state of glorious uncertainty'. To Annabella's questions about himself Byron responded tersely: occupation, 'nothing'; plans, 'I have none'; health, 'very well'. Augusta was pursuing his suit with the 'shy antelope', Lady Charlotte Leveson-Gower, whose frequent epistles were full of 'sentences which were *not* to be answered, or if answered, replied to in a *particular* manner, Ec., with a hundred little things' which persuaded Augusta that a match was in the offing. Then suddenly in the second week of September with a scurry of fright the antelope was off into the undergrowth; she wrote 'full of alarms' concerning 'some family scheme . . . of a compact elsewhere'; she had been 'so foolish', the young man referred was on the point of arriving— 'what was she to do?' Writing to Lady Melbourne, Byron said that 'the little girl had no will of her own, and might not be aware of what she was doing'; he 'made X write a kind but satisfactory answer, taking it *all* on herself, and getting the other out of it completely.' Later in the same year the girl married Henry Charles Howard, afterwards the Earl of Surrey and in 1842 the 13th Duke of Norfolk. On receiving this confused withdrawal, Byron turned to Augusta: 'You see that, after all, Miss Milbanke is to be the person—I will write to her.' Augusta tried to dissuade him, remarking that Annabella had not the qualities to make him a satisfactory wife; but she took the letter, when he had finished, and reading it through, observed: 'Well, really, this is a very pretty letter;— it is a pity it should not go. I never read a prettier one.' 'Then it *shall* go', Byron replied; and the letter was despatched from Mansfield on 10th September.

Byron's proposal (for Annabella took it as a proposal, though it was rather a tentative feeler to discover how a proposal would be received) was no very ardent effusion of feelings; it was a very guarded epistle and, strangely for Byron, wordy. Once it had gone, he was characteristically a prey to regrets and second thoughts. Newstead would have to be sold— if Annabella accepted—to provide for the marriage settlement, and Newstead had never appeared so romantic and delightful— so desirable—as in these early autumn days, with the sun catching the first of the turning leaves in the park, and the lakes so placidly reflecting the changing clouds. The mood of the place was elegiac, and it was with sadness that Byron contemplated the rupture that must come with Augusta, the break in two lives which each passing day proved so admirably suited for the sympathy, comfort and happiness of the other. Nothing broke the outward calm, but within Byron was restless, ill at ease. On the 13th he seized on the hopeful prospect of a refusal, and wrote off to Hobhouse: 'If a circumstance (which may happen but is as unlikely to happen as Johanna Southcote establishing herself as the real Mrs Trinity) does not occur—I have thoughts of going direct and directly to Italy—if so, will you come with me?'

On Sunday, 18th September, Byron and Augusta were sitting at dinner with their sole guest, the local apothecary, when a gardener brought in and handed him his mother's wedding ring, which she had lost many years before and which he had just found in digging the garden beneath her bedroom window. At the same moment the post arrived, and seeing Annabella's letter Byron remarked, 'If it contains a consent, I will be married with this ring.' As Byron opened the letter, his face turned so ghastly pale that Augusta feared that he was going to faint. 'It never rains but it pours', he said, handing her the letter with Annabella's acceptance. She had sent him two letters, one addressed to the Albany, and there was a further letter from Sir Ralph. Augusta thought her letter 'was the best and prettiest she ever read'. The choice was made; Byron's comment was: 'The stars, I presume, did it.' The loyal Augusta could but look on—and hope. But what would *la tante* think of Annabella's acceptance? He wrote, enquiring, 'May I hope for your consent, too? . . . In course I mean to reform most thoroughly, and become "a good man and true" in all the various senses of these respective and respectable appellations.'

Augusta urged Byron to set out for Seaham at once, but he preferred to put off that journey. It was with a melancholy foreboding that he and Augusta took their last walks together through the Abbey rooms, in the great park and by the lakes. The beauty of the place filled them with infinite sadness; to part with so much, in exchange for a future so vague and uncertain. In the 'Devil's Wood' behind the Abbey, where 'the Wicked Lord' had placed his statues of leering satyrs, they carved their names on an elm-tree bole and the date, 20th September, 1814. The next day they set out, Augusta for Six Mile Bottom, from which she had been away almost three months, and Byron for London.

VII
The Byron Marriage
1814-1815

AUGUSTA, HOME again at Six Mile Bottom after so long an absence from the daily cares of the household and the petty personal concerns of her exigent husband (although it must be said that George Leigh had put no obstacle in the way of her being with Byron—doubtless with a mind to its pecuniary advantages), and once more in the domestic routine, had time to take stock of Byron's position and of her own. No one was less demanding than Augusta; there was little of possessiveness in her love for Byron. She looked above all for his happiness; but she knew him too well not to have doubts as to the wisdom of his choice of Annabella. Augusta could admire the intellectual and moral superiority of the girl whose letters to Byron she had read; yet she sensed, with an intuition which was characteristic of her, that Annabella was in love (if she was in love at all) with a Byron of her own imagination, with an innocently idealised portrait of the public figure of the poetic lord, so wayward but still so worthy of her redemption—a personage who bore little resemblance to the reality of the 'Baby' Byron whom she, Augusta, understood in the most capricious of his many moods and, understanding, adored. However, it was her nature to be sanguine; marry Byron must—she had no doubts about that; and the choice having been made, Augusta accepted it with her habitual loyalty, which henceforth extended beyond Byron to Byron and Annabella.

Lady Melbourne had given her consent to the engagement of her niece, one effect of which, in her worldly opinion, would be to withdraw Byron from the influence of Augusta, for whom she had a distrust tinged with jealousy. For Byron she had a sincere affection; while admiring his poetic gifts, she enjoyed the frankness and wit of his confidences; from these (in which he only showed part of his chameleon self) she misjudged him, supposing him to share her cynical but realistic attitude to the conventions of a society that formed its moral judgements largely on the maintenance of appearances. She did not realise that Byron, like the renegade hero Alp of *The Siege of Corinth*, on which he was engaged about this time, had elements in him which were at utter variance with that society. Lady Melbourne was also at fault in her judgement of Augusta, whom she hardly knew except through Byron's correspondence. She put the blame on Augusta for the liaison with Byron, seeing in her an astute and unscrupulous woman—although why, of all her acquaintances, she should single out Augusta for her censure on this score is perhaps only to be answered by her concern at the latter's undisputed hold over his strongest feelings. Now, when Byron was delayed in London from setting out for Seaham to visit Annabella and her parents (a delay which was chiefly caused by Hanson's preoccupation with his own family's affairs and his consequent failure to attend to Byron's side of the financial arrangements for his marriage), Lady Melbourne regarded this procrastination as Augusta's doing. To this charge Byron replied, on 4th October: 'X never threw obstacles in the way; on the contrary, she has been more urgent than even you, that I should go to S[eaham] and wished me to set out from N[ewstead] instead of London. She wished me much to marry . . . X has written to A to express how much all my relations are pleased by the event, &c. &c.' Lady Melbourne did not appear to be convinced (or, possibly, appeased) by Byron's protest, and three days later he returned to Augusta's defence: 'X is the least selfish person in the world; you, of course, will never believe that either of us can have any right feeling. I don't deny this as far as regards me, but you don't know what a being she is; her only error has been my fault entirely, and for this I can plead no excuse, except passion, which is none . . .'

Far from hindering Byron in his 'matrimonial scheme' (the cynical phrase is Hobhouse's), Augusta had on 1st October written a charmingly natural and friendly letter to Annabella:

'I am afraid I have no better excuse to offer for this *self-introduction* than that of feeling unable any longer to reconcile myself to the idea of being *quite* a *stranger* to one whom I hope *soon* to call *my Sister*, and one—may I be allowed to add—whom I already love as such. If I could possibly express how deservedly dear my Brother is to me, you might in some degree imagine the joy I have felt in the anticipation of an event which promises to secure his happiness.

'Grateful as I am, I feel that I never can be sufficiently so for the blessing bestowed upon him in the possession of esteem and affection such as yours, for which I justly consider him (as he does himself) the most fortunate of human beings.

'I have been most anxious to write to you for the last fortnight, but delayed it from day to day in the hope that my Brother would be at Seaham to *chaperon* the arrival of my letter & make excuses for the writer who is but too sensible of her inability to express her feelings on this occasion. But, on finding he is still provokingly detained in Town by business, & unable to fix a day for his departure, I have resolved not to wait any longer, and trust entirely to your indulgence for forgiveness.'

Annabella let Byron know that she had heard from his sister—'mine'—and hoped that she had responded appropriately, though she feared she had not; however, she looked 'to the kindness which prompted her to write, for a good-natured opinion of my answer'. Byron took this opportunity to proclaim Augusta's admirable qualities: 'She is the least selfish & gentlest creature in being, & more attached to me than any one in existence can be.' A few days later he answered a question of Annabella's, whether Augusta was shy: 'To excess—she is as I tell her, like a frightened hare with new acquaintances . . .' He refrained from telling Annabella that Colonel Leigh had informed Augusta that 'they were betting away' at Newmarket as to whether they would eventually be married or not.

Although Hanson's delays were the ostensible reason for Byron's not quitting London, he was nevertheless loath to leave, to commit himself to so decided a course of action, about which he was now having disturbing second thoughts—he was 'horribly low-spirited', as he confessed to Lady Melbourne. On his side the correspondence with Annabella flagged; it was perhaps on his insistence (possibly also to re-assure Lady Melbourne of her attitude) that Augusta wrote

115

again to Annabella on 15th October: '. . . the very kind reception you gave my first letter encourages me to hope you will not be less indulgent to my motive in writing again . . . [P]ray think of me as one most desirous to *deserve* your future friendship & affection, & believe me when I assure you that so far from standing in need of any of *my "candid indulgence"* for what you term yr "apparent insensibility", I can most fully appreciate the motives for your *doubts* & *fears* of being able to make my dear Brother happy.

'He writes me word that he hopes *very* soon to see you. It is most provoking that his departure to Seaham should have hitherto met with so many impediments . . .'

Annabella was so touched by the friendly sincerity of Augusta's letters that she invited her to accompany Byron on his Seaham visit; but she had to decline, which she did gracefully, giving the reason that at that moment she was nurse to her baby, governess to her oldest girl and something between both to her two intermediate children. She went on to recall seeing Annabella at Lady Glenbervie's in the summer of 1813, and expressed her disbelief in Annabella's 'indifference' to Byron even at that time: 'This is betraying *all* my partiality, but I am *now* not afraid to let it appear to you. Every-body who knew him a *little* would agree with me in thinking him clever agreeable & good-natured, but to you who will soon love him for qualities much more *love-able*, I may venture to speak as I think. You would not be surprised at my attachment surpassing that of Sisters *in general* if you knew all his kindness to *me* & *mine* . . . I am anxious *too* for his sake & that of the *family shyness* that his first arrival at Seaham should be over. I am sure you will be amused at his having expressed a wish that *I* would endeavour to describe *his* portion of this fatal shyness to you, & a great many other of what he terms the peculiarities of his disposition . . .'

With delicacy Augusta was forewarning Annabella that Byron's was no ordinary character and that he would need understanding and particular handling. On the 25th October he was still dragging his feet in London; the fault was mostly Hanson's, to whom he wrote on that day an angry letter, warning him that if the marriage now came to nothing, he would 'never look upon any one again as my friend, who has even been the innocent cause of destroying my happiness'. But this procrastination was in accordance with his own mixed feelings, and his bad conscience was shown by his having Augusta write to explain his non-appearance at Seaham, where Lord Wentworth, Annabella's maternal uncle, had postponed his departure to await his arrival. She wrote that she had heard from Byron 'in such evident agitation and lowness of spirits' at the dilatoriness of Hanson, but that it was very material that the business over disposing of Newstead should be settled before Byron travelled north. 'At all events I hope it will only convince you more forcibly that he is most anxious you should attribute his prolonged absence to no cause but the true one.' On the following day, 27th October, she wrote again, a long letter to say that she had heard from Byron, 'in better spirits', that Hanson was moving at last. She expressed her sorrow that Newstead would have to be sold, and then went on to speak of Byron's 'more love-able' qualities 'which *we have agreed* in thinking him possessed of'. Augusta concluded: 'I only want to hear that *B* is with you to be a very happy person.'

Finally on Saturday, 29th October, Byron left London, but instead of proceeding directly to County Durham he made for Six Mile Bottom, where he arrived in the evening. From his conversation and general air of dejection Augusta gathered how much in two minds he was whether to persevere in his 'matrimonial scheme'. She, however, was zealous in persuading him that it was the right and proper—indeed, the only—course; and Byron, always ready to acquiesce when Augusta felt strongly, took himself off late on Sunday and, 'proceeding very slowly' (as he admitted to Lady Melbourne), reached the Haycock Inn at Wansford that evening. Here he learned that recent visitors had been Lady Rosebery, eloping with her brother-in-law, Sir Henry Mildmay; in his unsettled state of mind he rather wished that he, too, had taken his courage in both hands and gone off with Augusta. Nevertheless he continued on his way, arriving at Seaham on Wednesday, 2nd November, and remained there for a fortnight, writing only once to Augusta in that period. She expressed her disquiet in a letter to Francis Hodgson: 'I have not heard from him for some time, and am uneasy about it; but it is very selfish to be so, for I know he is happy, and what more can I wish.'

117

If she had known the true state of affairs at Seaham, she would have had just cause for concern. What he kept from Augusta he confided to Lady Melbourne in a letter on 13th November: 'Do you know I have grave doubts if this will be a marriage now? Her disposition is the very reverse of our imaginings. She is overrun with fine feelings, scruples about herself and her disposition (I suppose, in fact, she means mine), and to crown all, is taken ill once every three days with I know not what . . . A few days ago she made one *scene*, not altogether out of C[aroline]'s style; it was too long and too trifling, in fact, to transcribe, but it did me no good . . . In short, it is impossible to foresee how this will end *now*, any more than two years ago; if there is a break, it shall be her doing not mine . . .' Byron, to cut short the endless inferences that Annabella drew from his slightest remark, had 'recourse to the eloquence of *action*', which had the effect of temporarily quieting her, but eventually led to exacerbation of her overstrung nerves and latent sexual feelings. Finally she asked him to leave, until they could be married. He departed in very bad humour, and on the journey south resolved to break off the engagement; but, on second thoughts, waited to talk it over with Augusta.

On 19th November he was back at Six Mile Bottom. Augusta had been in correspondence with Annabella and in consequence was not without some inkling that all was not well in that quarter. Annabella now feverishly regretted having sent Byron away and was all propitiation to him: 'Before you pass sentence on me finally, wait to see *me myself*. *Myself* is by no means the grave, didactic, deplorable person that I have appeared to you,' she wrote on 19th November, concluding: 'Remember me as your wife.' If there had been in Augusta any element of jealousy, this was the occasion when it might have prevailed over her disinterested, unselfish pursuit of what she conceived to be both Byron's and Anabella's welfare. She was the latter's staunchest advocate, and she was successful in shoring up Byron's wavering purpose. His letter in reply to Annabella on 20th November was so lacking in lover's fervour that it is possible that Augusta protested, for he added a postscript: 'I don't ask you to consider this as a letter, but merely a memorandum that I am thinking of you now—& loving you ever—my wife.' We feel that it was more Augusta's warm-hearted advocacy than Annabella's tortured, involuted letters that brought about the change in feeling which allowed him to write two days later from Cambridge, where he had gone to support his friend Dr Clarke's candidature for a professorship: 'Don't scold *yourself* any more. I told you before there was no occasion—you have not offended me. I am as happy as Hope can make me, and as gay as Love will allow me to be till we meet and ever my Heart—thine, B.' The following day Hodgson wrote an enthusiastic report to Augusta and to Annabella, telling them that the undergraduates had cheered Byron from the gallery of the Senate House, although applause had been specifically forbidden.

On 24th November Byron, accompanied by Hobhouse, returned from Cambridge to London, where he settled in once more at the Albany and took up again with some relish the pursuits of bachelor life which he was so reluctant to relinquish. His financial affairs were desperate: with £30,000 of debts, ready money was short, and Hanson, deeply involved with the attempts to 'lunatize' his son-in-law, Lord Portsmouth, was neglectful of Byron's affairs. The latter, who was settling £60,000 on Annabella, had re-opened negotiations with Claughton for the sale of Newstead, but it was soon clear that he would be unable to complete the purchase. Annabella, in the meanwhile, was writing affectionately to Augusta, who replied to a letter on 12th December: '. . . B does not tell me when he goes. You have of course heard that Mr. Claughton's proposals were inadmissable about poor dear Newstead, which may have detained him longer than he intended . . . I am delighted with your account of B.'s *conquests*, but above all it does my heart good to read what *you* think of him. From living so little in *the great world*, I have seen but few of his *intimate* friends. You know how those that are not that *may* mistake his character, & it has been my fate *often* when speaking of him & feeling quite animated by the subject to witness looks of surprise & compassion in my Listeners—as if to say, "Poor Thing! it is natural *she* should think him all perfection"— & you may imagine the happiness after this of communicating with one who loves him quite in my own way, & after my own heart . . .'

Byron, seeing that no money was forthcoming in the foreseeable future, at this stage offered to postpone the wedding: 'Will you wait? Perhaps the clouds may disperse in a month or two. Do as you please . . .' Annabella replied on 16th December: 'Dearest—Let us marry when the writings are done, and we will disperse the "clouds".' On the same day as Annabella was penning this, which in Byron's present mood appeared in the nature of a death warrant, he received a cheerful and (as usual) hurriedly written note from Augusta, so characteristically spontaneous as to point unequivocally the contrast between the two women,

'My dearest B +
'As usual I have but a short allowance of time to reply to your tendresses + but a few lines I know will be better than none—at least I find them so + It was very + very + good of you to think of me amidst all the visitors &c.&c. I have scarcely recovered [from] *mine* of yesterday. La Dame did talk so, oh my stars! but at least it saved me a world of trouble. Oh, but she found out a likeness in your picture to Mignonne [Medora] who is of course very good humoured in consequence + I want to know Dearest B + your plans—when you come + when you go—umph! when the writings travel, when ye Cake is to be cut, when the Bells are to ring, &c.&c.&c. By the bye, my visitors are acquainted with *A* & did praise her to the skies. They say her health has been hurt by studying &c. &c.&c.
'I have not a moment more my dearest + except to say
ever thine.'

And she signed with the flourish of swirls used by them both in their letters to each other.

It was not until Christmas Eve that Byron, furnished with a special licence from the Archbishop of Canterbury, and in company with Hobhouse, who was to act as his best man, could drag himself away from London. Hobhouse noted in his journal: 'I rode up to London, and at twelve set off with Lord Byron on his matrimonial scheme. At Chesterford we parted, he for Six Mile Bottom, and I for Cambridge.' Faced apparently with the inevitable, Byron could not forgo a final glimpse of Augusta. It was a dismal house-party; the Colonel was at home (which was a restraint on Byron) and, which was worse, he was suffering from a cold and cough that demanded Augusta's constant attention. On Christmas Day it was freezing without, so that Byron and Augusta were house-bound with the children and her peevishly irritable husband. To Augusta's experienced eye it was clear that Byron was more unsure than ever of the step he was about to take, and it needed all her persuasion to convince him to go through with the marriage. On Boxing Day, in a mood of deepest melancholy he left Augusta and drove to Cambridge, where he met Hobhouse at three, and continued that evening as far as Wansford. Hobhouse noted that 'never was lover less in haste'. The following day he reported in his journal that Byron 'owned that he felt considerable repugnance in marrying before his pecuniary affairs were arranged', that he was not in love with Annabella, and that he had wished at least to postpone the marriage, but that she had overruled him. 'The bridegroom more and more *less* impatient', he entered that night, and the following evening he reported that his friend's feelings towards Annabella had sunk to 'indifference, almost aversion'.

The Byron wedding took place in the drawing-room at Seaham at eleven o'clock in the morning of Monday, 2nd January, 1815; at midday Hobhouse handed Lady Byron into the carriage and the couple, accompanied by their servants, left on the bitterly cold drive to Sir Ralph Milbanke's house at Halnaby in Yorkshire, where they were to spend their honeymoon. As they passed through Durham the church bells rang out in their honour, to Byron's fury.

In the interval of a week which elapsed from Byron's departure from Six Mile Bottom until his wedding day Augusta needed all the reserves of her buoyant nature to resist the foreboding that assailed her. She wrote both to Byron and Annabella letters which reached Halnaby on the morning after their night arrival, and in the days which followed her frequent letters sought to alleviate the misgivings in her own mind as well as to give Annabella practical hints on handling the difficulties that she imagined she would be experiencing as a newly-married wife with a difficult husband. 'Dearest, first & best of human beings,' she began a letter to Byron in which she described the turmoil of her emotions at the hour of the ceremony, 'as the sea trembles when the earth quakes'—an expression which Byron found poetical. To Annabella she tried to give advice in dealing with Byron's 'black moods': 'I have no *doubts* of YOUR success AGAINST *Magician* (this is quite a *Newmarket* phrase excuse it)—how happy I shall be if I am right! . . . I wrote you some very imperfect congratulations on Monday, & am not a little impatient to receive the next account from Seaham which will *confirm* you my Sister . . . I never can express how much I wish you & my dearest B—all possible happiness . . . God bless you my dear *Annabella*. I have set the example, & beg for the future to be your most affecte *Augusta*.' Byron was too lazy to reply, but on 4th January Annabella wrote, inviting Augusta to join them at Halnaby. Augusta declined on the 9th, beginning her charming, sisterly letter 'My dearest Annabella': 'Your letter my dear Sister makes me both glad & sorry. The latter sensation is the consequence of not being able to *set out immediately* as my inclination would lead me to do, to see you & *our* B. I wish the distance was not so formidable in short I wish a great deal—& am in very bad humour when I reflect upon all the difficulties in my way, & which I fear are *unsurmountable* . . . I am amusing myself with ye thoughts of what B's countenance must have expressed during ye continuance of ye DURHAM PEAL. I am going to *scold* him so Adieu My dear Sister . . .'

Although Byron's letters at this time to Lady Melbourne and Tom Moore were of the customary cheerful kind ('Bell and I go on extremely well so far . . . .' 'So you want to know about milady and me? But let me not, as Roderick Random says, "profane the chaste mysteries of Hymen"—damn the word, I had nearly spelt it with a small *h*. I like Bell as well as you do (or did, you villain!) Bessy—and that is (or was) saying a great deal . . .'), yet Annabella's frequent letters to Augusta—they corresponded every two or three days—gave hints of Byron's eccentric behaviour, and worse; and these allusions increased, as she gained confidence in detailing them to the older woman. Augusta, on her part, with great subtlety and understanding of the girl whom she had not met, tried to warn her and to guide her in dealing with Byron's 'comical proceedings', the full extent of which she was not to discover until later, but which she guessed at at the time. Byron, his mind perplexed with his present financial difficulties and mistrusting the prospects of any immediate change for the better, found himself trapped into marriage (partly by his own weakness, partly by Annabella's insistence, and partly by Augusta's persuasion) with an intellectual, priggish and spoilt only child, as self-absorbed and egotistical as himself, but without his knowledge of the ways of the world. Moreover, she was entirely lacking in humour and in the normal intuitions of a woman in love. She had set herself the formidable task of 'reforming' Byron, and she maddened him from the beginning by the prim composure with which she went about her self-appointed work, drawing false inferences from his wild, incoherent (often wilfully misleading) remarks and offering patiently to share with him the burden of his 'crimes'. If ever there was incompatibility in marriage it was in the instance of Byron and Annabella; but admirers of Byron would be doing a gross injustice to both Byron and Annabella, if they attempted to absolve him from the cruelty of his behaviour during the honeymoon at Halnaby. His torture of himself and of Annabella became at times a mania.

Augusta, on 11th January, had written to encourage Annabella in confiding in her: 'What a *super-excellent* sister you are! I am only afraid you have adopted B's spoiling system, for you must have discovered that I am thoroughly *his* Enfant Gaté— but I try & *will* try *not* to be spoilt by your very great kindness.

'I think you may guess what will be my reply to your questions . . . oh yes, I will indeed be your "ONLY *friend*", but how can I thank you for considering me so kindly, all unknown as I am except by B's partial report . . . Your letters received this Morng. have been read and I know not how many times, & cannot be too often as they tell me of your happiness & dearest B's. I am more & more convinced of his good fortune *respecting you* & your fixed determination on ye subject of confidence & friendships is particularly adapted to his taste & comfort as far as I can understand both . . . I can easily believe that B. is not "blue-deviled" in his present abode . . . I am quite prepared to laugh with you at the "comical proceedings" of which I have some idea already. I agree with you that *you alone* (or at least such another "DETERMINED" person such as you) would have been proof against them. Thank Heaven! that the present rewards you for those little trials of the past, which none can fully understand who have not experienced similar ones . . .' And a few days later she reverted to these topics: 'I can laugh at this distance even at the continuation of the "comical proceedings"—it is so like him to *try & persuade* people that *he is disagreeable & all that*. Oh dear!'

Byron had been loud in his praises of Augusta to Annabella, causing her some twinges of jealousy, which she determinedly subdued—'Nobody understands me but Augusta'; 'I shall never love anybody as well as her.' Annabella must have reported his praises to Augusta, who replied on 20th January: 'My dear Sis, I wish I deserved half the kindness he feels & expresses towards me. I may think myself most fortunate that he has a Wife who is *not* "affronted" at such declarations as ye one you tell me of . . . No Brother can ever consider me as B. does, & you may imagine better than I can describe how he is loved in return—& his dear Wife who is so indulgent to "Guss" . . .'

Augusta was reassured by Annabella's letters; here was someone who could understand 'Baby' Byron, with 'his "comical ways", "façons de parler" & "grumps".' She could admit to Annabella now that she had once foolishly believed that she might have misunderstood him and that it might have made her unhappy. 'But now I give my fears to the Wind, & I am sure you do right "to laugh away all anxieties" for not even *I* can know him better . . .' It was on this more hopeful note that Augusta heard that the 'treacle-moon' (as Byron expressed it) at Halnaby was over and that they were accepting the Milbanke's invitation—in spite of Byron's desire to go alone to London—to return to Seaham. At the end of the month Augusta could write to Hodgson that her 'beloved B [was] very happy and comfortable'. 'From my own observations on their epistles, and knowledge of B's disposition and ways', she went on, 'I really hope *most* confidently that all will turn out very happily. It appears that Lady B. *sets about* making him happy quite in the right way. It is true that I judge at a distance, and we generally *hope* as we *wish*; but I assure you I don't conclude hastily on this subject, and will own to you, what I would not scarcely to any other person, that I HAD *many fears* and much anxiety founded upon many causes and circumstances of which I cannot *write*. Thank God! that they do not appear likely to be realized . . .'

Lady Melbourne, too, appeared reassured by the tone of

Byron's letters that all was going well, and she wrote to him him on 31st January, giving him the 'singular' opinion of one one of her friends that matrimony was the 'best chance of steadying his mind without weakening his genius'. She could not forgo a little dig at Augusta; accepting for herself the office of being his Corbeau Blanc (a reference to a story by Voltaire), she warned him against his Corbeau Noir, who was to be avoided: 'Remember that although you have no *Corbeau Noir*, actually *noir*, you may have one flying about, with many *black* feathers in her plumage.' Byron immediately rose to Augusta's defence: 'I suppose your "C— noir" is X, but if X were a raven, or a griffin, I must still take omens from her flight. I can't help loving her, though I have quite enough at home to prevent me from loving anyone essentially for some time to come.' In her next letter Lady Melbourne laughingly took Byron up on his peculiar usage of 'essential', and then went on: 'You wrong me about —. On one subject they [sic] are as black, and as hideous as any Phantasm of a distempered brain can imagine. But, that *essential* out of the way, I do not know anyone more fitted for your *Corbeau Blanc*, from cleverness, good-humour, and a thousand agreeable qualities—not forgetting the interest they take in you, and the knowledge they have of you, which renders them more able to manage and advise. Does this satisfy you? Does the end make up for the beginning?'

So established by this time was Annabella's confidence in Augusta that she confided to her gynaecological details and reports of her own sexual desires. At this period one of Augusta's chief worries was the sale of Newstead, which she feared would be regretted later by Byron, but she was well aware how pressing were his debts and that his income, apart from Annabella's seven hundred pounds a year, was virtually nothing. And, knowing Byron so well, she realised that life at Seaham in the bosom of the Milbanke family would soon bore him; she knew, too, that at Halnaby he had already made one frustrated attempt to get away and come south alone. Fearing that he might return without Annabella to Six Mile Bottom, she hinted at the end of January that her husband's absence might allow them both to visit her. On the 26th she wrote to Annabella: 'I am still in a *widowed* state, which makes our habitation one degree more capacious. B. will have described its dimensions and I hoped you would have arrived during the period—whenever you do, I need not say how welcome you will be.' She was trying to find them a 'Castle' near Newmarket, not because her 'hospitality' would be easily or soon tired by such guests, but the truth was that her house was miserably small. On 8th February she wrote: 'I can easily believe all you tell me of the melancholy state of *female hearts* where ever B— makes his appearance. I think I see him behaving VERY PRETTILY— it *is* well indeed! you are not given to Jealousy . . . There is nothing on earth so delightful to me, as to hear of or read praises of him.' And as a postscript she added:

'I am so glad he allows himself to dine—*improvement* the first!

'I am sure you will effect all you wish.

'I shall expect shortly to hear of his *rising with ye Lark*.'

However, the news of all this hopeful progress was rudely disturbed by Annabella's letter of 6th February in which she gave an account of Byron's having been overcome with fumes, when in a rage he threw water on the fire in his dressing-room. Augusta immediately diagnosed the cause of this manifestation of bad temper: 'What could possess B. to put out his Fire? It is astonishing how active the Lords of Creation are in doing *Mischief*. I think you must have been frightened at his *Stupor*. Oh! yes his own account of this exploit would I daresay be comic, but dearest Annabella don't allow him to play the fool any more in this way, & do hide YOUR *Brandy Bottle*—I suspect that he had stolen it again!' She then gave Annabella more excellent advice about dealing with his health and low spirits: 'You must have discovered that his ways of treating it [his health] are not what one could exactly desire—at least they used to fidgit me sadly tho' as I found remonstrances ineffectual I ceased to remonstrate. You must not mind all his ideas about his "predestined" Misfortunes. I must tell you that it is a family failing in ye *Bs* to have uneven spirits. I have even remarked it in a much stronger degree in some of us than in B—and when the *glooms* prevail I too well know the effects . . .' And three days later, on hearing further reports from Annabella, she tried to make light of them, although showing her concern: ' "Alas!" indeed! "Naughty B"! as the children used to say when he affronted them. I am not many degrees removed from a fit of despair at his *untoward* ways.'

With an absence of tact—or rather, out of a frustration tinged with bitterness—during this fit of 'glooms' Byron expressed more than once to Annabella his preference for Augusta, remarks which the former passed on to her. Praising Annabella warmly for the improvements in his health, Augusta replied: 'After being so liberal of my approbation I cannot resist saying that I am also glad poor "Guss" is not quite forgotten—altho' it must be confessed that she is introduced sometimes very mal-à-propos—or rather that she *would* be—to any less indulgent *Rib & Sis* than you are . . .' However, Byron's spirits soon revived, and Annabella had to report outdoor rambles and parlour games. 'Your "ramble-scramble tumble-cum-jumble" ', wrote Augusta, 'must have been delightful & I wish I could have been of the party, to have helped you out of the Bog or stuck there with you . . . Only think! of B playing Drafts! I never should have suspected him of such a thing . . .' Augusta's search for a house near Newmarket proved fruitless, and she had not heard Byron's plans from him—for he would not write. She feared their coming to Six Mile Bottom, and had tried to put them off with the excuse that her Aunt Sophia Byron might descend on her. Byron let Annabella know his desire to visit Augusta alone—her house could at least accommodate him— but she was determined to accompany him, and at length he reluctantly acquiesced. On 9th March they set out from Seaham for Six Mile Bottom, missing Lady Melbourne's letter informing them of her success in leasing for them the Duchess of Devonshire's house at No. 13 Piccadilly. This had been done despite Augusta's sound advice; the annual rental of seven hundred pounds was the equivalent of Annabella's whole income: 'Could not B— content himself with a *small* house in Town. Oh no—I know his *soaring* spirit—but why not—*till* he *could* have a *great* one! Don't you like *my* pretending to settle your affairs! . . .'

The Byrons journeyed south in easy stages and did not arrive until the evening of the 12th. Augusta was upstairs changing, when she heard the carriage drive up; and it was a few minutes before she could descend to greet them. Controlling her agitation, she shook hands with Annabella—whom she had not seen since Lady Glenbervies's party in 1813—then turned and embraced her brother. Byron, she noticed, was in a highly wrought-up state, more nervous even than she, which he attributed to a letter he had just opened concerning the sale of Newstead. Augusta then took Annabella upstairs to show her their rooms, and when they were in the bedroom Annabella, expressing her pleasure in being under her roof, kissed her warmly. Returning to the drawing-room, Augusta remarked to Byron what had passed upstairs; whereupon he taunted her, with a touch of malice which the situation did not require, for not having greeted her sister-in-law more graciously and affectionately. The undercurrent of tension remained all the evening; Byron ignored or snubbed Annabella, showing an undisguised preference to talk to Augusta. Finally, about nine o'clock, after he had hinted so broadly as not to be mistaken that her presence was unwelcome, Annabella retired to bed. It was not long before Augusta realised that her worst fears were more than justified. After drinking some brandy, Byron's mood of sullen resentment turned into a fury almost demoniacal. He inveighed against marriage, Annabella, George Leigh, his impossible financial situation, the futility of existence in England. Augusta, accustomed as she was to the vehemence of his denunciations, and making every allowance for his own admonition not to take his words too seriously, was shocked at the change that had come about in the little more than two months since she had seen him. When he attempted to embrace her, she gently but firmly extricated herself. He grew somewhat calmer before he took leave of her and went upstairs, but later she heard him shouting and cursing Fletcher as he undressed.

The next morning, when the three met, Augusta kissed Byron and Annabella in a tranquil and unconcerned manner. Byron, too, was quieter and more composed, but in the course of the day his black mood returned and he vented his anger at Annabella in cynical allusions and innuendoes addressed to Augusta. 'Well, Guss, I'm a reformed man, ain't I?' he asked with heavy irony, when the conversation turned to marriage. 'I *have* observed some improvements already,' she replied. From the outset his delight appeared to be (in his own words) 'to work them both well'. He would make personal and intimate comparisons between the two women, refer to their underclothing and make pointed allusions to their menstrual periods. His favourite amusement was to hint at secrets between himself and Augusta, greeting her in the morning with a mischievous reference to occurrences of the previous night: 'So you wouldn't, Guss . . .' A few days after their arrival a package was delivered from a London jeweller, containing two brooches, one marked A, the other B, with locks of hair and the sign XXX. In Annabella's presence he gave one of the brooches to Augusta, saying, 'If she knew what these mean! Do you remember our signs at Newstead?' as if to allude to something that Annabella was too ignorant or blind to guess. On another occasion he quoted his own words: ' "We must part, we must fly to—unite it again"—Do you recall when I wrote that, Guss?'

It was in the evenings chiefly that he exercised his cruelty on the two women. He would lie on the sofa and have them kiss him by turns, making clear his predilection for Augusta. In comparing his character on points of resemblance with Augusta's, he said, with deep significance, 'You know, Augusta, you're of an inflammable constitution.' He spoke of his affairs before marriage, especially of intrigues carried on while he was corresponding with Annabella—'And all that time you thought I was dying for you.' 'Ask Augusta if I have been a virtuous man', he said. 'I am afraid', replied Augusta, 'there is no such thing as a virtuous man in these days.' At about nine o'clock, if Annabella showed signs of staying, he would dismiss her with crushing irony: 'We can amuse ourselves without you, my *charmer*.' Augusta tried to mitigate his sadistic pleasure in belittling Annabella and to turn aside his praises of herself. Once, when he said to her, 'Augusta, you're my best, my only friend,' she replied miserably, 'I fear I've been your worst.' Every night she stayed up late with him, trying to moderate his drinking and violence. In the mornings, contrary to his habit, he would rise early, leaving Annabella, and repair to Augusta's bedroom.

Augusta and Annabella had experienced an immediate and instinctive liking for each other, and now they formed a sympathetic conspiracy of defence against Byron's outrages; a 'tacit understanding' was established between them. When the weather was fine, they went for walks in the afternoons. The older woman tried to comfort the younger, explaining Byron's moods by the desperation of his finances and more particularly

129

by his ruined digestion, caused by his starving himself and then gorging, which brought on pains that he tried to relieve by over-doses of magnesia. Augusta could not deny Annabella's belief that Byron had not loved her when they married, but she tried to support her in the hope that a persevering affection would awaken love in him. She spoke of habit having great power over Byron. Solicitous as she now was of Annabella's welfare, she saw that Byron's cruelty was in part anger at the impasse in which he found himself, fatally linked to a character such as hers; she observed also that Annabella was not the 'malleable' person that Byron declared her to be; there was a quiet resistance in her that boded no good for the future. It was a clash between two intractable, egocentric wills, which left little room for give and take.

By the second week of their stay the struggle to restrain Byron and comfort Annabella was so exhausting to Augusta, that she already longed for their departure. Byron, however, was very reluctant to move, and it was Annabella who noted that Augusta 'evidently did not wish to detain' them. On 28th March they set out for London to take up their residence in Piccadilly. As their carriage moved away, Byron waved his handkerchief to Augusta 'in the most passionate manner', until they turned from the drive to the main road and she was lost from view.

Left alone with the children at Six Mile Bottom, Augusta contemplated the wreckage of her hopes. Her love for 'Baby' Byron was undiminished (and together with it a love had sprung up for his young wife), but even her sanguine disposition failed to find much comfort in thoughts of the future. She had written to Francis Hodgson on 18th March, putting on a brave front to the true state of affairs: 'I've nothing but *agreeables* to communicate, on a subject of the greatest interest to you as well as to me. B. & Lady B. arrived here last Sunday . . . I hope they will stay some days longer with me, and shall regret their departure, whenever it takes place, as much as I now delight in their society. B. is looking particularly well, and of Lady B. I scarcely know how to write, for I have a sad trick of being struck dumb when I am most happy and pleased. The expectations I had formed could not be *exceeded*, but at least they are fully answered. I think I never saw or heard or read of a more perfect being in mortal mould . . .' On 31st March she wrote again, and although her remarks were veiled, they betrayed the change in her feelings: 'Byron and Lady B. left me on Tuesday for London . . . I am sorry to say his nerves and spirits are very far from what I wish them, but don't speak of this to him on any account. I think the uncomfortable state of his affairs is the cause; at least, I can discern no other. He has every blessing this world can bestow. I trust that the Almighty will be graciously pleased to grant him those *inward* feelings of peace and calm which are now unfortunately wanting. This is a subject which I cannot dwell upon . . . I think Lady B. very judiciously abstains from pressing the consideration of it upon him at the present moment. In short the more I see of her the more I love and esteem her, and feel how grateful I am and ought to be for the blessing of such a wife for my dear, darling B.'

VIII

The Byron Debacle

1815 - 1816

IN MARCH 1815, Augusta was appointed lady-in-waiting to Queen Charlotte. On hearing of the appointment, while still at Six Mile Bottom, Byron had suggested that she stay with them at 13 Piccadilly when she came to London to arrange her rooms at St James's Palace. Annabella now wrote to thank her for having them on their way south from Seaham and to repeat Byron's invitation, and Augusta answered this letter on 30th March: 'Dearest Annabella—I need not say that your letter is most acceptable to poor forlorn *me*. The contents (some of them at least) might have been more agreeable, but your kindness is not the less felt ... Dearest Sis I do not require your account of the view from yr Windows as an inducement to pay you a visit. You will perhaps be a better judge by & bye whether I shall not be a plague—& you must tell me *truly* if I am likely to prove so—you know I should not be "affronted" ...

'I have this Morng received a congratulatory Epistle from Lady Harcourt upon this appointment of mine, in which she says many fine things about the Queen's pleasure in appointing me (for the sake of my Grandmother & Mother) but one which surprises me about the Prince, that she believes "what determined the Q— most upon this occasion was its being the Regent's wish" ! ! ! ! ! !

'My *youngsters* do not forget "Aunt Bella" & "Uncle B" ... God bless you dearest Annabella—Kiss *"Duckey"*! for Sis & if possible give me a favourable report of the "Wind & the Weathercock"—Ever yr most affecte Guss.'

From this it appears that, if the Prince Regent had still no wish to employ 'that very helpless gentleman' George Leigh, he had no intention of victimising his family, and that this appointment at the court of his mother gave him the means of assisting them. Augusta's stepmother, the dowager Duchess of

Leeds, was still prominent in court circles, having supervised the upbringing of the Princesses.

The ten days before Augusta's arrival in London were, in Annabella's recollection some of the least unhappy days that she spent in Byron's company. Byron was pleased to pick up the threads of his former London life; on 7th April he met Walter Scott for the first time at Murray's in Albemarle St and the two men enjoyed each other's company for two hours, in spite of their widely different political views. He saw something of Douglas Kinnaird (who was at the time much occupied with the theatre) and called on Lady Melbourne. However, he had a premonition that no good would come from Augusta's visit; his uneasiness was such that he went out of the house at the hour when she was expected to arrive. On his return both women noticed his black looks, and he greeted Augusta coldly and Georgiana, who had accompanied her, hardly less so; but within a short time his attitude thawed towards his sister and all his old fondness returned. Yet that evening, in Augusta's presence, he uttered a warning that stirred all Annabella's latent suspicions: 'You were a fool to let her come. You will find it will make a good deal of difference to you *in all ways*', said in a manner which threatened a resumption of those relations which had marred their stay at Six Mile Bottom.

Augusta, sensing that the situation had not altered for the better, did all she could to bring comfort to Annabella, who was pregnant, and to protect her from Byron's cruelty. Soon after her arrival, Annabella was called to the bedside of her uncle, Lord Wentworth; she spent three nights with the dying man, until her mother reached London, when she received an affectionate note from Byron: 'Dearest—Now your mother is come I won't have you worried any longer—more particularly in your present situation which is rendered very precarious by what you have already gone through—Pray come home—ever thine'—and he signed with the flourish of swirls habitually used between Augusta and himself. It would be easy to see Augusta's guiding hand in this sign of anxious solicitude. However, Annabella's return to Piccadilly was not marked by any change in Byron's attitude to the two women; he showed a decided preference for Augusta's company and would send Annabella up to bed in the evening so that he could spend an hour alone with the other. Augusta had difficulty in restraining his drinking; but there were times when she could coax him out of his gloom or frustrated anger into a more benign mood. But to Annabella, waiting for Byron in her bedroom, the sound of their laughter as they came up the stairs together was no less galling—from the thought that it was only with Augusta that he could laugh—than the sound of his 'stride of passion' when he came to bed in hatred and loathing of her. One night, hearing her walking about in the room above, Byron sent Augusta up to see what was the matter. Annabella was in an agony of jealousy, but Augusta's calm innocence and kindness checked her tears and restored her to something like equanimity.

Augusta understood (in a way that Annabella did not appreciate) that much of Byron's unsettled state of mind sprang from the precariousness of his financial means. If Lady Melbourne had thought, in procuring for them the large establishment in Piccadilly, that Byron's creditors would be impressed by the apparent solidity of his affairs and not press for settlement, she had badly miscalculated. Further, Lord Wentworth's death in April gave rise to hopes that money would be available for repayment of Byron's large outstanding debts, and the claims thereafter became more pressing. Although the Byrons did little entertaining (the reason for this was partly Byron's dislike of Annabella's friends), they required a carriage and a staff of servants. The income from Annabella's marriage settlement merely covered the rental of the house: the rent, however, was still outstanding two years after the expiration of the tenancy. Byron lived from day to day under the fear that an execution would be made on the furniture and library and that bailiffs would enter the house. He was bitter against Annabella's parents for failing to come to their help, although (as Augusta, who defended them, patiently pointed out) Sir Ralph was in difficulties himself and was, in fact, attempting to secure them money on loan from Lord Melbourne. As a distraction from these pecuniary embarrassments Byron eagerly accepted a position, offered at the instigation of Douglas Kinnaird, on the management committee of Drury Lane Theatre. From the end of May 'the Manager', as Annabella slightingly named him, was assiduous in his attendance in the green room, reading scripts, soliciting Scott, Coleridge and Moore for new plays, settling disputes among the actresses and assisting in the supervision of the productions.

Augusta spent part of her days at St James's Palace, where she was required to learn her new duties as 'Bed-chamber Woman' to the ageing Queen Charlotte, who was now in her early seventies, living in semi-retirement since the madness of the King. She had been allocated a small flat in the palace, but in her anxiety over Byron and Annabella she preferred to remain with them in Piccadilly. Byron's behaviour had become increasingly erratic and unpredictable. On taking up his office at the theatre he had taunted the two women by remarking that he had every intention of using his position to secure himself a mistress among the actresses—'I am looking out to see who will suit me best.' Augusta received this threat lightly— he rather flattered himself that a conquest would be so easily achieved; but Annabella took his words seriously. Annabella could not fail to be jealous at Augusta's ascendancy over Byron, yet the latter was devotedly kind to her and always consulted her wishes in everything. When Byron attacked Annabella's parents—they were a constant butt for his malicious witticisms —Augusta invariably took their part, as she did when he abused the Carlisles. One evening he said to Augusta in front of Annabella, 'Lady Melbourne does not like you, Guss.' Augusta replied that she was unaware of any offence she had committed against her. At this, Byron approached her and whispered something in her ear which caused her to blush. At times he would threaten her, half seriously, half in mockery: 'I'll tell, Augusta.' On one such occasion she replied crossly, 'I don't care if you do.' 'Well', he expostulated, 'if I ever heard anything like the impudence of the woman!' Nevertheless it was Annabella who bore the brunt of his ill-humour; for four days he would not speak to her, and passed her with every mark of deepest aversion. This was more than Augusta would tolerate and she roundly told him that she would not stay in the house to see her so insultingly treated. There were times when he softened and was playful and affectionate towards his wife, but his moods were so volatile that one could never be sure what scene might follow. He was drinking a great deal, and brandy produced in him the most violent paroxysms of repugnance and hatred of Annabella, her parents and his now intolerable position.

Even Augusta was at a loss to know how to moderate his violence. She sat up late with him, as she had at Six Mile Bottom; here in the silence of the house she sometimes roused him from his melancholia and he would talk of his predicament with moderation and reason.

It was from these more rational conversations that Augusta realised into what an impasse the marriage had come. Byron declared his intention of first begetting an heir and then taking himself abroad. If he was to retain his sanity, he must separate from Annabella. Even on those days when the gloom lifted, Augusta saw too clearly that there were but small grounds for hope. Towards the end of June, when Augusta had been almost two months in the house, Annabella could bear the strain of her presence no longer and asked her to fix a time to go. A few days after the news had reached London of Napoleon's defeat at Waterloo, Augusta regretfully left Piccadilly and returned to Newmarket. When she had gone, Annabella felt remorse that her jealousy and her suspicions (for they were no more than that) of the nature of her relationship with Byron had been the cause of dismissing her so unkindly. Their correspondence was renewed in the former spirit of sisterly concern and affection.

Of Byron's intimate friends Augusta much preferred Hodgson; Kinnaird and Hobhouse she considered as unworthy associates who encouraged him to drink: Kinnaird's white brandy was famous—infamous in her eyes. Gradually she came to see Hobhouse's disinterested affection and loyalty to Byron. On 5th July, in reply to letters he had written to the latter from France, where he had gone to report on the Bourbon restoration, she replied on Byron's behalf: 'I am aware of your being very anxious to hear from my brother; and knowing him to be just now very lazy, I think the next best thing to hearing *from* him must be to hear *of* him . . .' Not trusting Hobhouse in the way she trusted Hodgson, she glossed over the true state of affairs in the Byron household: 'I returned home ten days ago, after more than two months séjour in Piccadilly . . . B is looking particularly well, eats very heartily of *meat*, bread and biscuit, allows himself half-a-pint of claret at dinner, when at home (and he seldom dines out), has abjured brandy and other spirituous liquors. Lady B. is *not* looking well or feeling so, but there is very good reason for this temporary indisposition. What a blessing it is that he has such a Lady B! . . . The only drawbacks to their present happiness and comfort are pecuniary concerns, and I grieve to say the remedy is to be the sale of Rochdale and Newstead on the 28th of this month. Alas! for the dear old Abbey! . . . The sale was a measure hastily determined upon in a moment of despair, and I can't help fearing . . . will be repented of if it takes place; but nothing can be urged successfully against it, and I have left off urging almost upon principle . . .' She went on to tell Hobhouse how the Milbankes' own difficulties prevented their assisting the Byrons. 'Lady B. is, of course, most anxious B. should be convinced of their good will, and whatever may be wanting on hers on this and other points just now, I feel sanguine that a little time and patience will set all right and enlighten his *now* prejudiced mind as to who are his *real* friends. They got out but little . . . . almost *too* little, but you know B. can't do any thing moderately . . .' These were the only hints she gave Hobhouse of the troubles in Piccadilly, and such blame as she gave was apportioned equally between Byron and Annabella.

On 24th July Hobhouse returned from France, and he accompanied Byron four days later to Garraway's, where Newstead was bought in at 95,000 guineas and Rochdale at 16,000 guineas. In the next fortnight Hobhouse saw Byron five times, twice dining with him in the company of Kinnaird and others. These were the occasions of which Annabella reported: 'Sometime after she [Augusta] went H[obhouse] returned from abroad. B— told me it was upon business . . . but the effect was that of making him adopt a system of estranging himself from me & pursuing every vice, less from inclination . . . than from a principle of destroying every better feeling—Drinking brandy.'

In July Byron made a fresh will, which, after arranging for the marriage settlement, left the residue to Augusta and her heirs. Annabella wrote, informing her: 'Dearest Lei,—I must tell you how lovingly B. has been talking of "dear Goose", till he had half a mind to cry—and so had I. The conversation arose from his telling the contents of a Will that he has just made—as far as I can judge, quite what he ought to make . . . you should have satisfaction in knowing that your children will afterwards have a provision ... it appears to me very judicious ...'

In spite of Augusta's new appointment at St James's, affairs had again reached a state of crisis at Six Mile Bottom, so that Colonel Leigh came up to London in the middle of August to try to recover the good graces of the Prince Regent. Annabella reported his lack of immediate success in a letter to Augusta's friend, the Hon. Mrs George Villiers: 'Col. Leigh returned here after the Royal audience ... The P.R. was very gracious, though not familiar, (Co. Thornton being present) and promised to give some place or appointment. For what is the Petitioner qualified? A puzzling question, which his R.H. may *fairly* take some time to consider ... He is himself so much elated by the favour of an interview, that he thinks no further exertion necessary ...' The Colonel, having retired from the army (he was not present on the field of Waterloo), was at a loss to know how to apply for his pension; eventually it was Augusta who applied on his behalf to the Secretary at War. And at this juncture, as if to cap the woes that fell on the unfortunate Leighs, when a relative died, leaving a bequest to George Leigh and his recently widowed mother, a certain Mrs Longe appeared and disputed the will. Augusta in her tribulations wrote to Byron, and he left London for Newmarket on 30th August. She had not wanted him to come, as she feared that her husband, who was at home, might try to borrow from him on the prospect of Newstead's selling.

Two days later Augusta wrote to Annabella: 'My dearest A—I've just got yr letter & thank you from my heart for all your kindness. I hear from G[eorge] that he has sent Mrs. Longe's paper to Lord Chichester ... I think Mrs. Longe *a* Devil & THE Devil! oh fie! but never mind I can't help it ... B. was quite well yesterday—he is as yet invisible this Morng— but I will obey you de bon cœur ... we had a little *Sparring* about *Brandy* last night—but I came off victorious—I'm not so sure however that the contest may not be renewed ...' She then went on to relate a discussion with Byron of Hobhouse's remark to him, after the former had seen Lady Milbanke, that she 'wanted him to sell Newstead hugely'. She continued: 'He [Byron] has confessed almost all his *naughty fits & sayings* but without seeming to have an idea that I might have heard them,

138

& of course I did not betray that I had. Upon ye whole I am pleased with him as far as relates to Pip—of whose merits he seems convinced as he ought to be, & of whom he talks quite pathetically as the "best little Wife" in ye World . . . B. is writing for himself & his own acct. will be much more agreeable than all I can write—So God bless you dearest Sis—Ever thine Guss—or Goose.'

In her perfect loyalty towards Byron and Annabella, she had defended the Milbankes when Byron had launched one of his customary attacks on them. The visit seems to have achieved nothing except adding to the rancour of Byron's mind, and he returned to London after five days' absence very ill-disposed towards Augusta.

Annabella was now well advanced in pregnancy, the baby being due at the beginning of December, and it was arranged that the lying-in should take place in London and not at Seaham, as was first intended, since Byron was not prepared to leave London (there was good reason for this from fear of a bailiff's execution) and Annabella would not go alone. Further, she would have her mother and Augusta with her, and as *accoucheur* she had booked the services of Dr Le Mann. In the first week in November she sent Augusta 'a few observations respecting the nature of my greatest fears for B', whom 'she daily understood better'. 'His misfortune is an habitual *passion for Excitement*, which is always found in ardent temperaments, where the pursuits are not in some degree organized. It is the Ennui of a monotonous existence that drives the best-hearted people of this description to the most dangerous paths, and makes them often seem to act from bad motives when in fact they are only flying from internal suffering by any external stimulus. The love of tormenting arises chiefly from this Source . . .' She attributed Byron's drinking to this origin, and his ennui to a 'vitiated stomach' arising from 'habits of Excess'. But her laboured analysis finished with a *cri de cœur* to Augusta: 'I know in what it must end if it encrease—and with such apprehensions you will wonder if I am sometimes almost heart broken before my time. My dear, dear A, do give me every opinion of yours on this . . .'

The lawyers' delays in securing the Milbanke loan finally brought about the long dreaded event on 8th November, when a bailiff entered and took up residence in the house. The next day Annabella wrote desperately to Augusta: 'God knows what I suffered yesterday & am suffering from B's distraction, which is of the *very worst* kind. He leaves the House telling me he will at once abandon himself to every sort of desperation—speaks to me only to upbraid me with having married him when he wished not—and says he is therefore acquitted of all principle towards me, and I must consider myself *only* to be answerable for the vicious courses to which his despair will drive him—and is driving him. The going out of the house & the drinking are the most fatal. He was really quite frantic yesterday—said he did not care for any consequences to me, & it seemed impossible to tell if his feelings towards you or me were the most completely reversed—for as I have told you, he loves or hates us together . . . Things never were so serious . . .

'P.S. I have waited to the last in hopes of some change—but all is inexorable pride & hardness. O Augusta, will it ever change for me—I scarcely know what I say . . .'

Two days later she wrote again, asking Augusta to come to Piccadilly in the middle of the following week, and adding: 'You will do good I think—if any can be done. My dearest A, I feel all your kindness.' She had stressed that, if Augusta came, she should not take her part against Byron or 'risk B's displeasure' for her sake.

Augusta, with the earlier scenes at Six Mile Bottom and Piccadilly vividly in mind, was deeply perplexed, undecided whether her presence now could alleviate a situation perhaps already irreparable. Colonel Leigh was opposed to her going, and in no pleasant humour at being left alone in the country with the children. In her indecision Augusta wrote to her old friend Mrs George Villiers, requesting her advice. The latter replied that she thought she should go, as she owed it to both Byron and Annabella to do them a service if she could. Finally, Annabella's plea that if any good were to be done, it was she who would achieve it, decided her. Bringing Georgiana with her, Augusta arrived in Piccadilly on 15th November.

Byron's greeting was not the most gracious, but as the evening advanced he became more open and friendly. In the following days Annabella recounted to her the progressive deterioration in Byron's behaviour in the last two months. He had con-

140

stantly professed his intention of giving himself to drink and women and had asked her to condone the offences, adding that he would continue in them whether she did or did not. He declared that he would have any woman who came his way and if Annabella were dissatisfied she was at liberty to do the same herself—it was a matter of complete indifference to him, and perhaps the easiest way to get rid of her was by divorce. About a month before he had taken as mistress an actress from Drury Lane, Susan Boyce; he had admitted this to her, saying that he would not bother to play the hypocrite. One night in bed he declared sarcastically that Annabella looked very respectable in comparison with the woman he had just that moment left. He threatened to bring his mistress home at night, and further asked Annabella to acquaint Augusta with all this, in a manner which suggested that he was acting in this way out of revenge towards her as much as towards Annabella.

For an even longer period he had been almost consistently drunk; if he stayed at home in the evening it was to drink brandy, which brought on 'paroxysms of rage and frenzy'. On one occasion he threw on the hearth and pounded to pieces with the poker a watch that he had possessed since boyhood and had taken to the East with him; on another occasion in an outburst of passion against Augusta he had burnt her picture. In his drunken state his language was vicious and obscene, and he had made revealing remarks which doubtless he subsequently forgot. He was aware, however, that these scenes of violence were most upsetting for Annabella, especially in her present condition; on more than one occasion he had asked if the child was dead.

If Annabella's letters had prepared her to expect Byron's present spiritual and physical state, yet it was very much of a shock for Augusta to be a witness of the scenes which occurred almost daily. There were lucid and even affectionate intermissions, but so little provocation was necessary to upset his equilibrium that scarcely a day went by without a violent outburst. Three nights after Augusta's coming to Piccadilly he nearly came to blows with the actor-manager Alexander Ray in the course of a drunken argument at Douglas Kinnaird's. One evening, arriving home late from some party, he found Augusta and Annabella waiting up for him. Seeing the latter so calm and indignant, he appeared suddenly to be overcome with remorse and flung himself at her feet, declaring himself a monster—she could never forgive him; he had lost her for ever. Annabella, deeply touched, said, 'Byron, all is forgotten; never, never, shall you hear of it more!' He got to his feet, and folding his arms, burst into laughter. 'What do you mean?' Annabella asked in surprise. 'Only a philosophical experiment—that's all,' Byron replied. 'I wished to ascertain the value of your resolutions.'

Some days after her arrival Augusta first met Mrs Clermont, Annabella's former governess and an intimate of the Milbanke family, who had come to London to be near her at her confinement. When Mrs Clermont spoke of the effect of Byron's erratic behaviour on Annabella, Augusta was obliged to admit that she was excessively shocked at his conduct and that she shared her apprehensions that in a paroxysm of drunken rage he might endanger her life. She spoke also to Fletcher, Byron's servant, who confessed that he, too, was alarmed by his master's violence and was afraid that he might employ the pistols which he kept loaded by his bedside. Augusta warned him to be on the watch. The possibility of Byron's using the pistols was not an idle one; a few days afterwards he discharged a pistol in Annabella's bedroom, but protested that it was by accident. Augusta resumed her habit of sitting up late with him in an attempt to get him to see reason and to restrain him from disturbing Annabella's rest by his noisy practice of smashing the tops of soda-water bottles with a poker or hurling them across the room. She learned from him of his intention of going abroad as soon as he was free; one of his complaints against Annabella was that the marriage settlement prevented him from selling Newstead and Rochdale for whatever figure they would fetch, so that he could use the money to leave the country.

If Annabella was wretched, it was clear to her that Augusta was even more so. One evening the two women were sitting together when Byron was out at the theatre. Augusta, in her despair, exclaimed, 'Ah, you don't know what a fool I have been about him', and she brushed back her hair from her forehead with a hand that trembled. Annabella rose, went over to her and kissed her on the forehead, then left the room.

About the end of November Sophia Byron, Augusta's and

Byron's maiden aunt, arrived in London, and in her anxiety Augusta sought her out. After hearing a detailed report of the state of affairs, Sophia Byron declared it her opinion that Byron was insane and that medical advice should be obtained. As the time for Annabella's confinement drew nearer, Byron's furies and rages grew more violent; if he went to visit her, his cruelty reduced her to tears. He threatened again to bring a mistress into the house, and it required all Augusta's firmness to dissuade him. Even the usually placid Fletcher had serious fears for the safety of the two women, saying one day to Augusta, 'I hope my Lord won't do you or my Lady any harm.' One night, after Augusta had gone to bed, she was so alarmed by Byron's violence below, that she came out of her room in fear that he was attacking Annabella. Fletcher would watch him until he was actually in bed, lest he should go into her bedroom. Finally, realising that she had no control over him, Augusta asked their cousin George Byron to come to live in the house. She also invited Mrs Clermont to stay; the latter and the nurse occupied rooms next to Annabella's, to prevent his disturbing her. Lady Milbanke, who had come up to London to be with her daughter, had been taken seriously ill and was confined to her bed at Mivart's Hotel in Lower Brook Street.

On 9th December Annabella, feeling her labour pains beginning, went to see Byron in the library; here there was another scene, which caused her the greatest grief, and she left the room in tears. Byron then went out to the theatre. On his return he asked Augusta how Annabella was and told her that he had enquired of Annabella whether she chose to continue to live with him. Augusta reproved him for asking such a question at such a time. 'Yes,' he answered carelessly, 'I am a fool—I always *mis-time* my questions.' It is unlikely that there was anything more than coincidence in his posing Annabella this question at this time (or was it an uncanny intuition?), for on that very day, with Augusta's knowledge and agreement, she had consulted Serjeant Heywood, an old friend of her parents, whether she should not leave the house and go to an hotel to have her child. Apparently he advised her to stay in Piccadilly, as it was there at one o'clock on the following day, Sunday, that she gave birth to a daughter, Augusta Ada. She was called the first after her aunt; the second was 'a very antique family name . . . not used since the reign of King John'. In its earliest days the baby was known as Augusta Junior, but this was soon dropped. Augusta wrote to Hodgson the next day announcing the birth of a daughter, and reported that 'B. is in great good looks', though he would have preferred a son, and she hinted that all was not well in the Byron ménage—'I would give half the world *at least*, that I could have an hour's conversation with you'. But any hopes she and Annabella may have had that the birth of a child would bring the parents together were speedily proved false. As Byron was later to write:

> The child of love! though born in bitterness,
> And nurtured in convulsion. Of thy sire
> These were the elements, and thine no less.

The bailiffs were still in the house; the money promised from the Milbanke loan was further delayed—in fact, it does not seem to have been paid until almost Christmas. Byron's frenzied rages and wild talk increased, so that to the inmates of the house he appeared indeed at times to be suffering from the delusions of insanity; yet at the same time, by the questions he put to Annabella, it seemed that he was acting with a fixed determination in mind. To Hobhouse he admitted that his pecuniary embarrassments 'drove him half-mad', and that it was essential for him to break up his present establishment. On 28th December Lady Milbanke, on the eve of her departure from London to convalesce at Kirkby, wrote to Byron, inviting him and his family to join Sir Ralph and her there. Byron intimated that Annabella and the baby should go, but that he should either live in London as a single man or, better, go abroad. Annabella found in George Byron someone who shared her facility in interpreting literally everything uttered by Byron, even when he was clearly influenced by drink. Augusta, although she could discriminate among his wildest ravings, had good reason to fear for his reason. Yet none of them dared suggest to him that he should seek medical advice.

Augusta, whose worries were increased by the illness of Georgiana, whom Le Mann was attending, was filled with pity and indignation as she observed the marks of Byron's deterioration, but she was helpless to check it; she was obliged to admit her failure and miserably resign herself to what would happen.

He frequently threatened suicide. His appearance was altered; his skin was a bad colour, he complained of pains in his head and body and one eye had become appreciably smaller than the other. She feared the outcome of his rages; on the occasions when he visited Annabella he left her in floods of tears. In his drunken outbursts his language was such that she had to ensure that Georgiana was out of hearing. Besides the brandy he was taking laudanum. The eventual crisis came on 3rd January. Byron went to Annabella's room, where she was in bed; the violent tones of his voice could be clearly heard by the nurse in the next room. Augusta was told later how he talked of his mistresses (she did not then know that she was also claimed by Byron to have been his mistress) and of his intention to continue to have them, though he was tired of Susan Boyce; how he would 'execute all the wickedness his imagination could devise'. 'A woman', he declared, 'has no right to complain if her husband does not beat or confine her—and you will *remember* I have neither *beaten* nor *confined* you. I have never done an act that could bring me under the law—at least on this side of the water.' After much incoherent and unkind talk, delivered as a threatening tirade, he left her sobbing. She explained to the nurse, who came to her when Byron departed, that her husband's mind was deranged. For three days he refused to come near her.

To Augusta he declared that it was his fixed intention that Annabella should leave with the child just as soon as she was fit to travel, although it was mid-winter. She pleaded with him, trying to reason him into a calmer state of mind, but her efforts were of no avail, and he remained implacable. On 6th January he read her a note he had written to Annabella, and asked her to take it to her:

'When you are disposed to leave London, it would be convenient that a day should be fixed—& (if possible) not a very remote one for that purpose. Of my opinion upon that subject you are sufficiently in possession—& of the circumstances which have led to it—as also to my plans—or rather intentions—for the future. When in the country I will write to you more fully. As Lady Noel [under Lord Wentworth's will the Milbankes had adopted the surname Noel] has asked you to Kirkby, there you can be for the present—unless you prefer Seaham.

'As the dismissal of the present establishment is of importance to me, the sooner you can fix on the day the better—though of course your convenience & inclination shall be first consulted.

'The child will of course accompany you—there is a more easy and safer carriage than the chariot (unless you prefer it) which I mentioned before—on that you can do as you please.'

When Annabella received this courteously cruel note by Augusta's hand, she burst into tears, saying through her sobs, 'I expected it, but I can't help feeling *this*—to think that I have lived to be hated by my husband!' The following day she answered with another note delivered by Augusta:

'I shall obey your wishes, and fix the earliest day that circumstances will admit for leaving London.'

Annabella had given no indication of the domestic crisis in her letters to her parents or in one written to Lady Melbourne on 4th January, in which she wrote: 'My confinement has been rendered so comfortable by Mrs Leigh's kindness and attention, which I never can forget, that I feel no inclination to break loose.' Now, under the strongest impression that Byron was insane, Augusta and Annabella determined to have medical advice, and they asked Dr Baillie, who had attended Byron for his foot as a boy and who was the brother of Annabella's friend, Joanna Baillie, to call. On the day of her dismissal, 7th January, Annabella wrote out an *aide-mémoire* for Dr Baillie:

'The principal insane ideas are—that he *must* be wicked—is foredoomed to evil—and compelled by some irresistible power to follow this destiny, doing violence all the time to his feelings. Under the influence of this imagined fatalism he will be most unkind to those whom he loves best, suffering agonies at the same time for the pain he gives them. He then believes the world to be governed by a Malignant Spirit, & at one time conceived himself to be a fallen angel . . .

'Undoubtedly I am more than any one the subject of his irritation, because he deems himself (as he has said) a villain for marrying me on account of former circumstances—adding that the more I love him, & the better I am, the more accursed he is. When he uses me worst he seems the more sensible that I do not deserve it—and speaks of me as the most perfect of human beings, with passionate affection—at times—at others he expresses loathing & hatred—and there is no sort of injury or outrage within the Law which he has not *studied* to inflict, against his feelings, & from what I conceive to be an insane principle. I am convinced that my removal will compose him for a time—and I wish to defer any attempt at restraint till its effects are seen—but should they be such, ought I to suffer him to fulfil his intention of going abroad to the spot with which I know his most maddening feelings to be connected, without restraint, if I can impose it ?'

Le Mann, Annabella's own doctor, whom she consulted at this time, sent her a volume of the *Medical Journal* with a mark against the entry *hydrocephalus*, as perhaps applying to Byron's case. At an interview on 8th January Dr Baillie was not prepared to venture an opinion, but he suggested that Byron might be persuaded to see Le Mann. Le Mann also would give no decided opinion without a consultation with Byron, and suggested that the symptoms might have been caused by a disordered state of the liver; further, 'that his brain might be partially affected unless the disease was speedily removed'. Annabella then paid a visit to Hanson, and stated her apprehensions so forcibly that the solicitor feared that she might put Byron under personal restraint. Hanson, who knew Byron much better than she, strongly deprecated such a course. Annabella asked him to try to persuade Byron to follow her to Kirkby, and, taking leave of him, declared her intention of returning to London 'at a minute's warning', if her presence was required.

Augusta was a miserable witness of all this activity on Annabella's part. Not that she opposed it, but the thought of Byron insane, and perhaps forcibly constrained, was more than she could bear. At first, learning of Annabella's dismissal, she had declared her determination also to leave the house. Annabella confided to Sophia Byron that Byron had 'intimated criminal dispositions' towards Augusta, but the two women agreed that, if George Byron could be persuaded to stay, it would be conducive to Byron's safety and comfort if Augusta remained to look after him—at least for a few days until Le Mann had seen him and pronounced an opinion. Annabella, fearing that she could not talk to Augusta of her departure with a 'decent visage', wrote her a note: 'With the expectations which I have, I never will nor can ask you to stay one moment longer than you are inclined to do . . . I am truth itself, when I say that, whatever the situation may be, there is no one whose society is dearer to me, or can contribute more to my happiness. These feelings will not change under any circumstances, and I should be grieved if you did not understand them. Should you hereafter condemn me, I shall not love you less . . . Judge for yourself about going or staying. I wish you to consider *yourself*, if you would be wise enough to do that for the first time in your life.' Annabella wished to prolong her own stay until Le Mann's visit on 15th January, but after another scene on the 13th, when Byron called her out of the room with such looks of rage that both George Byron and Augusta had the greatest fears for her safety, George Byron declared that he would not suffer her to remain any longer in the house without himself informing her parents. This was the only occasion on which Annabella apprehended an immediate danger to her life. She thereupon fixed her departure for the 15th.

On the evening of 14th January she went into the room where Byron and Augusta were sitting together, and, offering him her hand, said simply, 'Byron, I have come to say goodbye.' Byron rose, and taking up a position in front of the fire, with his hands behind his back, smiled at her. 'When shall we three meet again?' he asked. One report (not that of an eyewitness) says that Annabella replied, 'In heaven, I trust.' Then she left them. As Byron was not up when she departed next morning, this was the last time that Byron and Annabella ever saw each other.

IX

The Separation

1816

ON THE morning Annabella left 13 Piccadilly for Kirkby, Augusta, accompanied by George Byron, paid a visit to the solicitor Hanson. That afternoon she began a series of almost daily bulletins that kept Annabella in touch with all that was going on in London. Never once did she falter in her absolute loyalty to both Byron and Annabella. It is in these intimate, truthful, amazingly perceptive and tactful letters, at times revealing her despair, at all times her perfect naturalness and balance—written at intervals of running the household, ordering Byron nourishing meals, seeing that he moderated his drinking and followed his medical regimen, interviewing doctors and solicitors, attending to his correspondence as well as her own, and looking after Georgiana—that we see the full measure of the woman, and understand something of the reason why she won Byron's unfailing love. She reported that she had found Hanson 'very zealous and kind . . . Speaking very kindly of you on *the* subject, he said when he heard of yr departure "Well perhaps it is as well" & that ye only thing is to enforce medical advice. I told him of course all you desired & that Le Mann was to see him today—which he thought all right *but* wishes Le M. to call on him after, merely to give him a pretence to speak on ye subject to B—which he means to do most openly as to the danger he is incurring by his habits & not having advice when it is evident he so much wants it . . . H. seemed so positive *I* ought *not* to go for a day or two that I really think I cannot—tho I had packed up & am certain I ought to go home if possible—but *can I* after this. My poor dear A I fear you are not more happy than I am—or I would not mind any perplexity at least feel your being free from it a comfort.

'B. rose early—seems quiet, but complains of languor & feeling ill—asked how you were. I said pretty well & spoke as you desired *lightly* of yr feelings. He has not said much & that little in good humour. He talks of fasting today.'

Before the post was collected at five o'clock she added a postscript: 'Le Mann has been with B. who confused at first but afterwards talked openly rationally & goodhumouredly *avoiding always ye main point.* Le M. of course turned all on ye score of health—proposed Calomel, which at last was agreed to, or any other medicine advised. He begged Le M. to call again tomorrow. All was said that *could* with prudence & policy for a 1st visit . . . Le Mann votes for my staying a few days so I certainly must & shall . . .'

That evening Augusta accompanied Byron, their cousin George and Scrope Davies to Drury Lane. She reported the events in her letter to Annabella the next afternoon: 'I've not yet seen B., but he is at dinner, so Dieu merci does *not dine out.* I heard from Fletcher that his pills from Le Mann met with a *miss for tin* [in imitation of Fletcher's Nottinghamshire dialect] & were crushed, so he did not take them last night. I hear Le M. has been with him "some *time"* today . . . The Play last night affected him much even to tears, but G[eorge] said it was nothing to ye last time. He appeared very odd all the time there & I am perfectly sure that Scrope D remarked it from his looks & manner. B. set him down on our way home & proposed a *supper at Watier's* which made me *shake,* but ye other scarcely answered & most determinedly *held off* from everything of the sort. The Miss Cookes [the actresses] as usual was the principal theme. Very little has been said of yr departure & I always treat the subject lightly—but I really was annoyed at all the *folly* displayed last night & defy any body not to discover *something is amiss.* Mrs Clermont called this morning, & we had a confab; it is a comfort to me her being at hand I feel so deplorably responsible now you are gone. He went to Bed ear*lier* last night & drank wine instead of Brandy . . . Mrs Clermont agrees with me as to ye probability of his following you. Le Mann's plan is to gain his confidence before he hints at *ye main point* which I think very sensible . . . His manner of mentioning having seen L.M. to me was curious—perfectly unsuspecting & only childishly talking of being *torpid,* tho one saw much real apprehension & fidgets under it.' Before the post left, she added: 'I've seen B one moment. He told me he had seen Le M. who said his liver was very bad—shewed me yr letter and desires me to tell you the *misfortin* of the pills & that therefore his life is still in *abeyance*.'

From Woburn on Monday evening Annabella had written to Byron: '. . . I hope you are *good*, and remember my medical prayers & injunctions. Don't give yourself up to the abominable trade of versifying—nor to brandy—nor to any thing or any body that is not *lawful & right* . . . Ada's love to you with mine—*Pip*.' Arriving at Kirkby on Wednesday evening, she sent another affectionate letter beginning 'Dearest Duck', with playful allusions to the comfort of the lavatory and the '*sitting*-room or *sulking*-room', and ending 'Love to the good goose & everybody's love to you both from hence. Ever thy most loving Pippin . . . Pip-ip.' On this same day Augusta sent off her bulletin: 'I am sorry to say the pills are still *untaken* & that Perry's dinner is *today*. He is going but with a resolution to be "*moderate* on account of his Liver" of which he talks to everyone. No Brandy last night or the night before. In ye course of the Eveg. George & I were quite struck with his ill looks—so much so we cd not help asking if he felt ill—he said yes, *very*. Went at 9 to the Play with S. Davies—I really think ye only inducement was the *Cookes* & there seems no promise of success *there*. He came home early but sat up late & upon desiring me to give me his watch off the chimney piece, added "don't touch that Pistol instead". I own I was not quite happy at perceiving one there & asked carelessly *why*. He said he had observed a man lurking about the street door & did not like it! However he proceeded quietly to bed, saying he would not take ye pills because of his dinner today . . . You are mentioned by him with great kindness. I always long to write down at ye moment for *my Liver* does not admit of much *memory* at present—but one thing was, "Tell her as I told Murray that she is the only woman I could have lived 6 months with." Your letter was read many times but with what reflections I could not exactly discover. "Why does Pip object to my *versifying*"—"What a letter nothing in it but what I'm to do or *not* to do—& so on." ' She added a line before the post: 'Just seen Le M. who has been an hour with B—*very favorable* as far as it goes—he has promised him not to drink much to-day, & is very tractable.'

151

Alas for good resolutions and fair promises. The dinner with James Perry, editor of the *Morning Chronicle*, had gone with a swing, as Augusta reported the following day: 'I write very much down in the dumps. B returned between 12 & 1 this Mng with Hobhouse—both drunk—sent me & George to bed, & call'd for Brandy! Fletcher says H. drank none but B replied to his declarations to that effect "So much the better—there will be the more for me"—& drank two glasses—would not take his Calomel & in short so far so bad! One comfort is *H* looks really dying—God forgive me, I hope He will take him to a better world—but however B. frown'd to such a degree at me to go away that this dear friend (I mean fiend) either was or pretended to be quite shock'd—said he wd go—& when B pursued me out of the room to apologise for his frowns (when by the bye he tumbled flat on his face up the staircase) H said to George all sorts of *tendresses* of course to be repeated to me—I was *all the Angels* in ye world & fortunate for him I was married! Fletcher has just informed me he left the house door open at 3 o clock in ye morng. & "lucky we had not all our throats cut!"'

Although Annabella had had in mind separating from Byron before the birth of Ada, the thought that his actions might be the result of insanity led her to postpone any decision until she had heard from the medical advisers. But in a letter to her friend Selina Doyle, written from Woburn on the first night of her journey (a letter turgid almost to the point of incomprehensibility), she indicated that it was but a delay, for she referred to her undertaking 'the responsibility of that Measure, which Duty, not Timidity now determines me to postpone for a short time'. On Wednesday she wrote to Augusta and to George Byron informing them that her mother and father were both of her opinion that the patient should come to Kirkby where he could enjoy the advantages of air and exercise—'*I* deem the change of scene of the greatest consequence—and this place particularly eligible.' Annabella asked George Byron to acquaint Hanson with the contents of her letter. She thought Byron might be persuaded to come in order to beget an heir, and asked Augusta tactfully to hint at this delicate reason. So far it appeared that she had not divulged to her parents a full account of Byron's behaviour. However, on the following day, for some reason which is not clear, she did inform them of at least part of his eccentricities, and Lady Milbanke impetuously decided to come to London to seek medical and legal advice. Then Annabella received a letter from Selina Doyle (in answer to hers from Woburn) which mentioned 'outrages' and 'ill treatment', and this letter, it would appear, was seen by her parents, who forced from her a confession. Thereupon she began a statement of what she had suffered at Byron's hands for her mother to take to London with her.

Augusta was unaware of this change in the tide of events. As George Byron was deep in plans for matrimony—'he is gone to *pop* to M[ary] P[ole] this morning, in a troubled state of nerves'—Augusta reported that she herself went to see Hanson, who agreed with Mrs Clermont that it would not be prudent to press matters too precipitately with Byron about going to the country. He was still talking of going abroad, possibly with Hobhouse. Returning from Hanson on Thursday morning, she wrote to Annabella: 'I can't discover from Fletcher that any thing of abroad was mentioned last night. Whatever was the subject of conversation I could have heard it & so could George from the top of the house—so loud! B's head is very bad this morning Fletcher says. I really have told you as nearly as possible all that has passed about you since yr departure . . .' She then gave an account of Le Mann's report of Byron's liver complaint. 'Le M. talked *very* seriously of the drinking which he owned to . . . Le Mann says the pains in his loins &c are all Liver. His memory failed him this Eveg to such a degree he exclaimed at it himself.' On Friday, after seeing that Byron had a wholesome mutton broth for dinner, she wrote both to Annabella and (a most tactful letter) to her parents: 'At the same time we can't help requesting you to suspend any *positive determinations* for the present. The case is ye most difficult that could be imagined. That *malady does exist* can't be doubted but it is not such as yet as to admit of control. Mr. Le Mann thinks much good might be done by a perseverance in medicine & regular habits—but who can enforce them!'

Both Hanson and Le Mann urged Augusta to stay, and even Colonel Leigh was seized with 'such a comical fright' that Byron might follow her if she went home that he asked her to remain in London. Annabella as late as 28th January besought her not to leave. However, if Augusta thought Byron's behaviour was caused by 'malady' and not 'depravity of heart', Lady Milbanke was of the contrary opinion, considering him 'bad not mad'. On Saturday, 20th January, she left for London to consult the prominent lawyer Sir Samuel Romilly. With her affairs now in the hands of her formidable mother, Annabella's tortured and sadly perplexed feelings suffered violent convulsions. 'I am not fit to have management of myself, not to be left alone . . . ', she wrote to Augusta '. . . God bless you and *him*!' On the 21st she confessed: 'Indeed I have done nothing except on the strictest principle of Duty, yet I feel as if I were going to receive sentence from the Judge with his black cap on. In short, I feel—I feel—as if I were in the regions below, to speak of them genteelly. Then I have dreadful *head*-aches—[not?] to mind other aches, and altogether growing a little rebellious. O that I were in London, if in the coal-hole.' The next day she added: 'A little more crazy still. Nothing but Conscience to comfort me, and just now it is a Job's comforter.'

Still in the dark as to what was going on, Augusta wrote on the 19th that George Byron had been accepted by Mary Pole and was considering coming to Leicestershire to see if Bosworth House would be a suitable residence, but that his mother-in-law-to-be was making objections. 'Poor G.B. is in sad consternation, tribulation, &c at Mrs. *Fool's* objections, which only regard his want of *monies*. She wants them to have £600 a yr. more! & to wait a year or 3 years in hopes I suppose of finding a *mine*—& he swears he won't wait—& the young lady that she will never marry another—& so on, quite en regle—but worst of all they want to see ME! to talk it over. Heavens & earth! as if I had not enough to do without such an addition! . . . G.B. still wishes to know if Bosworth House is vacant—will you enquire for him without saying exactly why . . .' Later that evening, Byron and George having gone out to the theatre, she reported that 'B is in very good sorts—complains a little of the pills being *inactive*, but has promised to take them again tonight. He has a cold & soreness of his face & head which I have remarked before after a fit of tip. He dined on mutton broth—has talked of you & *Miss* & says he is sure *you want him terribly* . . . I hope dearest you are not tormenting yourself with repentance & scruples—for I do think your having gone will somehow be of use, & so does Le M. B. asked him yesterday what effects *ye Liver* had on people—if it did not make some *hypochondriac*. This is the most he has said on *the main point* . . . I wish I could but see you for I am afraid you are in a very uncomfortable state, & suspect Ly N. may not continue so calm as at first. I really think if ye present system is preserved in it may produce good, & that it is all that can be done at present.' Her fears of Lady Noel's remaining calm evinced a remarkable prescience. And in the same letter she showed how aware she was of the possibility of rumours spreading in London, when she told Annabella that she was to sit for the painter Holmes, 'who will report to Ly C[aroline] L[amb] & the *Round House*— a fine affair in their imagination your absence—& my stay!'

In the meantime Annabella was writing to Mrs Clermont that 'Heaven knows I am desirous enough never to see him again if it could be *decently effected*', and to her mother, warning her to seek advice, not to take measures, and not to let Augusta or George Byron know of the statements which she had furnished her for the lawyers—'*Half*-measures won't do with him, I think he may be *awed* by decided ones.' But her mind was again thrown into a turmoil of indecision by a reassuring letter from Augusta, with the postscript: 'Le Mann is sanguine still . . . B came home very well last night—no brandy—& he took ye Calomel again & I have ordered a Fowl for his dinner.'

However, pressed by her mother and Mrs Clermont not to accept any reconciliation, Annabella's mind veered once more to follow her strange notion of duty; how different the outcome might have been if she had listened to the warm humanity and common-sense of Augusta's counsels. Annabella had warned the latter in a letter of 19th January (which in her confused state of mind she misdated) that her mother would be arriving in London, and Augusta met Lady Noel on the 22nd. That morning Mrs Clermont had called on Augusta and George Byron and had told them that in her own opinion Sir Ralph, after hearing from Annabella the misery of her married life, would not let her live with Byron again, or see him, if he could prevent it. George Byron vouchsafed to Mrs Clermont the uncalled-for information that had he known Annabella before her marriage, he would have tried to prevent it, realising Byron to be unfit for married life. Only the evening before Augusta had reported cheerfully of his improvement: '. . . staid at home —no brandy—& said very seriously he should go to Kirkby in Feby. & that "they must *keep* us for 6 months". Of course I said nothing to discourage such a plan. I have seen him but a moment today when he was eating a stewed knuckle of Veal with broth and rice.' But her interview with Lady Noel the next day must have shown her for the first time that she was already waging a losing battle to preserve the marriage; only by the plea of insanity could Byron's behaviour be countenanced, yet she knew from Le Mann that nothing could be done by the family to authorise physical restraint without specific medical opinion, and that he (although he was convinced that there was some derangement) would not take it upon himself to declare that there was sufficient evidence for them to act on it.

Augusta, in an attempt to win Annabellas sympathy by describing his mental and physical illness and perhaps to arouse her jealousy by referring to his attentions to women, reported: 'Ly N. seems to think *his* relations can't let him go on in this state, *yet* what *is* to be—what *can* be done! One of the things he did & said last night was desiring George to go & live at Seaham exactly as if it were his own! & even before dinner he said he considered himself *the greatest man existing*. G. said laughing "Except Buonaparte!" Ye answer was "God! I don't know that I do except even him!" ' Two days later she referred again to his physical illness: 'I found B. very bad with ye pain in his head when he sent for me yesterday before my dinner & after his . . . it seems now first over one eye then ye other, then between & over the nose & at times spasmodic . . . [He] made me go to the Play with him before which I had an opportunity of saying what I have long thought of & considered—that I heard from various quarters that his conduct at the Theatre was much observed & talked of—*Miss Boyce* even mentioned, & others hinted at. He tried to laugh at first wanted to know my authority which of course I did *not* give & took ye opportunity of mentioning also his want of discretion. He seemed very evidently *much* struck by my intelligence & to be sure he had not *flirted* when he returned to the Box, & Mr. Holmes has I find has been desired *not* to go to paint Miss Cooke.

'George last night spoke to him very sensibly & seriously of

Annabella, Byron's wife. Miniature by Sir George Hayter, 1812

Six Mile Bottom, Newmarket

you & what he was bringing on himself—ye same arguments *I* have gone over a thousand times & with ye same effects.

'I've seen him just now . . . His temper good, but he is much perplexed by a letter from Ly F. Webster again! & I'm to copy it for you & send it for *yr opinion & advice* if possible ! ! ! . . . Today he asked again after you, & *if you wanted* HIM.'

Later she continued her long account: 'B. has been at home this Eveg, & *very* well . . . This letter from Paris has set his brain into a sad ferment . . . He has already mentioned going with Hobhouse to Paris *to see* what *she means*. Is it not (hers) the most *barefaced* impudence you ever heard of? . . . B's first idea was "had she heard you had left Town?" or any reports about you & him—in short his poor head is quite off on this subject & *I* should like to knock *hers* agst the wall! . . .'

She told Annabella that she had repeated a thousand times what George Byron had spoken to him about the result of his present actions, and that at one point he said, ' "You think me *mad* on *that* subject." I replied you certainly don't speak rationally upon it. Surely if *control* is out of the question, ye next best thing is to try to make him aware *Malady does exist* . . .'

Augusta was seeing Lady Noel every day but, though she referred to her with tact to Annabella, she avoided commenting on their discussions. Annabella's letters were full of her own concerns, worries and ill health. To her remark that her father was even more severe than her mother Augusta replied that she was sorry to hear this 'because it will add to *your* worry . . . I foresee nothing but wretchedness for us all . . . Happy those! who can feel they don't deserve it—& that must ever be *your* comfort.' But by this time Annabella had fixed in her mind the necessity of a separation, and any effort on Augusta's part to rouse in her reactions of natural feminine jealousy or sympathy were unavailing.

On Friday, 26th, Augusta reported that Byron had gone to the Royal Society with Hobhouse '& came home . . . in the worst of humours & more mad than I've seen him since you [have] been gone. *Paris* is ye favorite theme. "H. is going abroad & will be his companion if he goes . . ."—& then H says I look as if I did not like him & thought he made B drink Brandy! and a good deal more in this style apropos of *nothing*! I was summoned as usual to attend him to his room where ye subject was renewed in a stronger manner by B. & at last I begged to know why there was this wonderful defence of H. when nobody had accused him? that as far as related to *my* opinion & the subject of going abroad I was quite willing & ready to give my objections *to himself* & repeat all I had said on the subject whenever he liked to hear. This produced no slight consternation. "I'll be *d*—*d* if you shall speak to him in my presence or out of it"—a great deal more in ye same way which is useless to repeat—all to defend H. from anything to do with his conduct about you & yours—that he (H) pitied you & said "poor thing!" In short my Dear A I was quite in an *internal* rage & calmly to all outward appearance looked steadfastly at B & asked him whether "He thought well of H?" You never saw such confusion—he is certainly VERY unpleasant tonight— says he will go off with ye first woman who will go with him— & constant allusions to Ly F[rancis Webster], to whom he has written a most improper answer. I don't know if it is actually gone, but it must do mischief if it does go & if by chance her Spouse gets hold of it I think it will cause an uproar. I am sent to Hanson tomorrow on all sorts of business—it is strange he won't go himself! & he has been FLIRTING if not worse at the Theatre tonight. To say the truth I think flirting is ye *worst* for everybody talks & stares of course.'

The honesty and good intentions of these reports from Augusta were lost on Annabella. On the same day as Augusta wrote this letter Annabella had heard from her mother of legal progress. Sir Samuel Romilly had advised that her father should write to Byron stating that it was 'impossible for him consistently with his *Duty* as a *Father* and his *principles* as a *Man*, to allow that Ld B. should be an inmate of his House, or allowing You to return to Ld B's'. Lady Noel informed her that both George Byron and Augusta thought her life had been unsafe with him, and reassured her: 'As to Your fears that *I* should be cajoled by *Sweet Words*, I can only say "old Birds are not caught by Chaff"—and in respect to Mrs. Leigh She has so committed herself before me and Clermont that *She cannot retract*, nor do I now believe She is inclined to do so—but it [is] I believe the wish of her heart that it should prove *Lunacy* not *depravity* without that excuse . . .'

Lady Noel had an appointment on the following day to see

Dr Stephen Lushington, an eminent civilian. She reported next day her interview with this 'most *gentlemanlike*, clear headed and clever Man', and that it was now decided that someone should be appointed by Sir Ralph to meet the person fixed on by Byron to draw up articles of separation. Lushington had also added the spicy gossip that Miss Boyce's 'Character' was so well known that Annabella's health would not have been safe if she had continued with Byron. Lady Noel did not give details of a meeting that she had had with Augusta and George Byron, as she found that Mrs Clermont had already done so. When Lady Noel had discussed the plan for separation with them, 'nothing [could] exceed their kindness towards you'; Mrs Clermont significantly added: 'I am only distressed when your Mother becomes harsh in speaking of *him* to Mrs. Leigh . . . I mention this that you may in writing to her speak kindly of Mrs. Leigh or rather as She *has deserv'd* from you & do not suffer any wild fancies to make you unjust . . .' Lady Noel, accompanied by Selina Doyle and Mrs Clermont, left London on the morning of Saturday, 27th January, before the arrival of Annabella's letter to her mother in which she wrote: 'I have been comforted & confirmed as usual by one of Mrs. Leigh's kind letters. She has been the truest of friends to me—and I hope you regard her, & *seem* to regard her as such, for I very much fear that She may be supposed the cause of Separation by many, and it would be a cruel injustice.' To Augusta Annabella had written on the 25th: 'Shall I still be your sister? I must resign my *rights* to be so considered; but I don't think that will make any difference in the kindness I have so uniformly experienced from you. I follow my Duty, and look to that peace which it can alone ensure—here or hereafter . . .' This was a solemn avowal from a young woman of twenty-three, and as a prophecy singularly ill-judged. However, as an admission of Augusta's kindness to her throughout her trials it was palpably fair; Augusta, notwithstanding her wretchedness on Byron's behalf, had never deviated in her loyalty and justice to Annabella, and it was but right of the latter to acknowledge it.

Augusta replied to Annabella on the 27th: 'You will ever be my own dearest Sis! How can you be otherwise—*indeed, indeed* every day makes you if possible dea*rer*, & gives you additional claims on me. But I can't say half enough . . .' She then gave her report on Byron: 'He is at dinner but he staid at home last night & was tolerably quiet, tho singing wildly & irritable. He gave me an opportunity of saying much more of *derangement*, & took it very quietly . . . He talked as if in expectation of what is going to happen—said, "I think things can't go on as they are don't you?" that he only wished you wd take some step, & so on. *Paris* is uppermost certainly. He said jestingly I should be in such a fuss if he went there, to which I calmly replied, "No, my fusses can't be increased or diminished"—which seemed to strike him & he pressed me to say more. I declined, giving as a reason that it made no impression & therefore I had better be silent . . .'

Writing on 28th January, Annabella warned Augusta that her father's communication to Byron was on the way and asked her to keep it secret that she had anticipated it, 'as it would be prejudicial to me and mine'. Sir Ralph's letter, drafted by Lushington, arrived at 13 Piccadilly Terrace with Annabella's on the 29th, when it was intercepted by Augusta and returned unopened. Augusta acted in this way out of regard for Annabella as much as for Byron. She felt from her knowledge of the former and from an equivocal quality in some of her letters that she was not acting completely on her own initiative, that it was rather the pressure of others (certainly Lady Noel, perhaps Mrs Clermont) which was causing her now to act, and that, given more time to consider, she might repent of and retract from a step the consequences of which might be fatal to her future happiness. Also, knowing Byron as no other person knew him, she realised that lawyers' threats would be met with all the stubbornness of his pride and were bound to fail, whereas a plea for reconciliation, sincerely made, would awaken his generosity of feeling and perhaps—there was just the faintest hope—work on his awareness of his own responsibility in provoking the crisis. Augusta acted as a person of her instinctive, responsive and responsible nature would have acted; unmindful of herself, she was unwittingly instrumental in awakening suspicions that were to end disastrously for her.

Immediately she sat down to write to Annabella: 'For once in my life I have ventured to act in accordance with my own judgement—not without 10000 fears I assure you. But I do it *for the best* & I do hope at least it will not be productive of evil, as I only wish *a few days delay*, & that you would hear all that I have to say before you send the enclosed.

'It appears to me of the VERY *utmost* consequence for *you* & *your child* (for you must believe *that* to be my first consideration) that you should *pause*. See Ly Noel—hear what passed between Le Mann Sir H. Halford [a celebrated physician] & her. The former was with me too late to write by Saturday's post & [is] so very strongly *of my own opinion* upon this subject that I begin to think it can't be a foolish one . . . you must my dear A—believe that I can only wish *your good* in venturing to act as I have. Pray *assure* Sir Ralph of this & obtain my forgiveness if possible . . .' She informed Annabella that George Byron was leaving on the following day for Leicestershire, to see the house he had in mind to take, and would call on her parents, if they would receive him. '. . . My own feelings and wishes (as I have told you I believe repeatedly) are, that *the whole blame* should rest on [Byron], & if ever a shade of it *rested on you* it would break my heart QUITE . . . I'm now in such agitation at what I've ventured to do that I CAN'T write rationally . . .'

George Byron, bearing a letter from Augusta for Annabella, travelled north to Kirkby; but, since he was strongly opposed to his cousin's behaviour, his visit only served to strengthen the Noels in their resolution to carry through the separation. Augusta had written on 30th January: 'I shall tell George in few words what I wish which is nearly as I expressed myself yesterday—that you would *pause* a few days, consider the *probable* & *possible* consequences of this letter from ye effects on B—for they *must* affect *you* & *your child*. I am very strongly of the opinion *revenge* will be uppermost & this from my late observations. What revenge could he take so effectual as depriving you of the child! & *who* could prevent him. Can *we* all say that a man who is not deranged *sufficiently* to admit of being *controuled* is unfit to have the care of his own child! & what would be the consequences to that child & your own feelings! Don't fancy I mean you to follow my advice, only to consider of these things. I too well know & feel all you have suffered, but my dread is yr suffering *more*, & my knowledge of your disposition only adds to this fear . . .' She then went on to inform Annabella that Byron was seeing Lady Melbourne, who was trying to act as a peacemaker and 'to induce B. by all she *dares* urge to behave

161

well to YOU—talks of your merits & attachment to him in ye VERY strongest manner . . .' She concluded her long and most reasonable letter: 'I daresay my dearest A, I've omitted 1000 things but George must fill ye chasm . . . Le M. is of opinion that he will take some very wild step in the fit of irritation *the* letter may occasion.'

If Augusta's plea for a short delay to consider matters before taking the final step was frustrated, much blame must be attached to George Byron, who was openly a partisan of Annabella, declared that Augusta's fears of Byrons doing an injury to himself were unfounded, and, further, quite gratuitously offered to give evidence that Byron himself wished for a separation. His surprising disloyalty to his cousin countered Augusta's counsels of moderation and delay. Sir Ralph, accompanied by Mrs Clermont (whose thinking from now on was coloured by the outraged implacability of Lady Noel), left immediately for London to deliver his letter by hand. Lady Noel's fury poured out in two letters to Augusta: 'I cannot think You had a right to Stop the letter . . . *You were not to judge* . . . You have done infinite mischief . . . Your barbarous and hard hearted Brother . . . has broken the heart that was devoted to him . . .' Annbella, however, prevented these overcharged missives from being sent. But Lady Noel had the satisfaction of passing on some revealing information to her husband about the infamy of his sister, Lady Melbourne: 'Ld [Byron] has told his Wife that in 1813 he had *absolute criminal* Connection with an *old Lady*, at the same time as with her Daughter in Law—that *She* absolutely *proposed it to him*—and that he said "She [was] *so old* he hardly knew how to go about it." Ld *B*. has told this also to his Sister . . .' Honest, bluff Sir Ralph should know the type of people he was dealing with.

X
Stanzas to Augusta
1816

SIR RALPH arrived at Mivart's Hotel and sent his letter around by special messenger to Piccadilly Terrace on Friday, 2nd February. Byron, who had just ordered horses to set out for Kirkby on the following Sunday, was deeply surprised when actually confronted with what he himself had so often proposed. The real was more stunning and wounding to his self-esteem than the merely imagined. He read: '*Very recently* Circumstances have come to my knowledge, which convince me, that with your opinions it cannot tend to your happiness to continue to live with Lady Byron, and I am yet more forcibly convinced that after her dismissal from your house, and the treatment she experienced whilst in it, those on whose protection she has the strongest natural claims could not feel themselves justified in permitting her return thither . . .' Although Sir Ralph was willing to bring the whole matter before the public, he was loath to do so; and he now proposed that Byron should appoint some 'professional friend' to meet another of his appointing 'to Settle such terms of Separation as may be mutually approved'. Immediately on receiving this letter, Augusta wrote at Byron's dictation: 'My dearest Annabella—I am desired by B. to write you a line to ask whether the separation between you (proposed this day by your Father) is *your* wish—and if so, he will acquiesce, & that you need not be under any apprehension of intemperate feelings or conduct on his part those belonging to you. I need not say with what grief I write on this subject. God bless you & dear little Guss. Ever yr most affec Sis, AL.'

With this letter Augusta enclosed a note of her own headed '*Private*': 'I am desired to send ye enclosed, & have to add that he is *quiet*, & that a *temperate* answer is *begun*. To Sr R's letter he objects that it is *exaggerated*, though he admits his conduct not to have been good. But all this I expected. He particularly dwells in his defence to *me* on the effect of pecuniary embarrassments on his mind, & ("if he is to believe Le Mann") that he has "been labouring for some time past under illness which occasions fits of PARTICULAR IRRITATION". Remember this is for *you alone*—at least I should not wish it to be repeated as it was said to me *in confidence*. Towards you there is no feeling but kindness but much annoyance at the grief he sees he occasions me. Poor dear Soul! But I can't dwell on or bear to think of *you* my dearest dear Sis & all yr suffereings . . .' (This, as well as all other letters from Augusta, was handed over by Annabella to Lushington). The following afternoon, after taking Sir Ralph's letter to show Hanson (who was in fact out of town) she sent another bulletin to Annabella: 'Things are *I know not how*. No answer has yet been *sent*, tho' one was *written* last night & with fewer objectionable points in it than I expected . . .' She mentioned her alarm at Byron's appearance, and went on to express Byron's concern at hearing that Annabella had also been unwell, and to let her know that he had declared his intention of going to Kirkby on Sunday, if the letter had not come. 'God only knows what is best—from my heart I wish I did & *could* give either you or yours comfort . . . Le Mann is indeed a great comfort to me. Whatever his *visionary* ideas may be my dear A surely there is *good sense* in thinking a person in a state of mind & body *he* is convinced his Patient *is* in, ought not to be treated as one *sane & sound* . . .'

But it was all of no avail. Annabella had recovered from the paroxysm of grief which had prostrated her at the time when she imagined Byron would be receiving her father's first letter; duty had resumed its inexorable sway and there was no room now for affection or second thoughts. To Augusta she wrote: 'You are desired by your brother to ask if my father has acted with my concurrence in proposing a separation. He has.' The following day, thinking that Augusta might once more take matters into her own hands, Annabella wrote again: 'I hope, my dear A., that you would on no account withhold from your brother the letter which I sent yesterday, in answer to yours written by his desire . . .'

Byron replied to Sir Ralph without equivocation and with quiet dignity: 'To the vague & general charge . . . I must naturally be at a loss how to answer . . . Lady Byron received no "dismissal" from my house in the sense you have attached to the word . . . It is true that . . . I had suggested to her the expediency of a temporary residence with her parents: —my reason for this was very simple & shortly stated—VIZ. the embarrassment of my circumstances & my inability to maintain our present establishment. The truth of what is thus stated may be easily ascertained by reference to Lady B. who is Truth itself . . . During the last year I have had to contend with distress without, & disease within: —upon the former I have little to say . . . & the latter I should not mention if I had not recent & professional authority for saying that the disorder which I have to combat . . . is such as to induce a morbid irritability of temper, which . . . may have rendered me little less disagreeable to others than I am to myself. I am however ignorant of any particular ill treatment which your daughter' has encountered . . .' He then spoke with feeling and justice of Annabella's good qualities—'the most amiable of beings—& nearer to Perfection than I had conceived could belong to Humanity in its present existence.

'Having said thus much . . . I come to the point, on which subject I must for a few days decline giving a decisive answer . . . For the present at least, your daughter is my wife; —she is the mother of my child—& till I have her express sanction of your proceedings, I shall take leave to doubt the propriety of your interference . . . '

Annabella's unambiguous reply to Augusta quickly removed any doubt of her attitude from Byron's mind and her refusal to answer his friendly letters appeared to confirm her resolution. On Monday, 5th February, Hobhouse rode up from Whitton, and that evening reported in his journal: 'George Byron had been down at Kirkby, and found Lady Noel like a fury. Byron confessed he had often been out of temper with her (LadyB.), refused to live with her friends—told her she was in his way— but then he had a liver complaint and from one to four executions in his house at a time. I never saw him so much affected in my life.' On the 7th Byron revealed his own stubbornness by writing to Sir Ralph, 'inviting Lady Byron's return'. And on the same day Augusta, distracted with worry at the way events were shaping, wrote a hurried note to Francis Hodgson, who was in the country: 'Can you *by any means* contrive to come up to Town? were it only for *a day*—it might be of the most essential service to a friend I know you love and value: there is too much probability of a *separation* between him and his Wife—no time is to be lost, but even if you are *too late* to prevent that happening *decidedly*, yet it would be the very greatest comfort and relief to me to confide other circumstances to you and consult you; and so, IF POSSIBLE, oblige me, if only for 24 hours. Say not *a word* of *my summons*—but attribute your coming, if you come, to business of your own or chance. Excuse brevity—I am so perfectly wretched . . .' Then she added a postscript: 'It is probable I may be obliged to go home next week: if my scheme appears wild, pray attribute it to ye state of mind I am [in]. Alas! I see only *ruin* and *distruction* in *every* shape to one most dear to me.' Rumours were already rife in London, and Augusta's staying on in Piccadilly was causing so much comment that the dowager Duchess of Leeds had tried to persuade her to leave; but her loyalty to Byron and Annabella overrode any thought of her own reputation.

In reply to a cold letter from Annabella, in which she excused her not having answered his to her (her letters to Augusta she had 'deemed a sufficient answer'), Byron wrote movingly on 8th February: 'All I can say seems useless—and all I could say might be no less unavailing—yet I still cling to the wreck of my hopes, before they sink for ever . . .'; and he asked if he might see her— '. . . I will say & do nothing to agitate either— it is torture to correspond thus . . .' On the same day Augusta, too, wrote: 'My silence will not have been misinterpreted by *you*, but all I could have said within ye last few days would only have added to what I know you are suffering. You have better advisers than *I* can be, tho none more anxious for yr peace & happiness. *I am on the spot* however & feel it a duty to say that I am apprehensive of the most serious consequences from the manner in which *he* has taken this *sad* business to heart. He writes today to ask you to see him—*pause* ere you refuse *for God's sake* . . . when I think of you & your dear child & another VERY dear to me, I am distracted with the prospect, which offers nothing but *ruin, destruction & wretchedness* in the most alarming forms . . .'

But Annabella was now too deeply committed to consider retreat. Both Hobhouse and Hodgson wrote to her counselling reconciliation, the former a letter somewhat injudicious in the language used, the latter with tact and delicacy; but the results were the same—an unbending refusal. Lady Noel saw the hands of Lady Melbourne and Augusta behind Byron in 'playing a deep Game'—Augusta for the 'basest motives—profit'; she was plotting to gain custody of the child and an allowance as 'assistance to her poverty'. Mrs Clermont tried to reassure her about Augusta—'Lady Noel goes *too fast* in attributing to her any wrong intentions.' Annabella still believed in Augusta's disinterested sincerity, writing to her on 12th February: 'I cannot say how much I feel for you. Myself is a lesser grief.'

On the same day Hobhouse came to London and called at 13 Piccadilly. In his journal he reported: 'There saw Mrs. Leigh & George Byron—and from them learnt what I fear is the real truth that Byron has been guilty of very great tyranny—menaces—furies—neglects, and even real injuries—such as telling his wife he was *living with another woman*—& actually in *fact* turning her out of the house.

'George Byron suspected she would leave him & told him so, a month before she went—but she had no intention of doing it when she went from London.

'Locking doors, showing pistols, pouring reproaches at her in bed—everything he seems, to believe them, to have been guilty of! and they acquit him—how? by saying that he is mad—certainly—and that Mr. Le Mann says that it is the consequence of a torpid liver—which has already affected his eyes—made one smaller than the other & made him squint.

'Whilst I heard these things Mrs. Leigh went out & brought word that her brother was crying bitterly in his bedroom—poor, poor fellow.'

Returning later, he met Lady Melbourne, 'who abused Lady Noel violently'. He continued his entry in his journal: 'He had heard he was to be accused of cruelty drunkenness & *infidelity*. I got him to own much of what I had been told in the morning—he was dreadfully agitated—said he was ruined & would blow out his brains—he is indignant but yet terrified—sometimes says "and yet she loved me once" and at other times that he is glad to be quit of such a woman. He said if I would go abroad he would separate at once.'

The strain was almost more than Augusta could bear; Byron's

moods and resolutions veered like a weathercock. Hanson had advised him to refuse an amicable separation and to let the matter be thrashed out in the courts. After Hobhouse had left, she began a letter to Annabella, but she confessed 'that I really fear my nerves are scarcely equal to allowing me to write *clearly* . . . You desire me to state *explicitly* every thing I allude to as suppressed. B— is in the deepest grief & has been so ever since he received Sr Ralph's first letter. He seems DETER-MINED *never willingly* to resign you. What is the alternative my dear A? That as YOUR Friends ARE *determined* upon a separation this sad business must come before the Public. *Supposing* even that nothing is LEGALLY PROVED against him which can procure you this separation, what will the *world think*! won't his character be blasted for ever! He is convinced of this, & I am convinced not only will his reputation be sacrificed to this exposure but *his* LIFE. My dear A, don't suppose I judge from declarations to put an end to his existence in the usual strain of such—no, those who make them in general are ye last to execute them. But he has at different times but constantly expressed in very mysterious terms a *deep* & *dreadful* tho *vague* intention—to more than me, to those who know him better, who have stronger minds, better judgements—NOT to SURVIVE such disgrace. Remember most of HIS predeterminations have become *actions*. What would be your feelings SHOULD *this* be the consequence—or even his eternal disgrace in *this* world—he is in *every* way in *any* way a ruined man.

'I am called away . . . pray don't decide hastily in driving him to desperation . . .'

She went on with her letter the next day, Tuesday, 13th February: 'I had I believe mentioned to you what wd be the consequences of this sad business being brought before a public Court . . . I must now say I can't at least be mistaken in what *are* the consequences *already*. The whole Town is full of reports of the *worst* kind. B. is quite aware of it, but still determined never to give you up, without he is compelled.

'. . . B is this morning in such a dreadfully agitated state that I don't know *what* to do. I attribute it in great measure to some *pecuniary* concerns . . . He says . . . that he is still most anxious for an interview, which would not bind you to anything . . .

There is one thing my dearest A, you should be prepared for (if worse don't occur) which is about the Child. He seems determined to have it, & I understand *the Law* wd allow it to him when a year old. I see in short such a *host of evils in perspective* & not ye least of all what your feelings would be if *any one* was the consequence of yr separating from him. You will think perhaps *I* of all people ought not to dissuade you from it . . .

'B. has just got yr letter—Alas!

'He desires me to say they refuse him all explanation whatever—that is yr Father &c.'

Augusta expressed her anxieties in a letter to Francis Hodgson on the 15th: 'These legal measures sound most horrible—& I fear there is nothing but open war to be expected . . . It is a *sad, sad* business dear Mr. H. B. deceives himself & deceives others, but his conscience will occasionally speak. Heaven grant Your prayers that it may end better than we expect, but I dare not hope it . . .' She continued distractedly: 'All that I see hanging over us—in every shape—some of it *certain*—ye rest but too much to be dreaded—but *I* CAN *not* urge her to return, & expose herself to a repetition of all I have witnessed—& heard of. She must decide for herself.' Of all those engaged in the Byron separation Augusta alone saw the issues with the greatest clarity and fairness to both sides, yet her efforts only served to encompass a cruelly ironic retribution.

On Saturday, 17th February, when Annabella was already planning to come to London to interview Lushington personally, Augusta found time to write to her: 'I don't presume to *urge* or to *advise*, yet I have sometimes (perhaps too often) thought it my duty to *represent*, being on the spot, seeing, hearing & knowing what others cannot. If I have erred it is in judgement not intention. There are reports abroad of a nature *too horrible to repeat*. I had guessed them from G.B's *mysterious* manner & *excessive* annoyance for some days past. *He* G.B yesterday sent for Hobhouse, who I find last night informed B. of them, & HE B has desired me to inform you of them. Of course this has added considerably to his agitations. Every other sinks into nothing before this MOST horrid one. God alone knows what is to be the end of it all . . . I have told you before of *his hints* of self destruction. The night before last, I went as usual to his room to light his Candles & seeing a Draught on the chimney piece which looked *fermenting*, I said "What is this." "My Draught, to be sure—what did you think it was? Laudanum?" I replied jokingly that I was not even *thinking* of Laudanum & the truth—that I thought the Draught spoilt, which caused my inquiry. He immediately looked very dark & black (in the old way) & said "I have plenty of Laudanum—& shall use it". Upon my laughing & trying to turn off the subject he only repeated in the most awful manner *his most solemn determination* on the subject. I thought it but right to ask Fletcher if he could get at it, & put water to it &c., & consulted Le Mann, who said he wd exchange it for Extract of Hops if I could get at it. Fletcher says he has looked in the place where it used to be kept, & every where else, & that B. must have locked it up! THIS would be the means my dear A in preference to any other. The MOST dreadful report!—who knows what it may urge him to do. He said to me last night in an agony "Even to have such a thing *said* is utter destruction & ruin to a man from which he never can recover".

'In answer to yr letter I am alas! but too well convinced you are acting from *Duty*—from *Principle*. Heaven grant the consequences may be less fatal than I dread. Don't talk of reproaches from *me* my own Dear A—I never could think you *wrong*, but I would save you if possible the misery I'm sure you wd feel if any one of my anticipations are realized . . .'

Colonel Leigh came to London at this juncture, and accepting that Augusta's presence was essential in Piccadilly, agreed that she should stay on until matters were clearer. Then on the 20th Augusta made her final, equally fruitless, appeal to Annabella: 'I am always wishing to speak or write to you . . . but then comes the reflexion that perhaps I *ought* NOT—that it may be deemed dishonorable in me as B's Sister to endeavor to sway you. Yet surely none can have felt more truly all *your* sufferings & unhappiness than I do. All this is my reflexion at one moment. Ye next suggests another—that I never could forgive myself, if I had omitted any thing in my power to contribute to the *future* happiness of both.

'I do think in my heart dearest A, that *your return* might be the *saving* & *reclaiming* of him. You could but give it a trial, & if he persisted in his ill-conduct you would be fully justified in

170

then abandoning him. Your doing it now, I do think will be his ruin . . .

'Of all this my Dear A you are a better judge than I am. You may know more than I do, of the charges you have to bring against him. Most likely you are aware you will have to depose against him *yrself*, & that without witnesses yr depositions will go for nothing—ye same in regard to those who have only heard circumstances from you.

'*You* will I know forgive all I am saying for the distraction of my mind. I can't help repeating that it is my opinion yr return *might* be his *salvation*—yr *abandoning* WILL inevitably be his ruin. Surely it is my duty to tell you so . . .'

*

On 22nd February, the day after Hanson had sent to Sir Ralph Noel Byron's refusal to assent to a separation, Annabella arrived in London and put up at Mivart's Hotel in Lower Brook St, where the same evening her counsel Lushington called on her. At this interview Annabella disclosed to the shocked lawyer her suspicions of the nature of Byron's relationship with Augusta: that she strongly suspected incest, for which her evidence was Byron's behaviour towards her, his remarks in Augusta's presence and when alone with Annabella. At first Lushington deprecated the slightest intimation of her suspicions, which, having the appearance of malice, could only harm her case. Further, such charges could not be substantiated in court, where the wife was debarred from giving evidence. If the separation came to court the charge against Byron would be 'brutally indecent conduct and language', and here part of the evidence would be his behaviour towards Augusta, yet not seeking thereby to prove incest. But within a week of her arrival in London the rumours were so rife that Lushington advised her to cease communicating with Augusta. Hobhouse noted in his journal on the 29th: 'Mrs. Leigh has been forbid all intercourse with her at her lawyer's request. A story has now got abroad against *her and Byron* ! ! !' The source of these two principal rumours was the unbalanced Lady Caroline Lamb; the first, the report 'too horrible to repeat' of Augusta's letter of the 17th, was that Byron practised homosexuality; the present rumour was of incest with Augusta.

In defence of Annabella, it must be said that it was partly the fear expressed by Augusta that Byron would claim custody of the child that made her act against that person who had always shown her the most unremitting kindness. The divided state of her mind at this time is illustrated by her writing to Augusta's Aunt Sophia, who replied on the 29th to her suggestion that she should warn Augusta to leave Piccadilly: ' "It is a constant thorn in my side" and I know not how to relieve it—without *tearing* a Veil from her Eyes which might almost overset her reason . . . I have written and used every argument in my power to *persuade* her to go from London. Le Sposo and her friends have been equally anxious for it . . . if I could by any means have afforded a journey and visit to L[ondon] just now I would have *spoken* to Mrs V[illiers] who has great weight with her . . . I believe she remains NOW on account of The D[rawing] Room being shortly expected to take place . . .' These two women seem singularly to have failed to grasp the quality of Augusta's loyalty. She was well aware of the rumours. Writing to Francis Hodgson on 4th March, she declared: 'Now, I have borne patiently & indeed laughed at all I have heard of reports against myself—& it has been a good deal for some days past. *The world* perhaps has a right to talk . . .'

Lord Holland, at Lushington's suggestion, was called in at this point as a mediator, but his lack of success in persuading Byron to agree to a separation was unequivocal, Byron replying on 3rd March: 'I answer *NO* . . . With regard to "amicable arrangement" I am open to the most amicable of arrangements. I am willing & desirous to become reconciled with Lady B . . . to be forgiven where I may have offended—& in some points, it may be, to forgive. But I will sign no separations . . .'

At the end of February Annabella received a letter from Augusta's friend Mrs George Villiers; referring to the calumnious reports now circulating against Augusta, which she had indignantly rebutted, she gave as the reason for the persistence of these rumours Annabella's refusal to assign a reason for the separation. Further, Mrs Villiers thought it essential for 'poor Augusta's reputation' that Annabella should make 'known to your friends in general those sentiments of confidence, esteem and affection' which she was sure she felt for her. Annabella wrote a very guarded letter in reply, but refused as 'improper' to reveal the cause for separation. The ambivalence, the deep division in her mind with regard to Augusta, is evident from this point. Contrary to Lushington's advice, she arranged that Augusta should meet her at her hotel on 5th March. This would give the lie direct to those persons who said she had broken off communications with Augusta. But Annabella had a further motive in seeing her: she repeated to Augusta what she had said to George Byron the previous evening, that she was 'perfectly determined never' to return to Byron, and that in this determination she was influenced by no one. Reporting Annabella's decision to Hodgson that evening, Augusta wrote: ... She hinted (but this is *sacred*) that she had reasons which she hoped would die with her—why she *could never* consistently with her *duty to God* do so ... I can never describe Ly B's appearance to you—but by comparing it to what I should imagine that of a Being of another world. She is positively reduced to a Skeleton—pale as *ashes*—a deep hollow tone of voice & a *calm* in her manner quite supernatural. She received *me* kindly, but that really appeared the only SURVIVING *feeling* —all else was *death like* calm. *I* can never forget it—never!'

Augusta now set about persuading Byron to avoid bringing the matter to court, and suggested to him as intermediary their cousin Robert Wilmot, who had just then arrived in London with his beautiful wife—she had inspired Byron to write the first of his *Hebrew Melodies*, 'She Walks in Beauty'. Wilmot was vain, pompous and something of an ass; but Augusta was only to learn this later. She wrote to him, suggesting that he act for Byron in a fresh approach to Annabella. 'I have been giving him [Byron] my opinions on this subject, & have reason (from experience in *past* cases) to think it just possible they may have weight tho' *at first* they appear to be rejected ... B. thinks you the only proper person of *all* belonging to him, friends & relatives, to go to her from him ...' On his way to Piccadilly on the following morning, the 6th, Hobhouse met Wilmot and they discussed the case—the former arguing that in view of the rumours the matter should come to court, the latter holding for a peaceful settlement. When Hobhouse arrived he found Annabella's letter of the day before in which she claimed a promise that, if she proved that the proceedings stemmed entirely from her, Byron would consent to a private arrangement.

Hobhouse asked if this was so, and Byron admitted that Augusta had given the undertaking on his behalf. Hobhouse then changed his view and thought it only just for Byron to redeem his promise; but, after consulting Augusta, he considered that Byron and his friends 'had a right to demand, previous to any separation, a positive disavowal of all the heinous charges made against Byron'. Augusta declared to Hobhouse that so strongly was she persuaded of Byron's madness that, were he so, she would nurse him. Byron's reply to this pronouncement was to quote Goldsmith's mock elegy: 'The dog it was who died'.

The advisers on both sides spent several days drawing up proposals for the separation, and on the 9th Wilmot arrived with a disavowal from Annabella of the two specific charges of homosexuality and incest: 'the two reports specifically mentioned by Mr. Wilmot do not form any part of the charges which, in the event of a Separation by agreement not taking place, she should have been compelled to make against Lord Byron'. However, thoughts that a settlement was imminent were premature. Disputes about an immediate legal stipulation as to the disposal of the Kirkby estates, when they came to Annabella, caused angry scenes; Byron, backed by Hanson and Douglas Kinnaird, was opposed to stipulating in a legal form there and then; Hobhouse and Wilmot (supported by Augusta) felt that Annabella's party were only reasonable in requiring that legal form be given, binding Byron to act in a way that would be naturally right when the occasion arose. Finally it was agreed that Sir Samuel Shepherd, the Solicitor General, should arbitrate in the matter, but not before it seemed likely that the case would come into the courts.

When it appeared that the matter would have to be settled publicly, Annabella drew up, with Lushington, a memorandum of her motives in not acting earlier against Augusta: 'My principles of conduct in regard to Mrs. Leigh were these. When I could not help perceiving things which must suggest dreadful suspicions, I considered that in proportion to the heinous nature of the crime, a stronger evidence was necessary. I could not adopt a middle line of conduct. I must either have quitted my husband at once upon such a supposition, by which I should have injured her character irreparably—or I must repel the idea as much as possible and act in direct opposition to it. The last alternative, however difficult and painful, appeared to be my duty . . . But my belief has been so strong that *any* further corroborating evidence would fix it unchangeably.' She later made some additions to this document (giving further reason for her actions) which she signed for her lawyer on 11th March:

'Because Mrs. L. had from her first acquaintance with Lady B. always manifested towards her the utmost kindness & attention . . .

'Because Mrs. L. at times exhibited signs of a deep remorse . . .

'Because Lady B, conceived it possible that the crime, if committed, might not only be deeply repented of, but never have been perpetrated since her marriage with Lord B . . .

'Since Lady B's Separation from Lord B. the report has become current in the World of such a connection having subsisted. This report was not shared nor sanctioned by Lady B . . . it being intimated that Mrs. L's character can never be so effectually preserved as by a renewal of intercourse with Lady B. she does for the motives & reasons before mentioned consent to renew that intercourse—

'Now this Statement is made in order to Justify Lady B. in her line of conduct she has now determined to adopt & in order to prevent all misconstruction of her motives in case Mrs L. should be proved here after to be guilty, and if any circumstances should compel . . . Lady B. to prefer the charge in order that Lady B, may be at full liberty so to do without being prejudiced by her present conduct.' Annabella had thus forged a powerful instrument for use when she deemed it justified. She had her cake and could eat it at leisure.

Augusta strongly disapproved of Byron's stubborn refusal to stipulate about Kirkby, and was disposed to leave the house (having even ordered fires at St James's Palace) rather than 'witness or sanction such conduct'. However, she was dissuaded from leaving—which was in reality in conflict with her deepest feelings and would, she realised, make it appear that she was '*afraid* to stay & face ye reports'. On the 13th Hobhouse called at Piccadilly and 'found her in tears and great distress indeed . . . She thinks she ought in duty to her husband and children to leave Byron's house—she having stayed long enough to *give the lie* to all rumours respecting herself, which Col. Leigh has most handsomely *discredited* in every way . . .' Augusta, anxious that Byron would not attribute her leaving to pressure from her husband or friends, asked Hobhouse to mention it to him as if the suggestion came from himself.

On Thursday, 14th March, the day Annabella signed her statement, Augusta wrote to Hodgson in despair. She was at this time seven months advanced in pregnancy: 'All going on as bad as possible—a Court inevitable I *fear* & the *Citation* out immediately . . . I am nearly dead with worry & finding I can do no good I will stay no longer . . .' That night she went on with her letter: 'I have been for some days *bordering* on a state of distraction . . . I & all B's friends had hoped things were in train to be amicably—or at least *quietly* arranged—when the 2 legals met & Mr. Hanson would not hear of one of the proposed arrangements—that of B. pledging himself *legally* to do what was judged right by *Arbitrators* respecting a division of the Kirkby Property. . . I must confess that it does appear to me the most useless quibble I ever heard of . . . But what is more horrible dear Mr. H. is this . . . that there will come out what must *destroy him* FOR EVER in this world—even what will deprive him of all right to his Child, & so blast *his* character that neither Sister nor *Wife* who has lived under the same roof with can ever be considered as they have been again! What this mysterious charge can be is beyond ye utmost stretch of my imagination to guess. He *vows* HE knows not . . . Still my mind misgives me, & I have argued thus—if (as I firmly believe) he has been subject to paroxysms of insanity for some years may he not have committed some act which he would not even avow to his dearest Friend—scarcely to his own soul. His manner to me make me suspect it is so. He *now* confesses himself *insane*, seems anxious to have it established in opinion that he *was* so, & says openly it will be his defence . . .

'You won't wonder at my being half mad myself—to add to all my apprehensions of the future . . . I really lived for twice 24 hours in the gravest dread of a *Duel*—between Mr. Wilmot & B or Mr. H. or D . . .

'It is my present intention dear Mr. H. to leave this house on Saturday. To explain *all* my reasons for so doing—all my GRIEF AT so doing wd be difficult at this distance—but I am told it is positively a duty I owe myself, my Husband & Children not to stay to APPEAR to sanction B's conduct—that having

176

staid while there was a *possibility* of reconciliation to do all I could towards it, I had better *now* go. You well know what it costs me to leave my dearest Brother, but indeed I CAN'T express one HALF of what I suffer . . .

'One word more—all my fears of a *dreadful fatal event* have revived—the *dark hints* are again expressed *should any* charge be brought even without *proof* against him, that can blacken his character . . .' This letter suggests that there were rumours of threats of charges other than homosexual practices and incest.

On the following day, Friday, 15th March, Augusta and Annabella met, and on her return Byron signed a document empowering the appointment of an arbitrator in the matter of Kirkby. On the Saturday Augusta took up her rooms at St James's Palace. Earlier in the week the engagement had been announced between Princess Charlotte and Prince Leopold of Saxe-Coburg and the wedding was expected to take place shortly; Augusta's presence as a lady in waiting was necessary, pregnant as she was. (However, she may have returned for some nights to Piccadilly, not finally quitting the house until Hobhouse came to stay on 3rd April.) Byron wrote himself to Annabella on 20th March, enclosing the famous lines:

> Fare thee well! and if forever,
> Still for ever, fare thee well:
> Even though unforgiving, never
> 'Gainst thee shall my heart rebel . . .

Augusta and Annabella continued to communicate and see each other at intervals, but, although the expressions used were friendly, the warmth had gone out of their friendship. At dinner at the Wilmots' on the 25th Augusta refused to shake hands with Selina Doyle, and told Annabella that 'she did think Miss Doyle had been too forward in her interference'. When Sir Samuel Shepherd delivered his judgement on the 27th in favour of Byron's binding himself straightway in legal form, the latter's rancour burst forth in the cruelly biting lines on Mrs Clermont in 'A Sketch from Private Life':

> Born in the garret, in the kitchen bred,
> Promoted thence to deck her mistress' head . . .
> With eye unmoved, and forehead unabash'd,
> She dines from off the plate she lately wash'd.

Quick with the tale, and ready with the lie,
The genial confidante, and general spy . . .

At this juncture Lady Caroline Lamb intervened, asking for
a clandestine meeting with Annabella, which took place on the
27th at Mrs George Lamb's house. Annabella must have thought
she was going to obtain something of importance, to have sul-
lied her own proud perfection by associating with such an
abandoned creature as Lady Caroline, and in the event she
was not disappointed. Returning to Mivart's Hotel, she wrote
down the minutes of her conversation: '. . . She became
greatly agitated—and told me she would constitute me the
judge of what she ought to do—having been bound by a solemn
promise not to reveal these secrets—yet having felt it her duty
to have done so before my marriage in order to save me
from so dreadful a fate . . . I then said that I conceived *her*
promise was released by his infringement of *his* [promise never
to renew such crimes], and that she might now redeem all by
giving me the knowledge if as important as she signified to the
preservation of my Child—that neither on Earth, nor in
Heaven, would she, in my opinion, have cause to repent so
disinterested an action.' It is difficult to judge which of the
actions of these two women was the more despicable—the
betrayal or the casuistry which pointed to rewards in return
for such betrayal. 'She then confessed as follows, with an un-
feigned degree of agitation—That from the time that Mrs. L—
came to Bennet St. in the year 1813—Lord B— had given her
various intimations of a criminal intercourse between them—
but that for some time he spoke of it in a manner which did not
enable her to fix it on Mrs L—thus—"Oh I never knew what
it was to love before—there is a woman I love so passionately—
she is with child by me, and if a daughter it shall be called
Medora"—that his avowals of this incestuous intercourse became bolder—till at last she said to him one dav, "I could
believe it of *you*—but not of *her*"—on this his vanity appeared
piqued to rage, and he said "Would *she* not?"—assured Ly
C.L.—that the seduction had not given him much trouble—
that it was soon accomplished . . . Since *that* avowal—Ly C—L
—never suffered any intimacy with Ld B— though she had
been prevailed upon to forgive "other & worse crimes"—

178

'Of these she gave the following account—that he had . . . confessed that from his boyhood he had been in the practice of unnatural crime—that Rushton [his page] was one of those whom he had corrupted . . . He mentioned 3 schoolfellows whom he had thus perverted . . . Ly C. L— did not believe that he had committed this crime since his return to England, though he had practised it unrestrictably in Turkey . . .

'I almost disavowed the belief of Incest—appeared so much agitated by the other subject that I suspected Ly C L— discovered her statement to be only a confirmation of my own opinions. I told her Rushton was now with Lord B— . . .' Before Annabella left her informer, in the presence of Mrs George Lamb, she more than 'almost disavowed'—she declared that she had had '*no* belief'. This was a deliberate lie on the part of one who was, in Byron's expressed opinion, 'Truth itself'. On her return to her hotel she wrote off to Lushington: 'The result of my interview this morning was, I am most concerned to say, to change my strong impressions relative to the 1st & 2nd reports, into *absolute* conviction.' She now decided that it would be unwise to meet Augusta, who was to be acquainted with her present resolution 'with the least possible pain' through the medium of Mrs Wilmot, to whom she wrote: 'The difficulties and vexations which have, as you know, lately attended my direct intercourse with Augusta, who has been equally embarrassed by questions in consequence, make me request that you will be the medium of a communication that appears absolutely necessary. I must confess to her that under my present feelings I experience the *most* painful effects from our meetings, nor can I suppose them less distressing to her. In requesting, therefore, that she will spare me these agitations, which I find my health and spirits equally unable to support, I feel that I do not require from her a Sacrifice which I should regret to ask.'

It was not until 13th April that the misogynic Hobhouse heard of this rupture of relations. He entered in his journal: 'This has terminated, I believe, all correspondence between *My dearest Augusta* and *My dearest Annabella* ! ! Such are female friendships.' However, he was wrong in his belief; the curtain had but been lowered after the first act.

Hobhouse had taken up residence at 13 Piccadilly on 3rd

April. Life was not easy with Byron, and there were frequent quarrels after drinking. It was probably after one of these scenes at the beginning of April that Augusta wrote to Hobhouse, for whom she had now formed a deep regard: 'Do not forsake your most unfortunate friend—if you do, he is lost— he has so few *sincere* friends and well judging ones . . . I am grateful from my heart for your friendship and friendly forbearance towards his infirmities of whatever kind they may be. His *mind* makes him the most unhappy of human beings. Let us hope it may not always be so. God bless you. I thank you for all your kindness . . .' For Augusta her brother was still 'Baby' Byron, and anyone who was kind to him won immediately her affection and gratitude.

On 8th April Byron's books were put up for sale and fetched £723.12.6, Murray thoughtfully buying some for Augusta. That evening Byron, Augusta and Hobhouse attended a party at Lady Jersey's, the undisputed leader of the London *ton*. No sooner had they entered the room, after being warmly greeted by their hostess, than they were aware that they were the object of general attention. They were introduced to Benjamin Constant and his wife by General Flahault, who afterwards married the heiress Miss Mercer Elphinstone, who was also present and came up and spoke to them. Byron was then shocked to see Mrs George Lamb deliberately cut Augusta, as did some others of their acquaintance; the men turned their backs on them and moved away. He stood silently on one side, watching the expression of public disapproval on the part of people who so recently had courted him. At the first moment that they could decently leave, they were about to retire, when Miss Mercer Elphinstone came up to them and spoke to Byron: 'You should have married *me*, and then this would not have happened to you!'

It was only now that Byron realised what Augusta's loyalty to him had cost her. And what if public disapproval should extend to the palace and she lost the position on which the welfare of her family depended? The shock of this discovery showed him the depths of her devotion. Within the next few days his love for his sister found its expression in the deeply moving lines of the 'Stanzas to Augusta':

When fortune changed—and love fled far,
  And hatred's shafts flew thick and fast,
Thou wert the solitary star
  Which rose and set not to the last.

Still may thy spirit dwell on mine,
  And teach it what to brave or brook—
There's more in one soft word of thine
  Than in the world's defied rebuke.
Thou stood'st, as stands a lovely tree,
  That still unbroke, though gently bent,
Still waves with fond fidelity
  Its boughs above a monument.
Devoted in the stormiest hour
  To shed thy weeping leaves o'er me.
But thou and thine shall know no blight,
  Whatever fate on me may fall;
For heaven in sunshine will requite
  The kind—and thee the most of all.

Augusta confessed in a letter to Hodgson that her true reason for staying on in London was to be near Byron; but by mid-April her condition demanded that she return to Six Mile Bottom. On Easter Sunday, 14th April, Hobhouse went down into the country, so that 'Byron might have a free leave taking of his sister' at 13 Piccadilly. Byron had a strong premonition (which in the event proved true) that he would never see Augusta again. They spent the day together, and Augusta was disconsolate in the agony of her despair. Byron, too, broke down and wept at the misery of their predicament; the culpability was entirely his. Before she departed, Augusta gave him a copy of the Bible, which has been thought by some an act of superficial piety, and, knowing Byron's contempt for contemporary religion, a singularly inappropriate gift. Byron did not consider it so; he kept it always by his bedside; and eight years later it was beside his deathbed at Missolonghi.

After Augusta had left him, Byron wrote to Annabella: 'I have just parted from Augusta—almost the last being you had left me to part with—& the only unshattered tie of my existence—wherever I may go—& I am going far—you & I can never meet again in this world—nor in the next—let this content or atone. If any accident occurs to me, be kind to her,—if she is then nothing—to her Children:—

'Some time ago—I informed you that with the knowledge that any child of ours was already provided for by other & better means—I had made my will in favour of her & her children—as prior to my marriage: this was not done in prejudice to you for we had not then differed—& even this is useless during your life by the settlements. I say therefore—be kind to her & hers—for never has she acted or spoken otherwise towards you—she has ever been your friend—this may seem valueless to one who now has so many:— be kind to her, however, & recollect that though it may be advantage to you to have lost a husband—it is sorrow to her to have the waters now, or the earth hereafter, between her & her brother.

'She is gone—I need hardly add that of this request she knows nothing—your late compliances have not been so extensive, as to render this an encroachment:— I repeat it—(for deep resentments have but *half* recollections) that you did once promise me thus much—do not forget it—nor deem it cancelled —it was not a vow . . .

The next day Byron wrote Augusta a short note: '. . . I trust you got home *safe* and are well. I am sadly without you, but I won't complain . . . Then he added a postscript: 'I can't bear to send you a short letter, and my heart is too full for a long one: don't think me unkind or ungrateful, dearest A., and tell me how is Georgey and *Do*, and you and *tip*, and all the *tips* on four *legs* or *two*: ever and again, and for ever, thine.'

The signing of the separation deed had been held up by Hanson's fruitless delaying actions. Finally at half-past three on Sunday afternoon, 19th April, 1816, Byron signed, saying, as he did so, 'I deliver this as Mrs Clermont's act and deed.' On the following Tuesday Byron in his Napoleonic coach, accompanied by Scrope Davies and Hobhouse travelling in Davies' chaise with Byron's physician Dr Polidori, set out for Dover. On Thursday, 25th April, the party embarked, and the ship put out in 'a rough sea and contrary wind'. Hobhouse, running to the end of the pier, waved until he could distinguish Byron no longer. That evening he wrote in his journal, 'God bless him for a gallant spirit and a kind one.'

XI
Epistles to Augusta
1816

THE ADMIRATION of Fanny Kemble for 'Lady Byron's beautiful power of silence' has been shared by others; it is therefore to be regretted that there is so little evidence for it. Before Byron had left the shores of England she had divulged her secret, directly or indirectly, to her maid (Mrs Minns), Mrs Clermont, Sir Ralph and Lady Milbanke, Colonel Francis Doyle and his sister Selina, Wilmot Horton and his wife, and Dr Lushington. In a matter which had spread from the scabrous gossip of drawing-rooms to furnish the world at large with a subject of insatiable speculation it is to be imagined that some at least of this small band of initiates had broken the pledge that bound them. Some, we know, did not—Mrs Minns for one, and perhaps Lushington.

On 24th April, the day before Byron sailed from Dover and Annabella returned to Kirkby, the latter paid a visit to Augusta's friend, Mrs George Villiers, in London. There she gave a 'partial explanation' of the vacillation in her recent behaviour towards Augusta. Writing to Augusta the following day, Mrs Villiers reported the meeting: 'Nothing could be more warmhearted, kind, considerate, feeling and affectionate —Yes—affectionate to the greatest degree than everything she said about you ... Lady B's declining to see you arose entirely from the difficulties and perplexities of her situation. She was fully aware of *your* difficulties too ... in short in such a situation the only safe line was absolute silence, and to that she was determined to adhere till his departure ...' Now that Byron had gone, Mrs Villiers informed Augusta, Annabella would again be communicating with her. Since Annabella had already acquainted Mrs Villiers with enough information to justify her attitude towards Augusta, this letter is a curiously tendentious one to have been written by the latter's friend. Indeed, the position Mrs Villiers was to adopt was quite incompatible with true friendship. She appears to have come under the spell of this highly articulate young woman seventeen years her junior, and to have been flattered by Annabella's confidences. In such a *cause célèbre* it was intriguing to be one of the inner circle of those who knew; and to be able to offer advice (assuming that she did have the interests of both the younger women at heart) was irresistible to her complacency. The self-delusion of these two women, who loudly proclaimed to each other their laudable intention of saving Augusta's soul, is scarcely credible. They were not conscious hypocrites; it would have been more readily forgivable if they had been. Annabella was at least motivated ostensibly by the natural wish to secure the custody of her child, more profoundly by a consuming jealousy of Byron's love for Augusta. With Mrs Villiers there was no deeper motive than the pleasure to be derived from her gratuitous interference.

No sooner was she settled in at Kirkby than Annabella wrote off to Mrs Villiers on 6th May. Mrs Villiers had advised her to speak to Augusta quite unambiguously of her suspicions —rather, her knowledge—of Augusta's incestuous relations with Byron, but to this Annabella objected. More finesse was required. 'My great object, next to the Security of my Child, is therefore the restoration of her mind to that state which is religiously desirable. I differ from you in regard to the effects of an unequivocal communication. It is easier for the injured than the guilty to pardon, & I doubt if any woman would forgive to another such an avowal. I have sometimes thought that a tacit understanding existed between her and me— particularly when she thought *him* acquitted by Insanity, and seemed herself sinking under the most dreadful remorse—but her tone has since changed from penitence to pride. It is scarcely possible she could on various occasions have supposed me unconscious . . . and I do not conceive that the repetition of his words to me in private, could make a change in her feelings, if what passed in her presence did not . . .' This young woman—her twenty-fourth birthday was on 17th May— prayed to God to create in Augusta, eight years her senior, 'a spirit of humility and repentance'.

Replying, Mrs Villiers feared that she might be thought indiscreet; yet her tactful letter was an invitation (which Annabella was free to accept or reject) to further confidences. Why, she enquired, if Annabella had suspected Augusta's relations with Byron, had she invited her to stay in Piccadilly? It gave Annabella 'real satisfaction' in answering Mrs Villiers on 12th May: 'It must be remembered that my *Conviction* was progressively formed, and not till lately fixed—and though my suspicion had been awakened very early, it was not at the period you allude to, sufficiently corroborated to have been made a principle of conduct without risking a cruel injury to one who professed herself most affectionately & disinterestedly devoted to my welfare. There was no medium—I must either have treated her as guilty or innocent . . . During her last visit my suspicions as to *previous* circumstances were most strongly corroborated—above all by *her* confessions & admissions when in a state of despair & distraction. They were of the most unequivocal nature possible, unless she had expressly named the subject of her remorse and horror . . .'

Mrs Villiers response to this letter was calculated to arouse Annabella's jealousy. Repeating that she considered it was essential for Augusta's rescue that she be told 'by some proper person' that Byron had betrayed her 'in writing to two or three women', besides Annabella herself, she continued: 'With such knowledge absence would essentially save her. Without it I cannot but foresee a probable evil—that from the state of their circumstances he may propose to her to go abroad to him . . . You say she would never forgive you for such an avowal of your knowledge—but who is to suffer for her unforgiveness—not you—but her—& she has enough sense to see . . . & her affection for her children will I think prevent her attempting to make any resistance that shd produce an *éclat* which must terminate in *her* ruin and *theirs* . . .'

Annabella's formidable powers of analysis were well shown in her reply to these friendly suggestions. She decided on a compromise which would, she thought, 'effect all the desired ends without risk of any sort— . . . The measure which I propose to take appears to me to unite the following advantages —that it will make *herself* acquainted with my real opinions & feelings, without binding me to avow them publicly, should she be desperate in the first impulse—that it will nevertheless suspend this terror over her, to be used as her future dispositions & conduct may render expedient—whilst it leaves her the power of profiting by my forbearance, without compelling the utterly degrading confession of her own guilt . . .' Having prayed that God would bring Augusta to 'a spirit of humility and repentance', she was only too willing herself to act as the divine instrument.

*

Augusta, at home at Six Mile Bottom, awaited the birth of her fifth child in a condition of spiritual and physical prostration. Even her buoyant spirit was not proof against the black despair which had settled on her in those poignant last days in London. Her letters at the time to Mrs Villiers were filled with gloom and misery. From Byron she had received a letter written on 24th April, the day before his vessel left Dover for Ostend. In this he told her that a witness of Frederick Howard's death at Waterloo had informed him that the body was neither 'mangled' nor left in the hands of the French, and that Howard had died in no great pain. Byron wrote again from Ostend and Ghent, and on 1st May from Brussels: he was anxious to pass quickly through the Low Countries—'Level roads don't suit me, as thou knowest; it must be up hill or down, and then I am more *au fait*.' Hobhouse was in touch with her and sent her a copy of Byron's 'Stanzas to Augusta'. Writing to thank him, she said: 'I think them most beautiful, and I need not add, they are most gratifying to me, who doat upon dear B.' In spite of these reassurances that Byron's thoughts lay with her, she felt only too surely that he, who had been for so long the centre of her existence, was passing out of her life and that the future held out little in the way of security or hope. The children's health filled her with concern. George Leigh's affairs were in their perennial state of crisis; the house would have to be sold, and it fell to Augusta to find a buyer. Augusta feared that the reports against her, which were still loudly voiced in London, would reach the palace, and that her position at court was jeopardised. It was now that she realised just how much her life had been built around Byron; without him, without his physical presence, she was bereft of the person who gave point to her existence and whom she, with all the resources of her loving nature, passionately loved.

A son, Frederick George, was born on 9th May, 1816.

George Leigh wrote to Annabella to acquaint her with the news, and he received a polite reply in return, but Augusta had had no letter from her since the first week in April. On the same day as Augusta gave birth to her son Caroline Lamb brought out her gothic novel *Glenarvon*, with its highly romantic account of her affair with Byron and thinly disguised caricatures of members of the Holland and Devonshire House circles. *Glenarvon* became the talk of London; the Byron legend was not going to be allowed to die.

By the beginning of June Annabella considered that Augusta was sufficiently recovered to receive from her a long-thought-out letter informing her of her future intentions. On Monday, 3rd June, she wrote:

'My dear Augusta,

'Before your Confinement I would not risk agitating you, but having the satisfaction of knowing you are recovered, I will no longer conceal from yourself that there are reasons founded on such circumstances in your conduct, as, (though thoroughly convinced they have existed) I am most anxious to bury in silence, which indispensably impose on me the duty of *limiting* my intercourse with you—

'I should more deeply lament this necessary consequence of causes, —(on the supposition of which, whilst in any degree doubtful, it would have been unjust to act)—if your feelings towards me could give me the power of doing you any good, —but you have not disguised your resentment against those who have befriended me, and have countenanced the arts which have been employed to injure me—Can I then longer believe those professions of affection, and even of exclusive zeal for *my* welfare, which I have been most reluctant to mistrust?—And on *this* ground my conduct, if known, would be amply & obviously justified to the world. I shall still not regret having loved and trusted you so entirely—May the blessing of a merciful God be with you & those nearest you—I am truly interested in the welfare of your children, and should your present unhappy dispositions be seriously changed, you will not then be deceived in considering me as one who will afford every service and consolation of your most faithful friend—
'A. I. Byron.'

This extraordinary missive was thought by Annabella to be limpid in its clarity—'By avoiding all ambiguity of meaning I have precluded the occasion for further explanation,' she explained to Mrs Villiers. And as a precautionary measure (which showed she had profited by Lushington's lessons), she had an attestation added to her copy by her father: 'I attest this to be a true copy of a letter from Lady Byron to Mrs. Leigh, sent according to date—Ralph Noel.' Augusta would have to contend with a well-equipped member of the church militant, legalistic and bureaucratic.

Augusta's reply was dated 6th June:

'My dear Annabella,

'As I always mistrust the first impulses of my feelings, & did not wish to write under the influence of such as your letter could not fail to produce, I would not answer it by return of post. I cannot say that I am *wholly surprised* at its contents. Your silence towards me during so long an interval and when all *obvious* necessity for it must have ceased formed so decided a contrast to your former kindness to me—and to what *my Conscience tells me my conduct towards you deserved from you* that it could not but require some explanation . . . To general accusations I must answer in general terms—and if I were on my death Bed I could affirm as I *now* do that I have uniformly considered you and consulted your happiness before and above any thing in this world. No sister could ever have the claims upon me that *you* had—I felt it—& acted up to the feeling to the best of my judgement. We are all perhaps too much inclined to magnify our trials, yet I think I may venture to pronounce my situation to *have been* & *to be still* one of extraordinary difficulty. I have been assured that the tide of public opinion has been so turned against my Brother that the least appearance of coolness on your part towards me would injure me most seriously—& I am therefore *for the sake of my children* compelled to accept from your *compassion* the "limited intercourse" which is all you can grant to one whom you pronounce no longer worthy of your esteem or affection! But the time may come when your present conviction and opinions will change—in the interim I feel how hopeless would be every attempt to defend myself. The only person whose testimony could avail

ABOVE: *Augusta's inscription enclosing a lock of her hair for Byron, 1813.*
BELOW: *Byron's note on the outside of the packet. (Both reproduced from* Lord
Byron's Wife *by Malcolm Elwin, by permission of the Earl of Lytton, owner
of the Lovelace Collection of Byron Papers)*

*Tree-trunk at Newstead Abbey carved with the
names of Byron and Augusta, 1813*

Byron's epitaph placed by Augusta in Hucknell Torkard church

me in proving how strictly and invariably I have done my duty by you—I have heard from yr own lips you consider unworthy of belief. On the particular points of accusation—1st. my "not having disguised my resentment to those who befriended you—" I know of nothing but the change of manner to Miss Doyle, which was discussed between us ye last time I saw you—and, 2nd. "my having countenanced the acts which were employed to injure you"— ! ! ! really you must have been cruelly misinformed and I cruelly injured[.] I ask not however by whom —for I feel I *scarcely* could forgive them. Before you judge and condemn me on the first point—you ought to consider that I as well as *you* may have had provocation—that it was impossible hearing and seeing all I did I should not be under the influence of *some* degree of irritation—not against those who wd "befriend YOU" but whom I often thought condemned OTHERS *too severely*. I will not however say more at present than that you need not regret having loved & trusted me so entirely—& the *sincerity of my affection for you & exclusive zeal for your welfare* ALL to whom I ever spoke of you—and who witnessed my conduct can fully *prove*. I would not dwell a moment on having done what was only my *duty* and *inclination* but in *self-defence*—

'My "present unhappy dispositions"— ! I have indeed in *outward* causes sufficient to make any one *wretched* but inward peace which none can take away—It never occurred to me you could act but on the strictest sense of duty—therefore I'm convinced you do so now towards me.

'God bless you—for every mark of kindness which you have bestowed on me & mine of which neither time or circumstances can efface the recollection.

'Believe me gratefully & afly yrs
'A.L.'

Annabella thought that this was 'perhaps the best letter she *could* have written', remarking how bitter it was 'to correspond on altered terms with one whom we have not ceased to love'. An ambivalence of feelings towards Augusta was thenceforth to characterise their relations. Augusta, writing on 10th June to inform Francis Hodgson of Byron's arrival in Geneva, revealed her anxieties: 'Of myself I can tell you little that will give you satisfaction, except that I am pretty well, only weak and nervous, and no wonder, for none can know *how much* I have suffered from this unhappy business—and, indeed, I have never known a minute's peace, and begin to despair of the future.' Significantly she asked Hodgson if he had kept her earlier letters, and if she had ever written or spoken a word that detracted from Annabella's merits or showed that she was partial solely to Byron's side in the separation.

On 19th June Mrs Villiers wrote to Annabella: 'Did you tell her of his having betrayed her to others or do you think it possible to do this? Could she once be brought to *believe* this fact, I should hope much from it . . . She is ordered to come to London for the Pss. Mary's marriage which I am very sorry for—the *tourbillon* of that, & present exertions to sell the Six Mile will give her no time for reflection . . .' But Augusta had time enough to reflect, and gradually it was borne in on her (reluctant as she was to admit it at first, considering it part of his delusions) that Byron had indeed betrayed her. He had given her his solemn word of honour at their last meeting that he had not imparted their secret to a soul, and she had trusted him entirely. Now the realisation of betrayal shattered her reserves. Her state was pitiable, but Annabella and Mrs Villiers were relentless in following up their advantage. Augusta's letters thenceforth show the wreckage of her confidence and former dignity. On Wednesday evening, 3rd July, she revealed the confusion of her mind: 'When I begin writing to you my dear Annabella one thought crowds so fast upon another that I become quite bewildered—and every attempt I make to express myself is perfectly unsatisfactory to myself—I fear must be so to *you*—I regret this the more as all I hear from you only serves to increase my sense of the obligations I owe you—I shall not however say *much* of them—in the first place because I am *dumb* always when I feel deeply—and in the next it might only add to the appearance of *duplicity* which (with yr present opinions) you must believe me guilty of—I only wish *every past & present* thought could be open to you . . . I declare—after the strictest examination of my own heart, there is *not one act or thought towards yourself* I would not wish you acquainted with —You say my dear A—*I have been the cause of your sufferings*— if I have it has been *innocently*—this must be my only consolation—Had I even entertained the *slightest* suspicions of any "*doubts*" of yours—I never could or would have entered your house—perhaps I did wrong as it is to do so—but I was under delusion certainly . . . The little portion of peace now remaining is in the reflexion that I *endeavoured* to do right . . . Dearest A—*I have not wronged you. I have not abused your generosity* . . . I shall never *seek* to see you while it is *your wish* I should not— One ray of comfort & hope suggested itself in the thought that *we may meet again*—that *my future conduct* may conduce to it— Tell me—pray—of anything in that which could by possibility atone for the past—in pity—tell it me dearest A. that I may have one more chance of happiness—'

Mrs Villiers exulted in her new friend's success in rescuing Augusta in this world—'the next step *must* be to try with your kind assistance', she wrote to Annabella, 'to make herself more fit for the next—it is now in good train . . .' Augusta came up to London on 11th July and went to her rooms at St James's, where Hobhouse called on her two days later and found her sadly perplexed over what message to send Byron, whom he was about to visit at Geneva. On the 15th Augusta reported her indecision to Annabella: 'My dear A—I am perfectly unable to decide *how* to act for the best respecting *him* & his knowledge of what has passed between us . . . I wish you to reflect on what I had better do—I really *must now* entirely mistrust my own judgement—there are dangers to be apprehended *both* ways—at least I see many from his ignorance.'

Annabella admitted in her reply: 'I am well aware that the very fear of giving pain sometimes makes me appear unfeeling.' Then she continued: 'It seems to me that you dwell too much on the pain you involuntarily occasioned me, and not enough on the irreparable injury you did *him* by the Voluntary sacrifices (for to principles like yours they must have been *entirely* sacrifices) which you once made to his immediate indulgences.' Any stick served to flog a penitent into a full recognition of the heinousness of her offences, and Annabella's 'fear of giving pain' does not seem to have been too formidable a ban. Recuperating by the sea at Lowestoft, she was kept acquainted by the vigilance of Mrs Villiers with every change in the condition of the victim. On 18th July she reported: 'Yesterday, for the first time, she dined here, & was here between 4 and 5 hours, & I must say that in my life I never saw anything equal to her dejection—her absence—her whole mind evidently preoccupied & engrossed—& apparently insensible of being in society . . .' Mrs Villiers was of the opinion that Augusta should be stopped from writing to her brother, but Annabella thought this too precipitate a step; it should be postponed a while. '. . . I am now leading her on to promise she will never renew a confidential intercourse by letter—or any personal intercourse— I find it necessary to gain step by step, and to disclose my views less abruptly than with some.' To Augusta she wrote on the 30th: 'If I think you have something to atone for to him, much more do I think he owes you atonement. Till you feel that he has in reality been your worst friend—indeed, *not* your friend—you cannot altogether think rightly . . . forgive him— desire his welfare—but resign the pernicious view of being his friend more nearly . . . I should not advise you for his sake to restrict your correspondence further than by keeping always in view to *rectify* instead of *soothing* or *indulging* his feelings—by avoiding therefore all phrases or *marks*, which may recall wrong ideas to his mind . . . and let me also warn you against the levity & nonsense which he likes for the worst reason, because it prevents him from reflecting seriously . . .'

How abject was Augusta's spiritual surrender is shown by her obeying these odious injunctions. On 5th August she replied to Annabella: 'I assure you most solemnly—most truly —I have *long* felt that he has *not* been my friend—but from my heart I forgive him—& pray to God to forgive him & change his heart—to restore him to peace—& there is nothing I would not do . . . to contribute to his good—how far & whether I may ever be able to do so it is I think impossible to foresee— since *futurity* is veiled . . .' At this stage Annabella decided to come to London, where Augusta was delaying her return to the country in hope of meeting her. On 31st August the first of several meetings took place at which, so Annabella declared, Augusta made a full confession of having slept with Byron before his marriage but not subsequently. When the unfortunate woman was informed how she had been betrayed by Byron, her first reaction was never to write to him again, but Annabella advised against such a 'violent resolution'. She was informed also that Mrs Villiers knew her secret, but that in the largeness of her heart she forgave and pitied her for having been 'the

Victim to the most infernal plot that has ever entered the heart of man to conceive . . .' Mrs Villiers told Augusta that she must look on Annabella as her 'Guardian Angel'—and she humbly accepted even this humiliating irony. As a final desperate measure, she agreed to show Annabella all Byron's letters to her.

*

Byron was at first unaware of Augusta's agony at the hands of these high-minded women. Yet his conscience was uneasy. As each day his lumbering Napoleonic carriage took him further from England, his thoughts dwelt fondly on the image of Augusta, who had so devotedly loved him and had sacrificed so much to attend on him:

> And there was one soft breast, as hath been said,
> Which unto his was bound with stronger ties
> Than the church links withal; and, though unwed,
> *That* love was pure, and, far above disguise,
> Had stood the test of mortal enmities
> Still undivided, and cemented more
> By peril, dreaded most in female eyes;
> But this was firm, and from a foreign shore
> Well to that heart might his these absent greetings pour!

Proceeding slowly up the Rhine, he longed to have her with him; for him it would have been a 'double joy' if she too had shared the beauties of the scene.

> The castle crag of Drachenfels
> Frowns o'er the wide and winding Rhine . . .
> Could thy dear eyes in following mine
> Still sweeten more these banks of Rhine!'

From Coblentz he sent Augusta these loving stanzas and a bunch of violets:

> Though long before thy hand they touch,
> I know that they must wither's be . . .

By June he was settled near Geneva in the Villa Diodati, with the Shelleys and Claire Clairmont as near neighbours. Here his thoughts would constantly revert to Augusta, and he wrote the somewhat theatrical lines to her:

Though the day of my destiny's over
And the star of my fate hath declined . . .,
And the love which my spirit hath painted
It never hath found but in *thee*.

Although Hobhouse and Scrope Davies had joined him, he was worried by the letters he received from Augusta, and in his anxiety he poured out his love for her in the beautiful 'Epistle to Augusta':

For thee, my own sweet sister, in thy heart
I know myself secure, as thou in mine;
We were and are—I am, even as thou art—
Beings who ne'er each other can resign;
It is the same, together or apart—
From life's commencement to its slow decline
We are entwined—let death come slow or fast,
The tie which bound the first endures the last!

These memorable stanzas were suppressed on Annabella's advice and were not published until 1830.

On 27th August he replied to Augusta: 'Your confidential letter is safe, and all the others. This one has cut me to the heart because I have made you uneasy. Still I think all these apprehensions—very groundless. Who can care for such a wretch as C[aroline Lamb], or believe such a seventy times convicted liar? and in the next place, whatever she may suppose or assert—I never "committed" any one to her but *myself*... Really this is starting at shadow. You distress me with—no— it is not *you*. But I have heard that Lady B— is ill, I am so sorry—but it's of no use—do not mention her again—but I shall not forget her kindness to you ... do not be uneasy— and do not "hate yourself" if you hate either let it be *me*— but do not—it would kill me; we are the last persons in the world—who ought—or could cease to love one another. Ever dearest thine + B.'

In the first week in September Scrope Davies left to return to England, taking with him some presents from Byron to Ada and Augusta's children, and a letter for her: 'And so—Lady B. has been "kind to you" you tell me—"very kind"—umph— it is as well she should be kind to some of us, and I am glad she has the heart & the discernment to be still *your* friend; you was ever so to her . . . I am in good health, & fair, though very unequal spirits; but for all that—she—or rather the Separation —has broken my heart. I feel as if an Elephant had trodden on it . . . I breathe lead. While the storm lasted and you were all pitying and comforting me with condemnation in Piccadilly, it was bad enough & violent enough, but it's worse now; I have neither strength nor spirits nor inclination to carry me through anything which will clear my brain or lighten my heart . . .' He then confessed his liaison with Claire Clairmont. 'Now don't scold—but what could I do? A foolish girl, in spite of all I would say or do, would come after me, or rather went before for I found her here, and I have had all the plague possible to persuade her to go back again, but at last she went . . . Don't hate me, but believe me ever Yrs. most affecly B.'

Augusta's cryptic remarks in her letters caused him acute disquiet. On 14th September he wrote: 'If I understand you rightly, you seem to have been apprehensive—or menaced (like every one else) by that infamous Bedlamite [Caroline Lamb]—If she stirs against you, neither her folly nor her falsehood should or shall protect her. Such a monster as that *has no sex*, and should live no longer . . . I should never think of her nor her infamies, but that they seem (I know not why) to make you uneasy. What 'tis she may tell or what she may know or pretend to know—is to me indifferent . . . This country is altogether the Paradise of Wilderness—I wish you were in it with me—& every one else out of it. Love me, A., ever thine—B.'

On 17th September Byron set out in the company of Hobhouse on a trip to the Bernese Oberland. From Ouchy he wrote on the first night, nettled by Augusta's remark that Lady Byron was being kind to her: '*Of* her you are to judge for yourself, but do not altogether forget that she has destroyed your brother. Whatever my faults might or may have been—*She*—was not the person marked out by providence to be their avenger . . . I do not think a human being could endure more mental torture than that woman has directly & indirectly inflicted upon me—within the last year . . . I would return from any distance at any time to see you, and come to England for you . . .' He invited her & some of her children to come on

195

abroad to him, but he feared 'that very helpless gentleman', her husband, would prevent that.

'What a fool I was to marry—and *you* not very wise—my dear—we might have lived so single and so happy—as old maids and bachelors; I shall never find any one like you—nor you (vain as it may seem) like me. We are just formed to pass our lives together, & therefore—we—at least—I—am by a crowd of circumstances removed from the only being who could ever have loved me, or whom I can unmixedly feel attached to.

'Had you been a Nun—and I a Monk—that we might have through a grate instead of across the sea—no matter—my voice and my heart are ever thine —B.'

On his tour of the Alps Byron kept a journal for his sister, and that his mind was filled with thoughts of her is shown by such entries as: 'Shall go to bed, thinking of you, dearest Augusta.' At Brienz he wrote: 'They sing too that *Tyrolese air* and song which you love, Augusta, because I love it—and I love, because you love it . . .' 'May your sleep be soft, and your dreams of me. I am going to bed—good night.' And he completed his journal on the 29th: '*To* you, dearest Augusta, I send, and *for* you I have kept this record of what I have seen and felt. Love me as you are beloved of me.' Enclosing his journal, he sent a letter instructing Augusta, if the news was true that Annabella was going abroad and taking Ada with her, that she inform Annabella that on no account was the child to leave England.

Poor Augusta, back at Six Mile Bottom after her turn of duty at St James's Palace, was in a state of nervous collapse. Their financial affairs were as bad as ever, and although the Duke of Leeds had petitioned Lord Liverpool, the prime minister, in hope of employment for George Leigh, nothing had come of it, which was not surprising, since he was ill-equipped to do anything. In her heart Augusta knew that she loved Byron, and Byron alone; though he had betrayed her, she had already forgiven him; he would talk, rattle on in this reckless way; it was impossible for him, out of nature with him, to keep any secret. With all his faults he was so entirely lovable and needed so much to be loved. But to maintain her social position—as, too, the only bread-winner in the family—she had to prostrate herself before the implacable Annabella. She was forced into the equivocal position of seeking her advice and following her commands. This was the price she had to pay for her rehabilitation in society, a guarantee which was at Annabella's disposal to withdraw at any sign of equivocation or disobedience. The needs of her family demanded that she should be the victim. She showed all Byron's letters to Annabella, thereby arousing afresh in that unforgiving bosom the ravages of jealousy. Writing to Mrs Villiers in September, Annabella reported: 'She has shown me of her own accord *his* letters to her—having only suppressed them because of the bitterness towards me—they are *absolute love letters*—and she wants to know how she can stop them.'

XII

Death and Count Manfred

1816 - 1824

AT DIODATI on the shores of Lake Geneva ('dear placid Leman') Byron finished the Third Canto of *Childe Harold* at the beginning of July, 1816. In the poem the feelings which engendered the Wordsworthian echoes in praise of natural beauties alternated with other moods, unsettled, remorseful, agonised—'quiet to quick bosoms is a hell'. On August 14th 'Monk' Lewis came to stay, and delighted Byron with a reading of his translation of Goethe's *Faust*. Here were the seeds which germinated and grew into the dramatic poem *Manfred*. Some months later Byron wrote to Moore of the turbulence of his thoughts in June and July: 'I was half mad between metaphysics, mountains, lakes, love unextinguishable, thoughts unutterable, and the nightmare of my own delinquencies.' Deeply perturbed by Augusta's letters, his love for her was run through and through by self-reproach and remorse; and as usual with him his 'convulsions' ended only in 'versifying'. The magnificent scenery of the Bernese Alps, which so impressed him on his tour with Hobhouse in September, gave him the setting for a poetic catharsis deeper in its contents than anything he had hitherto attempted. And by means of the drama he flung defiance in the face of a hostile world. He considered that its publication would cause a 'pucker'. What effect it would have on Augusta and her precarious position in society (if the thought passed through his mind) he did not pause to consider.

He saw himself (Manfred) as a spiritual Prometheus whose gift to humanity in face of the cosmic powers was the exaltation of the unconquerable individual will. Although the scene was set among the Alpine peaks, the drama was in reality an internal one in the poet's own mind. As in all Byron's work the sentiment was often glaringly, here blatantly, personal, but the problems envisaged were universal or, better perhaps, cosmic—

man's destiny in the power of cosmic forces. Manfred in his castle summons up the spirits of nature, and from them demands not the satisfaction of ambition or of pleasure or wisdom, but simply 'forgetfulness'. They answer that this they are unable to give: what would he have that they are empowered to grant? Finally he requires to see before him the spirit of his own star of destiny, and this appears to him in the form of a beautiful woman. Manfred approaches to embrace her, but from between his arms the figure vanishes, and he falls to the ground senseless. A voice is heard in incantation:

> . . . I call upon thee! and compel
> Thyself to be thy proper Hell!

The second scene opens on a precipice of the Jungfrau, where Manfred stands contemplating suicide, but he realises that his destiny 'makes it my fatality to live'. An eagle passing overhead draws from him first a poem in praise of the beauty of the world:

> Beautiful?
> How beautiful is all this visible world!
> How glorious in its action and itself!
> But we, who name ourselves its sovereigns, we
> Half dust, half deity, alike unfit
> To sink or soar . . .
> Contending with low wants and lofty will,
> Till our Mortality predominates,
> And men are—what they name not to themselves,
> And trust not to each other.

A chamois-hunter appears and pulls him back from the cliff's brink.

The first scene of the second act is set in the chamois-hunter's cottage. On being offered a stoup of wine, Manfred starts back, seeing blood upon the brim; this is the beginning of the incest theme—

> I say 'tis blood—my blood! the pure warm stream
> Which ran in the veins of my fathers, and in ours
> When we were in our youth, and had one heart,
> And loved each other as we should not love,
> And this was shed . . . .

Manfred, leaving the cottage, descends to the valley, where beside a cataract he calls up the Witch of the Alps, to gaze upon her beauty. He speaks to her of the one he loved, who alone shared his sympathy:

> She was like me in lineaments; her eyes,
> Her hair, her features, all, to the very tone
> Even of her voice, they said were like to mine;
> But softened all, and tempered into beauty:
> She had the same lone thoughts and wanderings . . .
> Pity, and smiles, and tears—which I had not;
> And tenderness—but that I had for her;
> Humility—and that I never had.
> Her faults were mine—her virtues were her own—
> I loved her, and destroyd her!

The witch asks, 'With thy hand?' and Manfred answers:

> Not with my hand, but heart, which broke her heart;
> It gazed on mine, and wither'd . . .

The witch leaves him, and on the summit of the Jungfrau he encounters the Destinies and Nemesis. When they depart, borne away on their clouds to the hall of the mighty spirit of evil, Arimanes, Manfred follows them. In his refusal to bow to Arimanes the spirits recognise that Manfred is their equal. At his request and with the permission of Arimanes, Nemesis calls up the phantom of Astarte, the one being whom Manfred has loved.

> Astarte! my beloved! speak to me:
> I have so much endured—so much endure . . .
>   Thou lovedst me
> Too much, as I loved thee: we were not made
> To torture thus each other—though it were
> The deadliest sin to love as we have loved.
> Say that thou loath'st me not . . .
> Speak to me! though it be in wrath . . .

The phantom repeats his name and tells him that he must die on the morrow, but she will not utter one word of forgiveness or of love, and disappears—'Farewell! . . . Manfred!'

A spirit speaks:

He is convulsed.—This is to be a mortal
And seek things beyond mortality.

And another:

Yet, see, he mastereth himself, and makes
His torture tributary to his will.
Had he been one of us, he would have made
An awful spirit.

The following year in Rome and Venice Byron revised what he had written and added the concluding act, which was sent off early in May and published the next month, causing a considerable 'pucker', for Astarte was widely identified with Augusta. The first scene of the last act opens in the castle of Manfred, where an abbot attempts to persuade him to return to Christianity. Manfred declines to pursue the dialogue, and on his departure the abbot says:

This should have been a noble creature: he
Hath all the energy which would have made
A goodly frame of glorious elements,
Had they been wisely mingled; as it is,
It is an awful chaos . . .
. . . mind and dust—and passions and pure thoughts
Mixed . . .
All dormant and destructive . . .

In the third scene Byron refers again to the incest theme with a boldness that is staggering. The retainers are discussing Manfred:

. . . with him
The sole companion of his wanderings
And watchings—her, whom of all earthly things
That lived, the only thing he seem'd to love,—
As he, indeed by blood was bound to do,
The lady Astarte, his—
Hush! who comes here?

Manfred finally prepares to meet his death, defiant to the end:

. . . I stand
Upon my strength—I do defy—deny—
Spurn back, and scorn ye!—

As he dies, he proclaims his independence of the powers:

> What I have done is done; I bear within
> A torture . . .
> The mind which is immortal makes itself
> Requital for its good or evil thoughts,—
> Is its own origin of ill and end—
> And its own place and time . . .

Early in October Byron and Hobhouse left Diodati, and crossing the Simplon, arrived in Milan on 12th October.

*

Fearing for her character in the world, Augusta considered seriously Byron's invitation to join him. This was the step which Lady Noel and Lushington hoped she would take. But Annabella, for reasons which were mixed, dissuaded her, and she remained to face the music. If Augusta owed her social rehabilitation, and with it her position at court, solely to Annabella's continued acquaintance, the price she had to pay was nothing less than the most abject humiliation. The alternative was social and financial ruin for herself and her family. Annabella was bent on her 'salvation', 'to save her from the dangers around'. At the end of October Augusta had a letter from Byron in Milan, telling of his sight-seeing: 'What delighted me most is a manuscript collection (preserved in the Ambrosian Library) of original love-letters and verses of Lucretia de Borgia and Cardinal Bembo; and a lock of her hair—so long—and fair and beautiful—and the letters so pretty . . . And pray what do you think is one of her *signatures*?—why this + a Cross—which she says "is to stand for her name etc." Is this not amusing? . . . And he concluded: '*A thousand loves* to *you* from *me*—which is very generous for I ask only *one* in return. Ever dearest thine B.'

Poor Augusta was at a loss how to answer these loving letters, which she felt obliged to show Annabella; and for some time she did not reply. Then she received one from Byron, written on 26th October, in which he said he would not write again at all if he had to wait for so long for an answer. Two days later he did write again, having heard from her in the meantime. 'I really do not & cannot understand all the mysteries & alarms in your letters & more particularly in the last. All I know is—that no human power short of destruction—shall prevent me from seeing you when—where—& how—I may please—according to time & circumstance; that you are the only comfort (except the remote possibility of my daughter's being so) left me in prospect in existence, and that I can bear the rest—so that you remain; but anything which is to divide us would drive me quite out of my senses; Miss Milbanke appears in all respects to have been formed for my destruction . . . You know she is the cause of all—whether intentionally or not is little to the purpose—You surely do not mean to say that if I come to England in Spring, that you & I shall not meet? If so I will never return to it . . .'

The next letter (18th December) came from Venice and revealed his better spirits, his 'thorough wretchedness' having lifted about a month before. He informed Augusta of his love for Marianna Segati. 'This adventure came very opportunely to console me, for I was beginning to be "like Sam Jennings very *unhappy*" but at present—at least for a month past—I have been very tranquil, very loving, & have not so much embarrassed myself with the tortures of the last two years and that virtuous monster Miss Milbanke, who had nearly driven me out of my senses—curse her.' He asked if she had read his new poems with Murray. 'I want to know if you don't think them very fine & all that—Goosey my love—don't they make you "put finger in eye?"' He ended with a postscript, informing her that Claire Clairmont had returned to England 'to produce a new baby B'.

At the beginning of March, 1817, Byron heard that, unbeknown to him at the time, Ada had been made a ward of Chancery, and that there was not the remotest intention of taking her out of the country 'without the Chancellor's order'. Byron wrote indignantly to Annabella and, receiving no reply, to Augusta: 'I desire to repeat what I have said—& say. I forgive everything up to this—but this I will never forgive; & no consideration on earth shall now prevail on me to look upon her as otherwise than my worst enemy. I curse her from the bottom of my heart, & in the bitterness of my Soul; & I only hope she may one day feel what she has made me suffer. They will break my heart or drive me mad, one day or the

203

other; but she is a Wretch and will end ill. She was born to be my destruction & has become so. Ten thousand curses be upon her & her father & mother's family now and for ever.'

Augusta's perplexity, as the go-between of Byron and Annabella, and in the falsity of feeling that her position entailed, was evident in the tone of her letters to Byron. Her misery was increased by the discovery that she was again pregnant. From Rome he wrote on 10th May: 'You are sadly timid [he had substituted this milder phrase for 'a sad coward'] my child, but so you all shewed yourselves when you could have been useful—particularly [George Byron]—but never mind.' Then, back once more in Venice, on 3rd June: 'I have received all your letters, I believe, which are full of woes, as usual, megrims and mysteries; but my sympathies remain in suspense, for, for the life of me I can't make out whether your disorder is a broken heart or the earache—or whether it is *you* that have been ill or the children—or what your melancholy & mysterious apprehensions tend to, or refer to, whether to Caroline Lamb's novels—Mrs. Clermont's evidence—Lady Byron's magnanimity—or any other piece of imposture; I know nothing of what you are in the doldrums about at present. I should think all that could affect *you* must have been over long ago; & as for me—leave me to take care of myself . . . I can battle my way through; better than your exquisite piece of helplessness G[eorge] L[eigh].'

In mid-June, when the 'pucker' over the publication of *Manfred* was at its height, Byron was threatening to dissolve the separation and bring the whole matter to the public courts. Augusta was driven nearly frantic with anxiety and fear. He wrote to her on 19th June, adding a significant postscript: 'I repeat to you again and again that it would be much better at once to explain your mysteries than to go on with this absurd obscure hinting mode of writing. What do you mean? What is there known or can be known which you & I do not know much better? & what concealment can you have from me? *I* never shrank—and it was on your account principally that I gave way at all—for I thought they would endeavour to drag you into it—although they had no business with anything previous to my marriage with that infernal fiend whose destruction I shall yet see.' His fury mounted as he poured scorn on Annabella and the Noels, culminating with the threat—'But "let them look to their bond".'

The fears of Augusta, her relations, Annabella and Mrs Villiers that the incest rumours would be revived by *Manfred* were confirmed a week after its publication by a reviewer in *The Day and New Times* of 23rd June, who wrote: '*Manfred* has exiled himself from society, and what is to be the ground of our compassion for the exile? Simply the commission of one of the most revolting of crimes. He has committed incest! Lord Byron has coloured *Manfred* into his own personal features...' Augusta's half-sister, Lady Chichester, brought the paper to Mrs Villiers, who communicated with Annabella: 'It is too barefaced for her friends to deny the allusion. All that appeared to me practicable I have done with her own family, who have all spoke to me about it ... the allusions to Augusta are dreadfully clear.' Augusta's family—Lady Chichester, the Duke of Leeds and Lord Francis Godolphin Osborne—and her friends viewed it as another example of Byron's maniacal desire to damage those who were nearest to him and whom he loved most. Augusta was counselled in reply to a letter in which she asked Annabella's advice on how she was to treat the subject, when she wrote to Byron: 'You can only speak of *Manfred* ... with the most decided expressions of disapprobation. He practically gives you away, and implies you were guilty *after* marriage.' Annabella, writing to Mrs Villiers, pondered: 'What does the Queen think, I wonder?' The scandal did not apparently penetrate to court circles, and gradually the furore subsided. But Augusta had suffered so deeply that the effects became visible in her appearance; she began to age, becoming more careless in her dress, so that people came in time to forget the beauty of her youth; she was described later as a 'Dowdy-Goody'.

For nine months Byron did not write. On 19th November, in a letter to Douglas Kinnaird, he explained his silence: 'If you see Augusta give my love to her, and tell her that I do not write because I really and truly do not understand one single word of her letters. To answer them is out of the question, I don't say it out of ill-nature, but whatever be the subject, there is so much paraphrase, parenthesis, initials, dashes, hints— and what Lord Ogleby calls "Mr. Sterling's damned crinkum crankum", that, sunburn me! if I know what the meaning or no meaning is, and am obliged to study Armenian as a relief.' In this same month Newstead Abbey was sold to Byron's Harrow school-fellow, Colonel Wildman, for £94,500. Another link with England was there broken. Byron wished also to find a purchaser for Rochdale, and with the proceeds of the sales of the two properties to buy annuities for Augusta and himself.

On 27th November Augusta gave birth to her sixth child, Amelia Marianne (Emily). Although it had been originally intended that she was to be godmother to Ada, when the child was christened Augusta's name was discreetly dropped, Lady Noel, Sophia Tamworth, and George Byron being the god-parents. However, when the time came to christen Emily, Annabella accepted the invitation to be her godmother. But Annabella would not permit Ada to be in Augusta's company, and while the latter was in London early in 1818, Annabella kept away, fearing that Augusta's 'delusion might tempt her to put ideas into Ada's mind that might take root there—something of "poor Papa", &c.' Early in the new year the Six Mile Bottom property was sold, and the Leigh family moved to London, first to 26 Great Quebec Street, Montague Square, then to a flat which was given them in St James's Palace. When Queen Charlotte died, passing peacefully away at Kew on 21st September, 1818, Augusta was permitted to retain her apartment at the palace, and further was granted a pension of £300, which, however, did not begin until 1820.

Augusta's anxieties as to Byron's well-being were somewhat allayed by a letter which she received in March—the first since the previous June—telling of his activities, which were not of a kind to convey much comfort. Then in September came a a letter, enclosing one for Lady Frances Webster, who had paid her a visit in London. Byron gave an amusing account of his recent acquisition of a new mistress, Margarita Cogni, La Fornarina, and concluding with the remark: 'You see Goose—that there's no quiet in the world—so be a good woman—and repent of yr sins.'

At the end of May, 1819, there arrived a letter from Venice which ruffled the apparent outward calm of Augusta's life and violently stirred up all the welter of her deeper feelings for Byron:

'Venice, May 17th, 1819

'My dearest Love, —I have been negligent in not writing, but what can I say? Three years absence—and the total change of scene and habit make such a difference—that we have now nothing in common but our affections and our relationship.—

'But I have never ceased nor can cease to feel for a moment that perfect & boundless attachment which bound and binds me to you—which renders me utterly incapable of *real* love for any other human being—for what could they be to me after *you*? My own XXXX we may have been very wrong—but I repent of nothing except that cursed marriage—& your refusing to continue to love me as you had loved me. I can neither forget nor *quite forgive* you for that precious piece of reformation but I can never be other than I have been—and whenever I love anything it is because it reminds me in some way or other of yourself... It is heart-breaking to think of our long Separation—and I am sure more than punishment enough for all our sins. Dante is more humane in his "Hell" for he places his unfortunate lovers (Francesca of Rimini & Paolo, whose case fell a good deal short of *ours*—though sufficiently naughty) in company—and though they suffer—it is at least together. If ever I return to England, it will be to see you—and recollect that in all time—& place—and feelings—I have never ceased to be the same to you in heart. Circumstances may have ruffled my manner & hardened my spirit—you may have seen me harsh & exasperated with all things around me; grieved & tortured with *your new resolution*—& the soon after persecution of that infamous fiend who drove me from my Country & conspired against my life by endeavouring to deprive me of all that could render it precious—but remember that even then *you* were the sole object that ever cost me a tear, and *what tears*! do you remember our *parting*? ... When you write to me speak to me of yourself—and say that you love me—never mind commonplace people and topics ... They say absence destroys weak passions—and confirms strong ones—Alas! mine for you is the union of all passions and of all affections—Has strengthened itself but will destroy me ...'

Shortly after this affecting letter arrived, Annabella met Augusta in London, where she was on a visit from Tunbridge Wells, and thought Augusta looked 'repressed and oppressed'.

The latter mentioned a letter from Byron but did not divulge its contents. Some days later she enclosed it with another to Annabella, 'for I have endeavoured in vain, in *thought and deed*, to reply to it ... in short he surely is to be considered a Maniac ...' She now asked Annabella for her 'advice and superior judgement' as to what she should do. Annabella replied that Augusta had two alternative courses open to her: to break off all communication with him or to take no notice of having received the letter. Augusta's letter in response to this shows how fearful and vacillating her spirit had become under these blows and constant stresses. She favoured the 'gentler expedient', but how would she answer Byron when he asked if she had received the letter?—and this he would certainly ask. A few days later she wrote again: 'No one can be more fully aware of the *Precipice* on which I stand than I am—but situated *as I am*—I feel that—if once I gave way to despair I could never shake it off & should be unfitted for every thing—as this would be adding to the evil I do all I can to avoid it— & I hope it is not presumptuous to *trust* in that Power who alone can shield & protect ...'

From Ravenna on 26th July (just after the publication of the first two cantos of *Don Juan*) Byron wrote again, a most considerate, kindly letter, with hardly more than a passing reference to her restrained reply. 'I am at too great a distance to scold you, but I *will* ask whether *your* letter of the 1st July is *an answer* to the letter I wrote you before I quitted Venice? What? is it come to *this*? Have you no memory? or no heart? You *had* both—and I *have* both—at least for *you*.

'I write this presuming that you received *that* letter. Is it that you fear? Do not be afraid of the past; the world has its own affairs without thinking of *ours* ... I do not like at all this pain in your side and always think of your mother's constitution. You must always be to me the first consideration in the world. Shall I come to *you*? or would a warm climate do you good? If so say the word and—I will provide you and your whole family (including that precious luggage your husband) with the means of making an agreeable journey. You need not fear about *me* ...' In the course of a long, informative letter he tells her of his falling in love with the twenty-year-old Contessa Teresa Guiccioli—hence his presence in Ravenna; and concludes: 'Write to me—love me—as ever Yours most affectly B.'

Later in the year, in December, there arose a far more serious threat: Byron announced in letters to Murray and Augusta his almost immediate return to England, arriving perhaps by the New Year. Protestations of undying love from abroad were bad enough, but Byron's physical presence was more than the two women most involved could bear. Augusta broke the news to Annabella: 'Luckily (or *un*luckily perhaps) I do not die easily—or I think this stroke would about finish me. However, my trust is in Providence.' Brought up by Lady Holdernesse in a conventionally Protestant background, Augusta in her troubles looked more and more to the consolations of religion. At this juncture Teresa Guiccioli was providentially taken ill, and the tender-hearted Byron could not bring himself to desert her bedside. He informed Murray of his change of plan: 'Let my sister be informed that I am not coming. I have not the courage to tell her so myself, at least as yet.'

Augusta's latent timidity and her very natural fears were increased by the fact that she was expecting another child (her seventh and last), which was born on 28th January, 1820, and christened Henry Francis. Nevertheless under the threat of Byron's return she showed that she still possessed a spirit of her own. In this crisis her fundamental loyalty to Byron reasserted itself. She had informed Annabella immediately she was apprised of his coming, and the latter replied in a letter full of dire warnings. 'It can scarcely be doubted, from the whole series of his correspondence, that you are his principal object in England.' She advised Augusta to let Byron know that she would not 'associate' with him, and to face his anger—'His revenge must be directed either against your *reputation* or your *pecuniary interests*'. These modes of revenging himself she must be prepared firmly to withstand. Further, 'You would not act consistently unless you acted from *Conviction.*—You would take half-measures, which must end in your ruin.—Anxious as I feel to support & comfort you in your recovered path of virtue, I could not hope to do so by an attempt to impose my own opinions.' Her advice was to inform Byron at Calais 'of the impossibility of your consenting to personal intercourse, after the letters you had at different times received from him, &c—

. . .' And in a postscript she added: 'If *my* reasons convince you, they become *yours*—if not, I have no wish to enforce them.' They did not convince Augusta, and the correspondence between the two women continued, even when it was known that Byron was not returning. Augusta gave her arguments why, should he ever return, she felt bound to receive him.

Supposing she should not decide to see him, she argued, 'what reasons could I give for it to my relations—friends—acquaintances but—*most of all* my Husband?' If he did attempt to resume sexual relations with her, then, and only then, would she say, 'Either this must cease—or our intercourse.' As for the pecuniary threat, the possibility of an alteration of the will to deprive her and her children '. . . pray do me the justice to believe that one thought of the interests of my children as far as *that* Channel is concerned never enters—I have only entreated—I believe more than once that ye Will might be altered . . .' She did indeed try to prevent Byron from leaving the residue of the estate away from the heir to the title—George Byron. In a letter to Kinnaird as late as October, 1823, Byron wrote that he had just heard from his sister, wishing him not to leave anything in his will to her children. He informed his banker friend that the Countess Guiccioli also refused to be a beneficiary. 'Is not this odd? *Two women* of different countries concurring upon the same point!' Yet at the end of 1819 Augusta in her deplorable financial position was already borrowing from Murray, Byron's publisher.

Augusta's main reason for her courageous stand was her deep affection for Byron, a love that went beyond any physical satisfaction. She explained to Annabella: 'I never have—I cannot now believe as you do in the *depth & strength* of what is manifested by fits & starts—when there is nothing else—surely it must be a dreadful idea that he *must* necessarily be wicked in *some* way—then dearest A—I do not feel that I could *without one effort* relinquish the hope—the change of making some impression on his better feelings—you will perhaps think me foolish—vain—I hope not the latter—but indeed do you think there is one person in Engd who would—who *could* say to him what from circumstances *I* might? it might be *lost now* but perhaps recur hereafter & it wd be a satisfaction to me at all events to have said it . . .' This attitude was very contrary to

Annabella's feelings and opinions, and she tried hard to dissuade Augusta, but the latter stood firm in her resolve—'what a grief it is to me that I cannot *implicitly* adopt your advice . . .' Augusta's intransigence won her a little relief from her persecutor; thenceforth their relations were less close.

*

Augusta's correspondence with Byron was intermittent throughout 1820. He was hurt by her cold response to his coming to England: 'You say nothing in favour of my return to England—Very well—I will stay where I am—and you will never see me more.' However, he wrote several times asking Augusta to press Annabella to allow him to sell out of the funds and put out his money in an Irish mortgage. In the course of the year he wrote several letters to his wife offering to show her his Memoirs and repeating his request for her to be kind to Augusta and her children, but it was not until the end of the year that she replied to him in a stiff note, the last she ever wrote to him: '. . . If the assurance . . . would conduce, —(as you state in a formal letter, & as appears from your reiterated requests) to calm your mind, I will not withhold it. The past shall not prevent me from befriending Augusta Leigh & her Children in any future circumstances which may call for my assistance—I promise to do so.—She knows nothing of this—.'

Byron replied: 'You have alluded to the "past" and I to the future. —As to Augusta—she knows as little of my request, as of your answer—Whatever she is or may have been—*you* have never had reason to complain of her—on the contrary—you are not aware of the obligations under which you have been to her. —Her life & mine—and yours & mine—were two things perfectly distinct from each other—when one ceased the other began—and now both are closed . . . She and two others were the only things I ever really loved—I may say it now, —for we are young no longer.'

It appears that once again Byron came to the Leighs' rescue, to extricate them for a time from their financial morass. From Ravenna he wrote on 19th August: 'My dearest Augusta —I have always loved you better than any earthly existence, and I always shall unless I go mad. And if I did *not* so love you —still I would not persecute or oppress any one wittingly—

especially for debts . . .' He then told her that he had cancelled Colonel Leigh's debt to him and offered further help. 'Whatever measure I can take for his extrication will be taken. Only tell me how—for I am ignorant, and far away . . .' In October Augusta heard again: 'How do you get on with your affairs? . . . How is all your rabbit-warren of a family? I gave you an account of mine by last letter. —The Child Allegra [Claire Claremont's daughter] is well—but the Monkey has got a cough—and the tame Crow has lately suffered from the head ache—Fletcher has been bled for a Stitch—& looks flourishing again—Pray write . . .'

In 1821 Byron stayed on in Ravenna paying court to the young Countess Guiccioli, and his letters tailed off, so that Augusta became worried. In June he replied to her anxious questions: 'What was I to write about? I live in a different world . . .' He had put Allegra into a convent. Venting his fury against the Noels, he wrote: 'Will you for the hundredth time apply to Lady B. about the *funds* . . . Don't forget this, that cursed connection crossed at every turn my fortunes, my feelings and my fame . . . I send you an Elegy on Lady Noel's *recovery* . . . I will reserve my tears for the demise of Lady Noel, but the old [bitch?] will live forever because she is so amiable and useful.' In September he sent Augusta some locks of his hair—streaked now with grey—to be set in a locket for Ada. A letter in October informed her that the exile of the Countess Guiccioli from Ravenna necessitated their all removing to Pisa. Of his love affair with the Countess he wrote that 'this is "possibly the last time of performance" . . . So you see that I have closed as papa *began*, and *you* will probably never see me again as long as you live. Indeed you don't deserve it—for having behaved so *coldly—when I was ready to have sacrificed every thing for you* . . .'

Through her own tortured and often painfully cryptic letters and possibly by way of Hobhouse and Murray who, seeing her from time to time, knew the precariousness of her social and financial position, Byron had become aware of Augusta's difficulties and was anxious to alleviate them. Writing to Murray in September, 1821, he referred to the state of her nerves. 'Lady Byron's people, and Ly Caroline Lamb's people, and a parcel of that set, got about her and frightened her with all sorts of hints and menaces, so that she has never since been able to write to *me* a *clear common letter*, and is so full of mysteries and miseries, that I can only sympathize, without always understanding her. All my loves, too, make a point of calling upon her, which puts her into a flutter (no difficult matter); and, the year before last I think, Lady F[rances] W[edderburn] W[ebster] marched in upon her, and Lady O[xford], a few years ago, spoke to her at a party; and these and such like calamities have made her afraid of her shadow. It is a very odd fancy that they all take to her: it was only six months ago, that I had some difficulty in preventing the Countess G. from invading her with an Italian letter.' (To please Byron the Countess used to tie up and preserve all Augusta's letters to him.) Another reason for Augusta's lowness of spirits was the publication of the cantos of *Don Juan*, the 'odious Don', as she referred to it to Hodgson; she considered it bound to sink Byron's reputation even lower with the English public. In a letter to Byron she described it as 'execrable' even in its composition, and added rather illogically that she had heard so much against it that she would not read it.

One of Byron's reasons for getting his money out of the funds was to secure a reversion for Augusta and her children, but this Annabella's counsellors would not allow him to do. From Pisa in March 1822, he wrote to Augusta, after Lady Noel's death in January had opened the prospect of an increase of income from the Wentworth property, which he was to share equally with Annabella: 'It has ever been my object (if I live long enough) to provide as far as I can for your children, as my daughter by Ly. B. is rich enough already, and my natural daughter also will have a decent provision. I shall try what I can to save or accumulate some funds for this purpose (if Fortune be favourable) and should therefore like to hear now and then from my "residee lega*toos*" as I am not likely to see much of them for the present.' It would appear that the Greek expedition prevented the fulfilment of these plans; he was still considering taking out annuities for himself and Augusta at the end of March 1823.

From Pisa, where he had been saddened by the deaths of Allegra and Shelley, Byron moved to Genoa in the autumn of 1822, the Gambas (Countess Guiccioli's father and brother) having been ordered to leave the state by the Pisan authorities. Augusta received a cheerful letter from him in November, telling of a deluge in Genoa and the activities of a preaching friar who predicted the immediate coming of the day of judgement, and who was not put out of countenance by its failure to arrive. In January he suggested a meeting in the spring either in England or Genoa. 'Hobhouse says your coming out would be the best thing which you could do, for yourself and me too—' Then in May came the news that he had offered his services to the Greek Committee in London and was 'to go up among the Greeks' in their struggle for liberation from Turkish rule. On 23rd June he informed her that he was to sail in about a fortnight. In fact his party sailed in the *Hercules* from Genoa on 16th July, and about 4th August anchored off Argostoli, the chief harbour of Cephalonia in the Ionian Islands.

In the early autumn of 1823 Augusta, distressed and harassed by sickness among her own children, heard that Ada was seriously ill. She sent a series of bulletins to Byron, who was now settled at Mataxata on Cephalonia. The first news of Ada's illness reached him on 30th September and it disturbed him to the extent of causing him to break off a journal he was writing, which he did not resume until he heard of her recovery early in November. On 8th October he wrote a long informative letter to Augusta, concluding with the request: 'I wish you would obtain from Lady B. some account of Ada's disposition, habits, studies, moral tendencies, and temper, as well as her personal appearance, for except from the miniature drawn five years ago (and she is now double that age nearly) I have no idea of even her aspect . . . Is the girl imaginative . . . Is she social or solitary, taciturn or talkative, fond of reading or otherwise, and what is her *tic*?—I mean her foible—is she passionate? I hope that the Gods have made her any thing save *poetical*— it is enough to have one such fool in the family.'

On the 15th February, 1824, at Missolonghi he had the first of his convulsive fits. A few days later he received Augusta's answers to his questions about Ada; she had transcribed long sections from Annabella's letter of December, written from Hastings, where she had taken Ada to recuperate. Then on the 23rd Byron began what was to be his last letter to Augusta, a letter that was never finished and that was found on his desk after his death. 'My dearest Augusta, —I received a few days ago yours and Lady B's report of Ada's health, with other letters from England for which I ought to be and am (I hope) sufficiently thankful, as they were of great comfort and I wanted some, having been recently unwell, but am now much better. So that you need not be alarmed.' He told her of his obtaining the release of some Turkish prisoners, including a pretty little girl of nine whom he had thought to send to England as a companion to Ada. He referred again to his illness: '. . . I should mention that my recent attack, and a very severe one, had a strong appearance of *epilepsy*. *Why*—I know not, for it is late in life—its first appearance at thirty-six—and, as far as I *know*, it is not *hereditary*, and it is that it may not *become* so, that you should tell Lady B. to take some precautions in the case of Ada. My attack has not yet returned, and I am fighting it off with abstinence and exercise, and thus far with success; if merely casual, it is all very well.' Here the writing breaks off.

On the morning of 9th April he received letters from England; one was from Augusta giving good reports of Ada and enclosing her silhouette, which he showed to the company, remarking that it was a very strange coincidence that Augusta herself should have been seriously ill at the same time as his fit. Afterwards he went out for a ride and was drenched in a downpour. That evening he was taken ill with a fever and rheumatic pains. His condition steadily worsened. On the 18th letters came from England, among them one from Hobhouse telling him of the progress of the Greek Committee and the enthusiasm of the public for the Greek cause, stirred by his presence in Greece. 'All friends make many enquiries after you, and hope you will take care of yourself in Greece, and will return here after the good fight has been foughten.' But he was too ill to read the letter or to hear its contents.

It was Easter Sunday. He lingered on until the following day, and passed away at six o'clock on 19th April, 1824.

XIII

Byron's Heir

1824 - 1831

LORD SYDNEY OSBORNE, Augusta's half-brother, who held a
government appointment in the Ionian Islands, had dispatched
by special express post a budget of letters and documents con-
taining the news of Byron's death. This was addressed to the
latter's business agent, Douglas Kinnaird, and it reached
London early in the morning of 14th May. Before eight o'clock
Hobhouse was awakened by a knocking on the door of his
Albany flat, and, opening it, was presented with a letter in
Kinnaird's handwriting and a packet of letters with the post-
mark of Corfu. Already fearing the worst, he broke the seal of
Kinnaird's letter, and his forebodings were quickly realised.
'My dear Hobhouse,' the letter ran, 'I can scarcely write to
tell you, yet delay is absurd & I know not how to soften what
your own fortitude alone can make you bear like a man—
Byron is no more—I send herewith these letters for you—
Pray come here as soon as you can . . . Much must be done—
but nothing till I see you . . .' That evening Hobhouse wrote
in his diary: 'In an agony of grief such as I have experienced
only twice before in my life . . . I opened the dispatches from
Corfu and there saw the details of the fatal event.'

In hurried consultation with Kinnaird and Sir Francis
Burdett it was decided that the latter should break the news to
Augusta at St James's Palace and take her the letter addressed
to her by Fletcher. With all her children ill, two of them
seriously, Augusta was in her now habitual state of nervous
confusion. Having received no intimation of Byron's earlier fit,
she was completely unprepared for the shock of his death. Her
state was pitiable. Reading through Fletcher's illiterate letter,
all the more poignant from its artlessness, its naive sincerity, she
was moved to fresh paroxysms of grief. Before Sir Francis left
her, she requested him to ask Hobhouse to call on her as soon
as he could. When later in the day Hobhouse arrived, he found

her, as he entered in his journal, 'in an afflicting condition. She gave me Fletcher's letter to read and I could not restrain my sorrow but again burst out into uncontrollable lamentation . . .'

One passage in the letter caused the wary Hobhouse a qualm —a reference to Byron's custom, since his fit of 15th February, of having Augusta's bible on his breakfast table every morning. This might be interpreted, if the news got out, as pointing to a late religious conversion, a thought that Augusta would have dearly liked to believe; but Hobhouse made her promise to be discreet in revealing it. In the weeks that followed Hobhouse was constantly with her; she followed his advice in all matters and found him the loyal, practical, considerate friend of Byron and not the disreputable member of 'the Piccadilly crew' she once had thought him. He, with Kinnaird and Burdett, were at once anxious to protect Byron's reputation, to allow 'no rumours prejudicial to his fame'. They saw that accurate reports got to the newspapers and they delivered personally into the hands of Murray and Mrs Fletcher the letters written to them by Fletcher. Kinnaird wrote off at once to Barry, Byron's banker-agent in Genoa, to see if a will, other than that with Hanson in London, had been deposited with him. Captain George Byron was informed of his accession to the title; on the same evening he went down to Beckenham to break the news to Annabella.

With the expedition to Greece the tone of the press towards Byron had for the most part changed; he was now by way of being a national hero. The obituary notice in *The Times* was typical of most: '. . . We know not how many of our country-men may share the feelings with which the news has afflicted us. There were individuals more to be approved for moral qualities than Lord Byron—to be more safely followed, or more tenderly beloved; but there lives no man on earth whose sudden depar-ture from it, under the circumstances in which that nobleman was cut off, appears to us more calculated to impress the mind with profound and unmingled mourning . . . That noblest of enterprises, the deliverance of Greece, employed the whole of Lord Byron's latter days—of his pecuniary resources, and of his masculine spirit. It was a cause worthy of a poet and a hero . . .'

Hobhouse was visiting Augusta on the 15th when the new Lord Byron came in—'he was much affected,' wrote Hobhouse,

'—he had seen Lady Byron & told me she was in a distressing state—she said she had no right to be considered by Lord Byron's friends, but she had her feelings'; and she asked if she could see the accounts of his end.

Hobhouse was determined to get hold of the Memoirs which Byron had given to Tom Moore, who had raised a loan on them with Murray for two thousand guineas. He saw Murray, who showed himself willing to give up the manuscripts to Augusta; at their first meeting she was told by Hobhouse that she owed it to Byron's memory to destroy them forthwith. This she was only too willing to do.

Augusta, writing to Francis Hodgson on 31st May, gave an account of these first days after the arrival of the fatal news: '... Did I tell I had received a long letter full of melancholy details relative to the last nine days, from his servant, Fletcher ... ? You shall read it some day ... I cannot bear to part with it at present. It appears to me that he had never entirely recovered the effects of two *fits* in February, and Fletcher remarks that they had made a great impression, and produced great alteration, not only to diet, but the more serious duties of a Christian ... *this* is my greatest hope and comfort ... Mr. Hobhouse, on reading that portion of F.'s letter, desired me *not to show it*, as many people might imagine that *terror* had made him *Methodistical* ... The last twelve hours were perfect tranquillity and apparent insensibility. Before that, and being aware of his situation, he appeared most anxious to give orders and express something to Fletcher; but, alas! intervals of delirium prevented his being understood further than that he desired him to go to his "child", to his "wife", and to his "poor dear sister", and *tell* them that ... This is indeed distressing to reflect upon ...'

She then detailed to Hodgson the wretched business of the burning of the Memoirs at Murray's house in Albemarle St on 17th May, and her part in it: 'You have probably seen in the newspapers long histories of *the Memoirs, and my name* mixed up with them, and I am anxious to tell you the *fact*. The first day, and the *very* day I received the fatal intelligence, that I saw Mr. Hobhouse, he said, "Now the first thing that we have to think of is to protect Lord B.'s fame; there are those Memoirs", and proceeded to tell me who had them now—*Mr. Moore,* and

218

of a long squabble between Moore and Murray about them, which is of no consequence. The next day he came with a written agreement in his hand, to state to me that Mr. Moore would pay Murray back the 2,000 guineas he had received from him for them, and give them up to me and me only; and, Mr. H. observed, "I should recommend you, Mrs. L., to destroy them", which he need not have done, for I was too well convinced that it was the only thing to do, from the little I had heard of them . . .' She then reported that she later had had a note from Wilmot Horton to the effect that Moore protested against the destruction of the Memoirs and wanted them sealed up and deposited for safe-keeping. (If only this advice had been followed!) Augusta went on: '. . . I told Mr. Wilmot that if I was to have a voice in the business (which I by no means wished), that it was my opinion and unalterable determination that they should be destroyed, and immediately . . . So the parties, Messrs. Moore, Murray, Hobhouse, Col. Doyle for Lady B., and Mr. Wilmot for me, and Mr. Luttrell, a friend of Mr. Moore's, met at Mr. Murray's; and after a long dispute and nearly quarrelling, upon Mr. Wilmot's stating that it was my wish and opinion, the MS. was burnt, and Moore paid Murray the 2,000 guineas . . . Of course, whoever succeeds to my brother's property would consider it incumbent on them to remunerate the *loser* . . .' Alas, as so often in money matters, Augusta's desire to do right by Moore was beyond her power of fulfilment, when later she found herself Byron's heiress.

On 10th June Kinnaird reported to Hobhouse and Hanson that a thorough search by Barry at Genoa had not disclosed a new will, and on the 19th the two executors named in the 1815 will, Hobhouse and Hanson, deposited this document at Doctors' Commons, and it was proved on 5th July. Byron left some £100,000 to Augusta and her children, but there were outstanding debts to be paid and the settlements—£64,000 on Annabella and £16,000 on Ada—had to be secured. At an outside estimate Augusta received £25,000 in trust for herself and the children, and a further £4,000 in 1828, the remainder of Annabella's marriage settlement, which was only paid after the death of Sir Ralph Noel. In addition there would also be the reversion of the £64,000 settlement on Annabella's death.

On the night of 29th June the *Florida* with the 'dear remains', as Augusta referred to them, arrived in the Thames, and on 1st July Hobhouse went to Rochester and boarded the ship next day. It was not until the 5th that the *Florida* had proceeded up river, where the customs authorities gave permission to land and the undertakers brought the body ashore at Palace Yard Stairs and carried it to a house in George Street, Westminster, where a room had been hung with black and decorated simply with the Byron arms 'roughly daubed on a deal board'. Augusta waited all day in the expectation of seeing Fletcher, but the customs people kept him on board the *Florida* for several days before releasing Byron's effects. Permission for burial in Westminster Abbey having been refused by the Dean of Westminster, Augusta's original wish was adhered to, and plans were made for the funeral in the family vault at Hucknall Torkard.

Writing to Hodgson on 8th July to tell him of the funeral arrangements—he wanted to be present—Augusta described her visit to George Street on the 6th to see the body. '. . . He was embalmed, so it was still possible; and the melancholy comfort that it bestowed on me *never* can be expressed. There are few who can understand it, I believe; for my own part, I only envy those who could remain with and watch over him till the last . . . It was awful to behold what I parted with convulsed, absolutely convulsed with grief, now cold and inanimate, and so altered that I could scarcely persuade myself it was him— not a vestige of what he was. But God's will be done! . . .

'I have seen Lady B., which was a great trial. She was much agitated. I believe I told you how handsomely she has behaved to my cousin the present Lord B. I am glad to hear you approved of what I have done about the Memoirs . . .' When she arrived back from George Street, Hobhouse called on her, and it was arranged that the funeral should set out from London on 12th July. Byron was lowered into the family vault at Hucknall on the 16th.

If Augusta's gloom was relieved by the thought that Byron's making her his heir would help solve the Leighs' perennial financial crisis, she was not long in discovering that the deed was looked on with very different views by George Byron and Annabella. By them it was regarded as the wages of sin. Annabella, a rich woman with more than £8,000 a year of her own, at once took it into her head to be magnanimous: she made over to the new Lord Byron the annual sum of £2,000 to which she was entitled by the provisions of the will. Her action got into the papers. *The Morning Chronicle* interpreted Annabella's disposal of her jointure as 'a proof at least' of her approval of her late husband's 'disposition to the female branch of his family'. On 7th July Augusta wrote to Annabella: 'If I understand you rightly dearest A, I fear you have been annoyed by the concluding sentence of the Paragraph in the Newspaper giving an account of the Will. I mean that which states your having given up yr Jointure to G.B.—as '*a proof at least*' &c &c &c . . .

'I am very sorry that you have been annoyed by it . . . My wishes & feelings on this point must be so well known to *you* that it is needless to repeat them—it is a most painful subject to me—but at the same time it is my duty I am sure to be grateful for the very unexpected blessing (& the *very* undeserved one) of thinking that my Children will not be Beggars—

'Your mention of the arrangements you have *so* kindly made with G.B— is the *first* communication *I* have had on the subject except from public report—I think it *Most* extraordinary that he has never named it to me or to his own sister.'

The considerateness and humility of Augusta's letter went some way to mollify Annabella's pique; but, as so often with her, there was a sting in the tail of her reply. 'I am very far from wishing to deny now what I have more than once said to my husband—that it was his duty to provide for you and yours—how far *exclusively* is a question which I am relieved to be under no necessity of discussing—and therefore certainly shall say nothing about the matter, whatever may be said for me.'

George Byron was more open in his animosity, and he soon had occasion on which he could let it be felt. Ever since the separation, when he was an inmate of the house in Piccadilly, he and his wife had been partisans of Annabella. If his sense of fairness had been outraged by what he had then witnessed of Byron's treatment of his wife, he had also seen the part played by Augusta in defending Annabella, mitigating Byron's cruelty and trying to avoid the separation. Subsequently, as part of her systematic campaign of self-justification (which had over the years turned into the persecution of Augusta), Annabella had informed George Byron of her suspicions of the 'atrocious crime' perpetrated by Augusta. When in September 1824 R. C. Dallas, whom Byron had liberally rewarded for his assistance in finding a publisher for *Childe Harold*, wrote to Augusta, informing her that he was about to publish some early letters of Byron to his mother and an account of his youth, both she and Hobhouse protested, and the latter obtained an injunction to prevent his publishing the book in England. Dallas's son then approached the new Lord Byron, who saw no objection and tried to persuade Hobhouse to relinquish his prohibition. Finally the letters were published in Paris, with a preface which could only wound Augusta, who was doubly shocked that George Byron should have apparently so flagrantly betrayed her interests.

Augusta, thinking that Annabella would share her view of George Byron's inconsiderate behaviour, wrote to her on 28th November:'. . . I wish too I had never loved G.B., sufficiently to make me more than angry at his late conduct—I think his sanctioning Mrs. Dallas's Book is an *outrage* to the living & the dead—such a production *I* never saw—putting aside what is said of myself by his Relation [his son] . . .' Dallas had attacked the will, and regarded Hobhouse's veto of publication as a means to gain more for the heiress. 'To add a few hundreds to the hundred thousands of pounds that Lord Byron has stripped from an ancient and honourable title which they were meant to support—not to give to his daughter, which would have put the silence of feeling upon the reproach of justice, but to enrich his sister *of the half blood* . . . Lord Byron, against all *moral* right, has applied the money procured by the sale of Newstead Abbey, to enrich his half-sister, and left the family title without the family estate which belonged to it.' Annabella could not well defend Dallas, so she defended George Byron's sanctioning the book by suggesting that he had sailed on a voyage—he took home to the Sandwich Islands the bodies of the sovereigns who had died on a visit to England—before he could have seen the completed publication.

The reply she received from Augusta must have startled her by its unaccustomed directness, showing her that the Byron blood, when roused, was still formidable: 'G.B. never saw the work entitled "Recollections, &c"—let *that* pass . . . No one I

222

think wd *dare* to affirm that he had given his sanction to the *Preface* & other parts of the "Recollections" which are not only offensive, but as I'm told *actionable*—if contempt was not what they best deserve—but to come to the point—what business had Mr. Dallas to publish letters of the late Lord Byron's . . . and what right had the present Lord Byron to Sanction such a publication which he did in the original book—which original Book I have read, NOW published in French . . .

'The *least* that can be said of G.B's upholding his Uncle in such a measure was that he was weak & good natured enough to wish to put a little Money in his pocket—& considering that Uncle's past obligations to my Brother, I think he might have had the *delicacy* to have *tried* at least to have prevented his adding to those obligations by such VERY *indelicate* & improper means—to have *protested against* it, if he could have done nothing more effective.

'Such is my opinion on *that* point . . . what I contend for is this, that it was *wrong* in George to listen one moment to the publication of *any* letters—at *such* a moment too! . . . You may say this was an error of judgement, & perhaps it was—I am *grieved* at it let it be what it would.' She concluded by stating that it was her misfortune 'to mourn over the LIVING loss of all I loved best'.

Annabella, secretly pleased at the way things were shaping, tried to plead for George Byron, but Augusta was firm in her disapproval: 'For the sake of *the Dead* I never can speak to him or be on terms of friendship UNLESS he takes the step which wd. be right.' His ship did not return to England until 1826, but when he was again in this country he received a letter from Augusta, admonishing him, 'for the credit & honor of the name you bear, & the title to which you have succeeded', to try to remove the stigma occasioned by Dallas's book. He replied angrily from Bath, but Augusta's next letter to him was returned unopened; and thenceforth there was a complete rupture between the heirs to Byron's title and fortune.

The revival of public interest in Byron matters, which was brought about by his sudden death at Missolonghi, served also to raise old scandals. The papers were full of his affairs. A little more than a fortnight after Sir Francis Burdett had brought her the fatal news, Augusta received a letter from 'the genial confidante and general spy', Mrs Clermont: 'I would not willingly have intruded upon your attention at this time, but that my character is again so shamefully traduced in various Newspapers—such calumny *must* not continue uncontradicted.' She asked, with scant ceremony, that Augusta should declare that she was innocent of interfering at the time of the separation, and concluded with something like a threat: 'This should be done as speedily as possible for reasons which it is unnecessary to mention.' Augusta immediately wrote her a reply, saying that she had invariably contradicted such calumnies and would continue to do so. Mrs. Clermont was at liberty to disclose this letter to whom she thought fit, with the exception that it must not be communicated to the newspapers.

If the amount of business to be conducted in relation to Byron's estate was a heavy burden to one who had much to do in running a house for a large family (six of her children were usually at home), Augusta now shared largely in Byron's posthumous fame. Count Pietro Gamba, Colonel Stanhope, Fletcher and William Parry, those who were witnesses of his last hours, all called on her. She heard through Hobhouse of an extraordinary letter from E. J. Trelawny, claiming a close friendship with Byron, which the latter had apparently overlooked in his own letters. Memoirs and reminiscences of Byron proliferated, beginning with Dallas's book and Medwin's inaccurate *Conversations with Lord Byron*, which came out in late 1824. Augusta was courted as the sister loved by the poet and defender of Greek liberty. While Annabella lived unobtrusively in the country, visited only by Fletcher, Augusta at St James's Palace was at the centre of all the public interest and acclaim. Hobhouse and Hanson as executors administered Byron's estate, but it was Douglas Kinnaird, a partner in Ransom's Bank, who tried to straighten out Augusta's very tangled financial matters. Colonel Leigh continued to live in his accustomed style, the demands of seven children (one, Augusta's namesake, privately nursed away from home) were heavy, and the debts accumulated over the years were more than even the new access of funds could stand. The slate was only partly erased, and soon Augusta was once more struggling to see how ready money could be found to meet the bills. She had borrowed from everyone on whom she could decently call; Kinnaird himself had come forward with a loan. The shifts to which she had been (and continued to be) put to raise these sums, and the continued state of anxiety in which for one reason or another she lived, had the effect of impairing her judgement. At forty, her age at Byron's death, she was much changed from the girl and young woman who had shown such good sense and practicality up to the time of the Byron separation. Byron's tempestuous influence on her life had left her without firmness or clarity in dealing with everyday affairs. In money matters the helpful but quick-tongued Kinnaird became exasperated with her—'I think she is half-witted', he wrote to Hobhouse.

Nor was Augusta's judgement of persons sounder. Her form of pietism saw in everything the manifestation of the divine will. Yet if her own will was crossed she could show herself extraordinarily stubborn. In the summer of 1825, when her eldest daughter, Georgiana, was sixteen, there appeared in London for the purpose of studying law a distant Cornish cousin, Henry Trevanion. A second son of a family of landed gentry, he had little to recommend him beside his very presentable person. Augusta, always romantic, was charmed with the young man, thoroughly captivated by his manners and appearance; and when about the time of her seventeenth birthday in November Trevanion proposed to Georgiana, her mother was delighted with the match. There were two difficulties in the way of a quick marriage: Colonel Leigh's firm opposition and the lack of money.

On 9th December Augusta wrote to Annabella a long letter, among so many other topics at last finding her way to the point —what had 'really absorbed the greatest portion of my thoughts of late . . . You will perhaps be much surprised to hear it is a *proposal* of *marriage* to Georgey! The Proposer is a Relation, his name *Trevanion* . . .

'The young Man is studying the Law & has talent to make the most of his Profession—exceedingly clever & in other respects the only person I know *worthy* of Georgey . . . he was introduced to me . . . by his Father about last July twelvemonth & I've seen much of him since from liking him & finding him so far superior to the *common herd*, but without the slightest idea till lately that Georgey was likely to attract him or indeed any body—She is such a *quiet* being—with very sound &

excellent sense & good judgement, but not brilliant in any way, & I should have said too *awkwardly shy* to be admired. The present state of things is that the Father ... is approving in ye kindest & most flattering manner but doubting whether there will be *de quoi* to enable to marry at present.

'I (who from experience) have a *horror* of long engagements & who see little chance of delay bringing any speedy material improvement, am strenuous for the thing being brought to pass as soon as possible. They are young—but they are both very steady, & have any thing but extravagant notions.'

Augusta concluded this rambling letter with a prophecy both ill-founded and in the event grimly ironical. It was, she wrote, 'something which wd make me *too* happy ... As far as one can judge, it promises all the happiness *this* world can give —& in case of anything happening to me, it wd ensure a sort of protection to her sisters.'

However, by early January 1826, the difficulties still persisted; Augusta was now determined to ignore her husband's disapproval and to raise the sum of £2000 to set up the young couple. To Annabella she wrote: 'I cannot at this distance describe to you the sort of *unheard of Misery. The Lovers* are both looking like Ghosts, & as for *the Law* there will be no studying that while this state of things lasts . . .' At this juncture Annabella, remembering perhaps Byron's injunction to be kind to Augusta and her children, came to their assistance with a loan. On her father's refusal to attend the wedding Georgiana was given away by Augusta's friend, Colonel Henry Wyndham. The only members of the family present at the St James's, Piccadilly, on 4th February, 1826, were Augusta and her younger daughter Medora.

After the event Augusta wrote to Annabella: 'A Line— dearest A to tell You our Marriage thank God! is happily over & in parting with dearest Georgey I feel I could not to ANYone in the world with such perfect confidence *as* to Henry Trevanion. I have seen him *daily hourly* for 3 months—in Moments of Sickness, Sorrow, anxiety & suspense—all most trying predicaments to the Lords of the Creation—& which Shew the *real* Character—& his has only *risen* in my estimation!

'I cannot express *all* I feel to you for your kindness on this

226

occasion to which we owe *so* MUCH! but indeed I *am* grateful
—so are they—'

It was soon discovered that Henry's health would not allow
him to continue with the law. Further, the promised allowance
of £900 a year from his father turned out to be £450. Augusta
had borrowed in order to set them up in a house. Henceforth,
with the arrival of grandchildren, their maintenance fell largely
on her already diminished resources.

*

Among those many persons who were let by Annabella into
the open secret of Augusta's 'crime', it was usually considered
that the latter's penury was the result of paying out large sums
by way of blackmail. There is no evidence to show that this
was so. In February 1826, Hobhouse received two begging
letters from a stranger who signed himself J. Wilmington
Fleming, informing him that poverty, unless speedily relieved,
would necessitate his selling to a publisher some 'extracts from
the confessions of a Lady of Rank relative to Lord Byron—
which certainly do not set his private life in a very amiable
view'. When Hobhouse ignored these missives, and a further
one which allowed him to identify the 'Lady of Rank' as
Caroline Lamb, the would-be blackmailer appealed to Augusta.
In this letter he revealed the nature of the extracts: 'The
Manuscript relates Lady Caroline's first interview with Lord
Byron—his subsequent approaches—his attacks upon her weakness—his opinion of Lady Byron—and that Lady's account
of the usage she received from him on her last visit to Lady
Caroline previous to her separation—with other subjects pain-
ful to a relative's feelings and interesting to the Public.'

If Fleming was threatening to disclose matters directly
concerning Augusta, it was extraordinary that he did not say
so—the 'subjects' were 'painful to a relative's feelings' indeed,
but much more so to Annabella's. Augusta was not perturbed
about herself; she wrote immediately to Hobhouse, and the
following day, in a letter to Annabella about domestic matters,
which included the difficulties in raising a loan, she merely
mentioned the matter quite casually—certainly without showing concern for herself. 'Mr. Hobhouse has not written nor
answered a note I sent him last night, enclosing a most extra-

ordinary letter I had received, offering me the refusal of a *publication* of Extracts from Ly C. Lamb's Journal! ! ! ! ! ! I cannot think what he is about.'

Sorry for the misery which could cause such action, Augusta, rather than leave the letter unanswered, sent Hanson to inform the blackmailer that she 'could have nothing whatever to do with any such things'. Thereupon he wrote again, and she enclosed both his letters when she next wrote to Annabella, thinking that she also might be approached: 'Of the truth of the Statement concerning the contents of the Journal *I have not the least doubt*—from all I *know* from those who have read it —& I believe it is shewn a qui voudra lire! That woman is a perfect *Demon* & one of the few I never *can* be charitable to.

'I cannot believe her *mad*—but EXCESSIVELY BAD ... & it was a happy moment for me to meet her last night ! ! ! when coming away with ye Dowr D[uchess] of Leeds from Ly Salisbury's. We were waiting for the Carriage in the *Cloak Room* —she suddenly jumped before us like *Beezlebub* MAD or DRUNK! accosted the D to her horror & to my dismay! ... Imagine after that, her accosting me & absolutely thrusting her hand almost into my face! I believe I *just* touched it & made her the most profound curtsey! then she made off somewhere—thro' a trap door I believe—for the whole apparition was to me like something from the lower Regions! & I half expected like the man in Der Freichutz to find the *Fiend's Mark* on my hand— not my brow!'

The result of this considerate warning on Augusta's part was that Annabella spread it around that it was Augusta who feared the exposure. The irony of Lady Noel's warning to Annabella in 1816—'Once more take care of X.—if I know anything of human nature she does and must hate you'—was that Augusta was by nature incapable of hating anybody; whereas Annabella's deep-rooted jealousy and animosity towards her were masked under an overt personal friendship, while she could not forbear from injuring her. Annabella's powers of self-deception were scarcely credible. If Augusta had hatred or enmity in her character she might have remembered at this point a letter she had received from Byron, written from Diodati on 14th September, 1816: 'You know I suppose that Lady Bn ... has also been (during or since the separation) in correspondence with that self-avowed libeller & strumpet, [William Lamb's] wife. This you may depend upon though I did not know it till recently.' When Augusta had shown her this letter, Annabella was at pains to deny the 'correspondence'; a denial which was in a sense true, but in fact Caroline Lamb had written to her (and she had acted on the 'strumpet's' advice). And what she did not reveal, for it would have besmirched the saint-like purity of her conduct, if it had been generally known, was that she had had a meeting with one of 'the worst women in London' (her own phrase) on 27th March, 1816, when her 'suspicions' concerning Augusta were 'changed into *absolute* conviction'. To have Fleming now referring to that clandestine interview was so disturbing to Annabella that she was determined to make out that the threat was in reality against Augusta.

Annabella wrote immediately in reply to Augusta, advising her to get Murray to see Fleming and offer him money for his copy, and another letter to Mrs George Lamb to inform William Lamb, Caroline's husband. However, she found William Lamb far too aloof and indolent to have any intention of intervening, so she advised Augusta to consult Wilmot Horton. She herself wrote to Mrs Villiers a letter in which self-deception (if it was such) merges with falsehood: '. . . I have again had occasion to try to be useful to A— on a very unpleasant business —which I will confide to you—' She concludes this mendacious letter with her reason for aiding Augusta in 'such impending danger': 'A promise of kindness, *sealed by death*, must ever bind me.' Self-delusion, or hypocrisy, could hardly go further. All her efforts were, however, rendered unnecessary; Fleming disappeared from the scene, possibly into a debtor's prison.

*

Of Byron's friends Augusta had formed a particular regard and respect for Hobhouse, who always treated her tactfully and kindly (though somewhat magisterially on occasion) as her friend's beloved sister. Her correspondence over the years with Francis Hodgson was marked by an openness and affection, as with one who shared her regard for Byron and her own brand of Protestant piety. Scrope Davies had known her in London before his hurried retreat ('down-diddled', as Douglas

Kinnaird described it) to Bruges to escape the creditors for his heavy gaming debts. From there he communicated with her from time to time. After Byron's death Augusta sent him one of his rings, and he wrote to thank her: 'Pray do give me the history of the ring which poor B. wore—When did he get it? what is the stone? On which hand and on which finger did he put it. These are all trifles but what is not interesting about the departed when they are such as he was . . . Your account of the last moments of B. has been more interesting to me than all the letters, papers, conversations, declarations, and affidavits the world has produced.'

As the writings on every aspect of Byron's life multiplied, Moore's claims to write his *Life*, as some compensation for the loss of his two thousand guineas at the burning of the Memoirs, were supported by such powerful figures as Lord Landsdowne, Lady Jersey and the Hollands. Augusta, encouraged by Hobhouse, who was jealous of Moore's relations with his late best friend, and possibly out of deference to Lady Byron, who disliked Byron's friends on principle, was violently prejudiced against Moore and opposed to his writing the biography, although she realised that there was some justice in his claim to do so. Byron had, after all, given him the manuscript of the Memoirs to make use of as a kind of delayed legacy for his son. Augusta, although she had never met him, had not a good word to say for Moore, referring to him in her letters in a most slighting way—'that despicable little Moore', usually heavily underlined.

In September 1825, she wrote to Annabella, describing a visit to Holland House: '. . . & who should be there but Mr. Moore ! ! ! whom I had been thanking My Stars for the last year & $\frac{1}{2}$ that I did not know (even by sight) . . .' She thought that the occasion had been arranged by Lady Holland. Moore gave an account in his journal of their meeting: 'In the evening, to my great surprise and pleasure, Mrs Leigh appeared. Could not help looking at her with deep interest; though she can hardly be said to be like Byron, yet she reminds one of him. Was still more pleased, when, evidently at her own request [here Moore seems to be in error], Lady Stanhope introduced me to her: found her pleasing, though (as I had always heard) nothing above the ordinary run of women. She herself began first to talk of him, after some time, by asking me "whether I saw any likeness". I answered, I did; and she said it was with strong fears of being answered "No", that she had asked the question. Talked of different pictures of him. I felt it difficult to keep the tears out of my eyes as I spoke with her. Said she would show me the miniature she thought the best, if I would call on her.' This last remark seems to have been made purely out of social politeness, for she was always not at home when he subsequently called.

At length, on Hobhouse's advice, Moore made up his quarrel with Murray and, after many difficulties had been overcome, began in late 1827 to collect his material for his *Life*, not for Murray but for Longman's. The incident which hastened the settling of these differences and delays was the publication in January 1828 of Leigh Hunt's mean and unworthy *Lord Byron and Some of His Contemporaries*. Murray thereupon closed with Moore for 4,000 guineas and gave him the use of all the Byron papers in his possession. Augusta liked and respected Murray, but her suspicions of Moore's motives remained. The first of the two volumes of the *Life, Letters, and Journals of Lord Byron* appeared in January 1830.

Another of Byron's friends, his business agent, Douglas Kinnaird, was in close touch with Augusta over the administration of the will and the attempt to put order into her hopeless financial affairs. Late in 1829, attempting yet again to raise money on a mortage with the help of a Colonel D'Aguilar, she fell out with Kinnaird, and he—already a sick man, dying of cancer—suddenly resigned his trusteeship. Augusta appealed to Hobhouse, who wrote to his friend on her behalf. Kinnaird replied: 'It will be a great weight off my mind—and I hope I need not assure you that I should consider it one of the greatest misfortunes of my life that you should feel a difficulty in justifying any part of my conduct towards Mrs Leigh.' Although he has a notoriously short temper, he denied that he had 'ever had an angry word with her', and asked Hobhouse's advice how he should make up the quarrel—'Should I leave a card?' It does not appear that his health permitted him to do this before he died on 12th March, 1830.

Kinnaird's death left vacant the office of one of the two trustees to the Byron marriage settlement; hitherto one trustee had looked to Annabella's interests and the other to Augusta's.

Now Annabella proposed—as she had the legal right to propose
—that her legal adviser, Lushington, be appointed to the
vacancy. This was a strange choice. He had acted against
Byron in the separation and had the poorest opinion of Augusta.
Not unnaturally the latter wrote (on 28th November, 1829) to
enter a protest to Annabella: 'As regards your nomination of
Dr. L. as trustee, I have to observe that he is a perfect stranger
to me; that in a matter where my own individual interests are
concerned it is of the highest importance to my comfort that I
should be on terms of friendly intercourse and even intimacy
with the Party; and that possessed as you are already of a
Protector to your interests in the person of Mr Bland, I had not
thought it unreasonable to hope that you would allow me a
similar advantage in the appointment of some individual personally known to me, and in whom I could confide entirely . . .'
In a postscript she suggested that Lushington in the circumstances would refuse the office, and asked that he be shown her
letter. In fact, unknown to her, Annabella was acting thus on
Lushington's advice. Further, Annabella, by an act of extraordinary discourtesy, informed Augusta that the matter was
decided and could not be altered—through the medium of her
solicitors. After some days, Augusta not having replied, Annabella sent her a condescending little note.

Augusta then gave expression to her deeply wounded feelings:
'I will not be so unjust to myself as to affect an acknowledgment
with reference to late events which I cannot feel—on that
subject *I never can have but one opinion*—and no future advantage
I may ever derive from the late nomination can compensate to
me for the appointment itself—the manner of communicating
it—or the misery, harassment and vexation which all the
measures connected with it have occasioned.' This letter was
passed on to Lushington for his comments, which included:
'You have already extended your forgiveness to Mrs. Leigh to so
unparalleled an extent that I must in candour say that all she
can feel, write or say in this transaction is comparatively of no
moment. Any personal contact with her is I think a degradation . . . all the anxiety you have had will be well repaid by the
cessation of such intercourse.' Augusta was not without reason
in protesting against his being a trustee where her interests
were involved.

Annabella complained of her independent behaviour to Mrs Wilmot Horton on 30th December, 1829: 'I have had a good deal to annoy me lately. Think of Mrs. Leigh's having, after all my endeavours to serve her, accused me of the most unfriendly conduct! . . . She cannot, I think, believe what she says, after all the reason she has had to know how sacred I have held the promise to be "kind still to Augusta". I grieve that she deprives me of opportunities of *acting* up to it in future. It is impossible for me to admit of personal intercourse with her after such wilful misconstructions.'

At the beginning of January she informed Augusta of her intentions, but offered to give her news of Ada's health when it was asked for. Augusta's reply on 15th January was not at all submissive. At this point the publication of the first volume of Moore's *Life* was giving both women cause for concern. Moore had dealt tactfully with Annabella, but he had had the temerity to suggest that the passage of time had already softened many of the harsh accusations made against Byron at the time of the separation. This was more than the self-righteousness of Annabella would stand. In spite of the advice of Lushington, Doyle and Wilmot Horton, who all contended that Moore should not be replied to, she composed her *Remarks* (published in the second volume of Moore's *Life*), ostensibly to defend her parents against the charge of undue influence on her actions in separating from Byron; but in reality this had the effect of raising over again the true reasons for the separation and Augusta's connection with them. Wilmot Horton honourably besought her to show the manuscript to Augusta before it was printed; this she did not do, but sent her one of the first copies, which she then distributed to George IV, peers, bishops, many middle-class friends, as well as some unknown to her, and even to bookshops.

While she was engaged on the composition of the *Remarks*, a letter came from Augusta asking after Ada's health and including some tentative enquiries as to her own sentiments. She answered this by imperiously demanding Augusta's 'unqualified assent' to four propositions:— that she had no right to interfere in the appointment of a trustee; that she did not doubt Annabella's desire to promote her interests and had no reason to complain of how the appointment was arranged or announced; that she had no grounds for suspecting Lushington's disinterestedness. The fourth head only repeated the second part of the second assertion. If she dissented, she was to show it by her silence. Augusta replied on 24th February: 'I dissent essentially from the contents of your letter, but I will not do so "in silence" lest that silence should be misinterpreted.' She was voluble, and urgent, in her rebuttal of Annabella's exacting demands, and she concluded her long letter with a paragraph which touched on the quick all Annabella's pride, complacency and 'high-mindedness': 'I can forgive and do forgive freely, all and everything that has agonised, and I may say all but destroyed me. I can believe that you have been actuated throughout by a principle which you thought the right one, but my own self-respect will never allow me to acknowledge an obligation where none has been originally conferred...' Annabella was almost speechless with indignation—'self-respect' indeed! Writing to Mrs. Villiers she overflowed: '... I can never pass over her insolence in offering me forgiveness...'

Augusta received her copy of the *Remarks* through the hands of Mrs Villiers at the beginning of March, just after the death of her namesake, the mentally retarded Augusta Charlotte. Mrs Villiers called several times (since she was in constant communication with Annabella, it is presumed she wanted to be able to report back), but Augusta was not at home to her. All the old scandals were revived, not only by the *Remarks*, but also by Thomas Campbell's ill-advised eulogy of Annabella in *The New Monthly*. Hobhouse was contemplating an answer to these, but early in April he saw Augusta, who, although she denied some of Annabella's assertions, requested him to make no answer.

The effect of all these gratuitous disclosures is shown by a letter from Drury, a son of Byron's Harrow headmaster, to his friend Francis Hodgson: 'What a mess has Tom Moore by his inadvertency stirred up about Lord Byron!... The character of Byron will be condemned for ever among his haters, and among his lovers strange suspicions must hover about, unless Lady B. or Lushington break silence.'

Hodgson replied to this: 'I have indeed too fully seen the late wretched matters about poor dear Byron and his ruined memory! My God! how cruel, how utterly revengeful, is the letter [the *Remarks*] of his *widow*! Do you for a moment give her credit for being actuated by regard to her parents' memory? If so, that would have been the prominent part of the letter . . . but it occupies a most inadequate space; and the rest shows her real reason for breaking silence: *pique* at being described as so ill-suited a wife for Byron . . . when this is so evidently the real cause of her speaking out, her laying it on filial feelings is as shallow as it is hypocritical . . .' Hodgson was, indeed, partly correct, but Annabella's reasons were not so shallow. Augusta's own opinion she now expressed to Hodgson. 'I have always thought', she wrote, 'that there was nothing in the whole world but the welfare of one's children which could induce one, or justify one, in abandoning one's husband! She may have considered this point, but she ought to have behaved differently . . .' A great rift had now come between the two women.

On the appearance of Moore's second volume in 1831 Augusta wrote to Hodgson: 'I long to hear what you think of this book . . . What will Lady B. do or say? What can she? And yet if she is quiet she must *writhe* under the torture! But she may thank herself either for her own sufferings, or the contumely which will rest on his memory. A few *gentle* words, instead of that despicable tirade on the last volume, would have secured her the esteem and pity of all the world . . . I know nothing of her or dear Ada, except *second hand*.

'On the 10th Dec. (Ada's birthday) I could not resist sending her some little token of my remembrance. I selected a Prayer-book (the Book of Common Prayer, in two volumes, with the Lessons bound up with it). I had them nicely bound, and *Ada*, in Old English characters, engraved on the back, and wrote her name and the date inside, put them up directed "To the Hon. Miss Byron, with every kind and affectionate wish", and wrote over this, "With Lady Byron's permission." In another outside envelope directed them to Lady B; sent them booked by coach; . . . and . . . have never heard one word since.'

XIV
Medora Leigh
1831 - 1849

THE PASSING of the years had softened Hobhouse's earlier misogynic views, and in July 1828 he married Lady Julia Hay, daughter of the seventh Marquis of Tweeddale. By 1831, when on his father's death he inherited the baronetcy, he was making his name as a reformer in Parliament and was well known in society, where he frequently met Augusta. On 1st July, 1831, he entered in his journal: 'I have been listening to a sad story from Colonel Leigh and his wife. Trevanion who married their eldest girl has seduced their second daughter 17 years old and had two children by her. The girl told her father that she and the young man read the Bible every morning.

'Strange to say the poor wife still clings to her husband and says she will follow him to prison—and stranger still Mrs Leigh seemed to me to be afraid of using harsh measures with this pious profligate—The poor girl is very fond of the man—she is hid in London—her father carried her off with a constable and an attorney from Colerne in Wilts. The man is wandering about London trying to find her, with a pistol in his pocket.

'The young girl was Lord Byron's favourite niece. I recollect her a little blue eyed chubby creature whom he used to fondle. What a fate. . .'

After Henry Trevanion had married Georgiana in 1826, a marriage which Annabella materially assisted in making possible, she had lent the couple Bifrons, a house that she had taken near Canterbury but could not bring herself to live in. In March 1829, when Georgiana was expecting her third child, Augusta in an evil hour resolved to send Elizabeth Medora, who was not yet fifteen, to live with the Trevanions. Apparently Henry was to supervise her education, and it fell out that he and Medora were often left alone together. Towards the end of the year the Baroness Grey and the Rev. the Hon. W. Eden paid a visit to Lady Byron, George Byron's wife, to

236

inform her of the scandal which was the talk of Canterbury. Medora had been seduced by Henry, with Georgiana's connivance, and was with child by him. The Reverend Eden had taxed them with the facts, which they admitted. Augusta was not told, but Lord Byron and Annabella provided money—the Trevanions had only enough income to live on—and the family, with Medora, crossed to Calais, where the girl gave birth to a son, in February 1830. The child was left behind in charge of the doctor, when the Trevanions and Medora returned to England in May, but it only lived a few months.

Medora then went back to her mother's flat in St James's Palace, and the Trevanions moved into a house in Cadogan Place belonging to an aunt. Augusta, who had not seen Medora for over a year, was quite unsuspecting of the nature of her relation with Trevanion, and tried unsuccessfully to get her to go out into society, as she had done previously. Since Augusta was excessively fond of Trevanion, she encouraged him to call almost every day, often going out herself and not returning until after midnight, leaving the young couple alone in the drawing-room. If she was unsuspicious of the cause of the change in Medora, she at last became aware of a wildness in Trevanion's behaviour and questioned him about it. In reply he wrote her a strange note and then tried to explain himself in a further letter, which he gave Medora (whom he used to call Nell) for her mother:

'My dearest Moé, —I owe some explanation for the pain I gave you by my wild note—I took laudanum—I promise you not to do so again—would to God that had been all! Your affectionate kindness distracted me with hopes that are now no more—and Nell had half my consent yesterday to have disclosed the fatal cause of my misery—it shall now and ever be a secret. She cannot speak without the consent I have revoked in my note last night, and you are too dear and good to ask of her a confidence the breach of which involves—my life. Never again allude to the subject if you have love or pity for your unhappy H.T.'

This missive should have alerted Augusta's suspicions, but she simply read it, returned it to Medora, and never again referred to the subject.

So things went on until February 1831, when Medora found

herself once more with child by Trevanion, who 'begged and entreated' her to confide in Augusta. He composed a letter, which Medora copied and signed; in it and a further one, written after they had seen her, they attributed the blame for their predicament to Augusta, whom they could not 'respect', and accused of 'acting on a system of distrust'. After reading these terrible letters, Augusta burned them. Her long, tortured letters in reply are expressive of the shocked confusion of her mind. Before her interview with the couple she wrote to Trevanion.

'It would be impossible in the *first* instance to speak to you my dearest—without such emotion as would be painful to us both—and I therefore take up my pen, but only to break the ice! for I feel equal (and in some respects greater) difficulty than I should in speaking.

'You know how I have loved and regarded you as my own Child—I can never cease to do so! . . . Show me how I can comfort and support you—confide in me dearest—too much suffering has been caused by want of confidence. What *might not* have been prevented could I have known, guessed, even *most remotely* suspected—but—I would not breathe a word if I could help it to give *further* pain! . . . Much do I blame myself! but as He who knows our hearts knows my trials, and the circumstances in which I've been placed, and that I have always acted to the *best of my judgement* for the welfare and happiness of others, I trust I shall find pardon! . . .

'I am convinced, dearest, that as I have opened my heart and feelings to you, you will comfort me! I need not point out to you the means! your own heart will dictate them . . .

'Heaven bless, comfort and guide you!'

Trevanion and Medora's means of comforting Augusta were to lay entirely the blame for their relationship on her. The day after their first talk with her Augusta wrote again to her son-in-law:

'Your note just received is to me *inexplicable. When* and *how* have you "*witnessed me acting on a system of distrust*"? When you answer this, I may be able to meet your accusation—certainly a most unjust one! I will not say *unkind*, for I can make allowances for the effects of your present state of mind upon feelings so sensitive as yours. Dearest—I wish I *could* comfort you.

'... Now, dearest, to reply to that most heart-breaking letter put into my hands yesterday— ... do not mistake me by supposing that I have so little consideration for the weakness of human nature as to think of "a *too precipitate* execution of my purpose"—a purpose on the accomplishment of which depends my only hope of consolation! You say, *you do not respect me*— you would *still* less respect me if I did not entertain such a hope, and do my utmost by the most judicious means I can think of to accomplish that on which the *eternal* welfare of that unhappy Being depends! and the PRESENT welfare—(nay, I may say *existence* and *sanity*) of so many others depends! ... I thank you from my heart for your *pledge*—I *accept it*—and *I trust to you implicitly*. Consult dearest G[eorgiana] on the *most judicious means* of proceeding in such a cruel predicament. I have explained to her my ideas on some *minor* points of *prudence*, which are perhaps more essential than you think—for it is a hateful word where more important interests than merely worldly ones are at stake, but where the ruin of so many may be the alternative of its observance it becomes a serious consideration.

'Now Dearest—let me implore you to be comforted ... That you are tried, SEVERELY tried, I feel—and I pray God to support you and comfort you and guide you! ... Do not accuse yourself, dearest, and make yourself out *what you are* NOT!'

The unfortunate Augusta in her utter bewilderment could only fall back on prudence and providence. She was still quite deluded by the specious Trevanion, whose worthlessness had been apparent to Colonel Leigh, more adept in the ways of the world. The foolish fondness which shows through every line of her letter to Trevanion is changed into something at least more realistic in the letter she wrote to the only little less culpable Medora:

'As in conversation upon painful subjects one is apt to express oneself strongly, and lest you might misinterpret such expressions, and mistake *that* for unkindness which would be but the effects of agitation, I must write to you, my dearest, what the fullness of my heart and my anxiety would dictate every moment to you!'

Augusta told Medora of the pain the discovery had caused

239

and implored her—'*on my knees I implore you*! to use every *effort of your soul* to cope with those temptations which assault you! . . .' She must know her duty, and perform it.

'Reflect that you are—no, not now—Great God avert it! that (how shall I write it?) you have committed *two* of the most deadly crimes! recollect who you have injured . . . not only your own Soul, but that of another, you think *more* dear than yourself. Think *whom* you have deprived of *his* affection! Think of others on whom *shame* and *disgrace* must fall, if even now you are not *outwardly circumspect* in your demeanour! Think of his Family—of *yours*—of your unmarried and innocent sister —of the broken heart of your Father, for that, THAT would be the result . . . Pardon me if I inflict pain on you—I must in this case "be cruel to be kind!"—for *could* I forgive myself, did I neglect to rouse you to the consideration of such consequences!

'To repeat *my* ardent desire to be of comfort to ALL is needless! Heaven guide me, in its mercy, *aright*—in the labyrinth in which I am involved! . . . Dearest, listen to one thing—which is certain and inevitable—a continuance (by which you must not understand that I require *impossibilities*, or *do not* and *will not* allow for the weakness of the human nature and the strength of its temptations)—but an obstinate continuance in this DREADFUL affair—or the least deception, will either *upset my reason* or *break my heart*. You imagine perhaps that *this* is a way of speaking and feeling—that my disposition is such that no *lasting* impression can be made on my feelings—but I have lived through so much I am like flint or steel at bottom, with only a light surface—but—do not *flatter* yourself that *I* should survive . . . I have suffered *much*—long (neither you or ANY human Being knows *how* much, but—I never knew sorrow like this! . . . Spare! oh spare me, Dearest! Spare yourself and all you hold most dear! Depend on it your efforts will be rewarded, and in your Mother's heart, surely you might find comfort.'

Augusta concludes this frantically anguished letter with a pious wish, which itself reveals the change that was already coming over a society increasingly coloured by evangelical morality—a hope that Medora would continue with Augusta's plan for her to be confirmed at Easter! But now she thought that Medora's preparation would be better conducted by a clergyman rather than by her mother. Poor Augusta had little to hope for apart from the intervention of providence.

There followed angry scenes between mother and daughter. Medora refused to be confirmed, and insisted in March that she should accompany Trevanion and Georgiana to the house they had taken in the village of Colerne near Bath. Georgiana herself expressed the strongest wish that Medora go with them, as she feared Trevanion's violence. Fearful of the consequences if Colonel Leigh should get to hear of what had occurred, Augusta, when Medora threatened to swallow the contents of a bottle of laudanum, which she brandished in her hand, finally was driven to a reluctant consent. The Wiltshire interlude, however, lasted only until June, when Georgiana wrote to Augusta, declaring that she was unable any longer to endure the *ménage à trois*. Augusta, not willing to face her husband, whom she had 'fearlessly opposed' in bringing about the unfortunate marriage, informed her friend, Colonel Henry Wyndham, and it was he who broke the news to Colonel Leigh. The Colonel acted quickly; in the company of a solicitor, a Bow Street officer and a woman who (Medora declared was 'intended to represent a lady's maid', he drove down to the country in his carriage and carried off Medora to London, where he placed her in the custody of a Mrs Pullen in Lisson Grove. She was there a virtual prisoner, locked and barred in a room overlooking Regent's Park, when Hobhouse heard of the sad affair from the Leighs.

Medora was not long in effecting her escape. Again with the connivance of Georgiana (who, contrary to what Hobhouse thought, wished nothing better than to get rid of her husband), Trevanion managed to find her address and get messages to her, sewn by Georgiana in linen returned from the laundry. Mrs Pullen was won over, the doors were left unlocked, and Medora escaped in the first week of July, with Trevanion, to Normandy, where they lived together as M. and Mme. Aubin. The child appears to have been still-born. Georgiana, as she had given her word to do, grounded her suit in the Ecclesiastical Court for a divorce from her husband, but it was dismissed, as the collusion was too evident.

To Augusta (as to others who knew the facts) it seemed that she was under the curse of the Byron heredity. Of the girls

Emily alone, who was fifteen in 1832, showed herself sympathetic and affectionate. The older boys—George was now twenty and Frederick sixteen—both revealed signs of turbulence and irresponsibility. George was in the army and Frederick the navy. The third son and youngest of the family was then aged twelve. It was not, therefore, surprising that, when the Countess Guiccioli visited England with her elder brother Vincenzo (Pietro, Byron's companion, had died in Greece in 1827) in the summer of 1832, she saw Augusta but once, when they spent three hours in each other's company. The Countess referred delicately to her fear of disturbing Augusta in a letter to John Murray in November of that year; which also reveals how well known Augusta's misforunes were:

'If you happen to see Mrs. Leigh do me the favour to tell her how much I regret not to have seen her from a so long time—and present her my best compliments. To say you the truth I fear that in the present state of her domestic annoyances to *receive visits* would be to her rather a troublesome than an agreeable thing, and for this reason only I differed [*sic*] day after day to call again upon her ... I hope to see her once more when I come back to London ...'

It is doubtful whether these two women whom Byron loved most did ever meet again.

In June 1833, after some two years of silence, Augusta received a letter from Medora, in which she wrote that she was ill; she declared that it was her present earnest desire to leave Trevanion and enter into a convent at Carhaix in Brittany. With this end in view, she added an urgent request for a regular sum of money to provide for her *pension*. Augusta, besides her own growing-up family, had to support Georgiana and her three children; to do this she was already making inroads into the capital, which secured Annabella's settlement, by realising on the reversions; nevertheless she declared herself willing to try to let Medora have the sum of sixty pounds a year.

Medora entered the convent, but within a month found herself again pregnant; with the Abbess's consent she left the convent (the Abbess forwarding her letters from Augusta and saying nothing of her removal) and went into lodgings apart from Trevanion, where she gave birth to a girl, Marie, some

nothing from the latter, wrote to her, appealing for confirmation of the report. Annabella's reply revealed how the years had forged from her latent jealousy an instrument of refined cruelty: 'Could I have believed that you had a Mother's affection for her, you would not now have to ask for information on that point. To say nothing of your previous conduct, —after she had, without any assistance of yours, freed herself from the tyranny of Mr. Trevanion, you left her unprotected and destitute, in a most alarming state of health, exposed to every temptation, and not even beyond his reach!... Your affectionate letters to her must appear a cruel mockery to those who know that you left her, for so long a time, only the alternative of vice or stavation.

'Her malady, the effect of physical and mental suffering combined, can be retarded ... only by extreme care and by her avoiding all distressing excitement. The former I can secure, but not the latter—I would save you, if it be not too late, from adding the guilt of her death to that of her birth. Leave her in peace!...'

This letter must have afforded Annabella exquisite satisfaction in writing. But the sequel was ironic; she had not counted on Medora. In her distress on receiving this untrue and tendentious account of her actions Augusta turned to Mrs Villiers, with whom she had not been on close terms since the latter had espoused Annabella's cause against her ten years previously. Mrs Villiers, knowing from Lady Chichester how unjust was Annabella's case, wrote a moving letter to her on Augusta's behalf. A long and very plain-spoken correspondence ensued. Mrs Villiers explained in detail that Augusta's income of £800 was unequal to the demands made on it, that Augusta had deprived herself of everything in order to provide for others, and that to do what she had done she had run herself heavily into debt. As was Annabella's habit, when once she had made up her mind, she remained implacable. On Mrs Villiers' advice Augusta composed the two statements, which were attested by Lord Chichester and his mother, and sent them with a covering letter to Annabella. The packet was returned unopened to Augusta's solicitors; on the envelope Annabella had written that she 'considered the correspondence terminated' by her answer to Augusta's first enquiry. Fresh appeals from

Mrs Villiers only elicited a compliment from Annabella on her able advocacy. The exchange of letters ended in an estrangement between the two, Mrs Villiers insisting that Augusta had done everything for Medora that was in her power to do and that Annabella's attitude was prejudiced and unfeeling.

In April 1841, Ada came to Paris with her husband, and Medora was treated by the Lovelaces as her sister. Then in June Annabella brought Medora and her child with her to England, where they lived at Moor Place, Esher, for just over a year. Annabella, on getting to know Medora better, was by this time having second thoughts about her character. She, who had always longed to be loved, began to see that Medora's over-demonstrative affection was not disinterested; in the first rosy hopes of arousing her love she had even allowed the young woman to address her by Byron's pet-name of Pip. In June 1842, when Medora's case was due to come up before the Court of Chancery, Augusta's counsel surrendered the deed of appointment just before the hearing. With this document in her possession Medora's attitude to her protectress changed abruptly. She considered that in some way Annabella had compromised her interest in favour of Augusta. Annabella, put on her guard by allusions dropped, realised that Medora was going to work on her mother for future advantage. 'In consequence I must,' she noted down, 'without disclosing my reasons, protect the mother by my arrangements.' She observed that there were 'but two holds on this character—Love of approbation and of money'. It seemed that Medora would use her parentage as a means to blackmail both Augusta and Annabella. Her frequent scenes of uncontrolled fury finally drove Annabella from Moor Place, but not before she had agreed to provide her with an income sufficient for herself, Marie, and her two French servants, Nathalie Beaurepaire and her husband, in the South of France.

In July, shortly before she set out for Hyères, the agreed place of retreat, Medora was paying a visit to the Lovelaces in St James's Square, when she almost ran into Augusta. That evening she wrote to Annabella:

'If dearest Pip I began my letter with anything else than what occupies me at this moment you might attribute the natural constraint of my letter to other causes, & I *know* you will sympathize at what I feel. I have this instant met my Mother. She was crossing the Square coming from York Street as the Carriage drove up to the door. I instantly recognised her—she is unchanged in face—& turned my head as if waiting for William who was ringing at the door. She could not have seen my face—my veil being down—& I saw her before she saw me—her sight and perceptions are not quick—& between the door being opened & my speaking to William, she had reached the Duke of Cleveland's before I got out—which I did quickly. She turned round and looked at the carriage— for I observed her from the little back window—probably from curiosity and thinking it might be you. She was followed by a dirty-looking rascally kind of servant out of livery who was playing with his glove, & was dressed in a dark brown kind of muslin gown with white pattern, a black silk shawl with long fringe and gathered round her as if she was afraid of losing it & a straw leghorn bonnet trimmed with white satin ribbons. Her large eyes are ever & indeed *unchanged*, her walk is most altered—she shuffles along as if she tried to carry the ground she walks on with her and looks WICKED. Oh, were there a thing I hoped to be spared it was this. If her curiosity were awakened it is lucky this took place at Lord L.'s door—be sure she fears him . . . I was very quietly dressed in my old dark silk gown black scarf & white bonnet—& she did *not* see my *face*, & I well remember how she never saw or knew any one & always used to say no one ever knew people or observed as quickly as me save "poor B."—& she used to rely on me for observation.

'This has shocked me—pained me, but it is over. I have drunk quantities of wine since, & now there is nothing left for me to suffer that I dread. Oh how dearly fondly I loved her, & had she only stifled the existence her sin gave me—but God *is* there—& I will do my best to bear as I have ever done but it is so long, so constant—God forgive her. Oh how horrible she looked—so wicked—so hyena-like—That I could have loved her so! Bear in mind one feeling the sight of her has given me yet more strongly—if for my good or that of Marie—intimidate her—she will grovel on the ground fawn, lick the dust— all—all that is despicable & bad. You she will not fear, you personally—but Lord L—, Dr. L—, or Wharton. Now we will

249

try and never mention her name—she will live for *years*. Oh could I only have loved the memory of my mother, but had death passed over me the chill—the horror—could not have been so great. Pity & forgive me if I involuntarily pain, I do not mean—but I *do* suffer . . .'

Pity and forgiveness! It was a mercy for Augusta that they did not meet. Before Medora left for France, Ada went to Esher to take leave of her. She described her visit: 'The last half hour I was there, I was compelled to hear a discourse on the bitterness of dependence and threats of throwing herself down the throat of the first man she could get hold of to marry . . . "At least I should not depend on *charity*"—and then came all sorts of vituperations.' Annabella had cause to regret her rashness in befriending Medora—the Byron-Leighs had a powerful, irresistible fascination for her—'The Serpent-race', she wrote to Selina Doyle, 'will finish my life, as they have certainly shortened it.' Yet she was to outlive almost all of them.

By 1843 Medora's letters to Annabella from the South of France had become full of complaints, demands and vague menaces. She had disclosed what she considered the truth of her birth to her two servants; and when in March she arrived in Paris, unknown at first to Annabella, she also informed a French lawyer, Monsieur Berryer, a Captain de Bathe, who had helped her, and a Mr Bulwer at the British Embassy. She borrowed money 'once or twice' from Selina Doyle's sister to pay for the hotel and to settle bills. When Annabella heard of her presence in Paris she dispatched a friend, Dr King, to offer to increase her allowance to £300 a year on one condition that she should resign all control over herself and Marie to Annabella. This offer Medora emphatically declined, and Dr King returned to England. Medora attempted to gain possession of the deed of appointment, which she had left with Lord Lovelace, but he refused to send the document to Paris. Annabella then ceased communicating with her, and stopped payment of her annuity of £150, but placed this sum in the hands of trustees for her future use, provided the deed was not sold and that she did not 'return to her life of vice'.

As Annabella had no intention of considering Monsieur Berryer's intervention on behalf of 'Mlle. Leigh', and had informed him of this in a polite letter, Medora accepted Captain de Bathe's offer of financial help and, accompanied by him, arrived in London, where she took lodgings at 8 Church Row, Old St Pancras. Medora's servants, the Beaurepaires, were already in London and attempting to blackmail both Annabella and Augusta by disclosing what they knew of Medora's birth. Victor Beaurepaire was threatening an action against Annabella for 'loss of character', in that she had represented Medora as 'a respectable widow' and had falsely given her name as Madame Aubin. On Lushington's advice, rather than allow the matter to be made public in the courts the blackmailer was bought off. In September Annabella received from Beaurepaire a letter, written in illiterate French, addressed to 'The Lady Noel Byron, femme de mauvaise foi, Moore Place, Esher, Surrey'. It stated that a reward was offered for any information concerning 'the unfortunate Elizabeth Aubin, natural daughter of Lord Byron', aged twenty-nine years, and of her daughter, aged nine years, who had been 'abandoned' by her adoptive mother, 'the very wicked Lady Noel Byron' and by the 'virtuous princess', her half sister Lady Lovelace, and by her 'rascal of a brother-in-law the Seigneur Harpagon de Lovelace'. Anyone with information of these unfortunate creatures, 'who were in the greatest misery', should get in touch with 'Mrs. Leigh her mother' at St James's Palace, where he would receive the promised reward of a hundred lashes or a hundred strokes of the 'knout' or 'schlague', whichever he preferred. Finally Beaurepaire threatened to assault Lord Lovelace in the street, so that at Bow Street he could make a full public statement.

Captain de Bathe introduced Medora to his solicitors, one of whom, a Mr Thomas Smith, who as a young man had met Byron in Greece, took over the conduct of her affairs. He interviewed Dr Lushington, who informed him that Annabella declined to have anything to do with her; but he gave it to be understood as his personal advice that Sir George Stephen might be able to do something for Medora, if she saw him and 'conducted herself well'. Sir George eventually offered financial assistance from Annabella on Medora's accepting three conditions: firstly, she must surrender the deed of appointment to trustees on Marie's behalf; secondly, she must sign an account of the sums she had already received at the time when she declared herself 'abandoned'; finally, she must return to France. Medora accepted the last two conditions, but stubbornly rejected the first. She had appealed for monetary help from her Leeds and Chichester relations. Hobhouse also received a begging letter, across which he wrote: 'Elizabeth Medora Leigh—stating herself to be a *child* of Lord Byron and starving—some imposter I *hope.*'

After calling several times at St James's Palace and being told that Augusta was not at home, she wrote to her mother a letter so intemperate in her accusations that Mr Smith refused to include a copy in his account of her case. Some indication of its contents may be gauged by her remarks in a letter to the Duke of Leeds, thanking him for his gift of ten pounds. Here she wrote that she had heard from Annabella 'all I had yet to learn of the infamy of the mother, once so dearly loved, that I owed my birth to incest and adultery'.

Suddenly in mid-October, without warning either Captain de Bathe or Mr Smith, Medora left London and returned to France with Marie and the deed of appointment. In May 1844, she raised a loan of £500 from a Captain Hugh Cossart Baker on security of the deed. Augusta heard nothing more of her until 9th September, 1849, when she was informed by her solicitors that Medora had died in the South of France. Subsequently it appeared that she had married, in 1844 or early in the following year, a retired non-commissioned officer from the French army. A son, Elie, was born in August 1845, both he and his half-sister Marie surviving their mother. Medora was only thirty-five at the time of her death.

XV
'Dearest Augusta'
1850 - 1851

Nowhere in the pattern of calamities that composed Augusta's life were the misfortunes more evident than among the members of her own immediate family. Early she had accepted the consequences of being 'abominably married' to that 'exquisite piece of helplessness' George Leigh. When in 1814 Byron had given her £3000 to help to settle his debts, he suggested that the Colonel 'think well of some plan of regulating his expenditure'. He does not appear throughout his life to have accepted Byron's sound advice, and the £300 which was his nominal contribution to the household expenses more often went, with other large borrowed sums, to meet his gaming losses. He had to have his valet, his carriage and his coachman. He was always self-centred and demanding, and there is evidence that his temper worsened with the years. The example of his way of life was not lost on his children; the three sons grew up feckless and took to gambling. As early as 1841 Mrs Villiers wrote of Augusta's concern for Frederick, the second son: 'Her son in the navy is a constant drain upon her, and one cannot wonder that she should try to the last moment to save him from the degradation which has not yet *fallen*, but is constantly impending over him.' Of the four girls Emily alone behaved with restraint and consideration; she would not go into society, feeling that money should not be spent on clothes, while the children (Georgiana's family) 'had not bread to eat'.

In the autumn of 1844 Augusta wrote to Byron's old friend Francis Hodgson, now the respected Provost of Eton, and reported that she had just seen in Sir Richard Westmacott's studio Thorwaldsen's statue of Byron, destined for Trinity College, Cambridge. She then referred to herself and her anxieties: 'I do become very superannuating, and always think of poor B.'s horror of "withering at top first", not from the same superabundance of brains but wear and tear of the few I possess . . . But you do and always will sympathise in my troubles for the sake of *him*, who is gone.'

Augusta attempted to meet the constant demand for money by borrowing on the security of the children's reversionary interests in Byron's estate. To do this she had to pay the exorbitant rates of interest demanded by the money-lenders, and the result was that her income was severely reduced. In 1846 Hobhouse, who was the sole surviving executor, could put up no longer with her constant requirement of fresh sources of supply; he filed a bill to permit the Chancery Court to adminster the estate—'for the numerous deeds executed by Mrs. Leigh had created so many claimants that he wished to be relieved from responsibility.' Lady Chichester wrote to Mrs Villiers of Augusta's efforts and struggles to provide for her family of locusts: '. . . Mrs. L. deprived herself not only of all the luxuries, but many of the necessaries of life to maintain them *entirely*.' She was obliged to raise loans from her relations and friends; Lord Carlisle, the Duke of Sutherland, the Duke of Norfolk, John Murray—'every friend they had', wrote Emily, 'had helped her Mother.' In these harrowing circumstances poor Fletcher's pension of £70 a year went unpaid.

At the end of 1848 a fresh demand—possibly a debt contracted by the miserable Frederick—brought Augusta to the humiliating position of addressing a letter to Annabella through the medium of Dr Lushington. Annabella's reply, also through Lushington, elicited a further letter from Augusta on 30th November:

'Dear Sir,

'I am very sorry to have given you so much and useless trouble.

'The subjects referred to in the letter addressed by me to Lady Byron, and which at my request you were so kind as to transmit to her—are such as I must decline to communicate through any person whatever.

'The time may come when Lady Byron will regret her answer, —it may easily be believed that no common causes would

have induced me AGAIN to address her after her having returned my letter unopened through her Solicitor.

I am Dear Sir

Your obedient and obliged

Augusta Leigh.'

In February of the following year she wrote again a most
humble, distressed letter to Lushington, informing him: 'A
combination of very unfortunate occurrences have placed me
in the *most serious* state of pecuniary distress, and which if not
IMMEDIATELY met, will—and *must* end in the ruin *of us all*. I
venture to turn to Lady Byron for assistance.' She did this with
the knowledge that she had no claim upon her 'except that
any Individual in distress would have upon her Benevolence
and her Charity'. Annabella, a rich woman with some £8000
a year of her own, was not to be moved even by such abject
humiliation; she replied that it was 'with very great pain'
that she must refuse; she was no longer disposed to 'be kind to
Augusta'.

On 3rd May, 1850, Colonel George Leigh died at the flat
in Flag Court, St James's Palace. After his death it was noticed
that Augusta 'had lately and rather suddenly become a very
sunk and aged person'.

Early in the following year the family situation had become
so desperate that Emily took it on herself to write to Lushington
in a further appeal to Annabella, who was her godmother:
'It is with many apologies that I venture to address you, but
the recollection of your kindness and the very sad position in
which circumstances have placed my Mother embolden me
to do so.

'I have twice written to Lady Byron upon former occasions
but from her silence I am afraid she may be angry and thought
me impertinent. The death of my Father, although it enables
us to retrench in many things that were necessary to his comfort, has at the same time deprived us of the £300 per annum,
leaving only £700 to pay debts and to exist upon.

'My Mother has been trying ever since last May to raise
a sum of money to enable her to make an arrangement with the
creditors. There is no channel that she has not tried, but alas!
all to no purpose, and I now turn to Lady Byron as our last

255

and only hope. When my Mother last applied to her, she seemed to think it would be of no permanent relief—but now we are so differently situated. Nothing would have induced me to make this application but my unhappiness at seeing my Mother in this wretched state, and her health is no longer equal to the continued anxiety that she has been existing in for so many years—and I may now say that ruin is now staring us in the face. I think it right to say that if Lady Byron would help us she would not be a loser by it, for my Mother's life has been accepted at an insurance office, and you are most likely well aware what an expense it would be to raise it there at her age . . .!

*

Since she had met him in 1848, Annabella was seeing much of a well-known Brighton clergyman, the Rev. Frederick Robertson, and over the years she had increasingly taken him into her confidence. She had revealed much of her private life and her thoughts to this ready listener. They met in Brighton on New Year's Day, 1851, and in the course of their conversation Annabella remarked: 'I thought Mrs Leigh my friend—I loved her—I love her still! I cannot help it. I shall see her once more in this world before we both die.' On 8th January she wrote to Robertson from Ockham: 'A hope has risen in my mind that through your ministry good might be done to that survivor for whom I am so deely interested . . . If you recollect, in our last conversation I said there was one whom I had not seen for years, but hoped before death to see again. That was the person whose *guilt* made a great part (*not* the whole) of my wretchedness . . .' Robertson was the worst of confidants for Annabella: he encouraged her in her self-deluding analysis of her own states of mind and in imagining that her interest in Augusta was a selfless furthering of the latter's redemption. In reality she was motivated by a deep-seated hatred and jealousy of Augusta, and a fervent desire to humiliate her still deeper, while she herself maintained her pose of beneficent magnanimity. Two years later, after the deaths of both Augusta and Ada (the latter buried at her own wish by the side of her father at Hucknall Torkard), Annabella wrote of herself: 'And now, after the lapse of forty years, I look back on the past as a calm

256

spectator, and *at last* can speak of it. I see what was, what *might* have been, had there been one person less among the living when I married. Then I might have had duties, however steeped in sorrow, more congenial with my nature than those I was compelled to adopt. Then my life would not have been the concealment of a Truth . . .'

One of Annabella's delusions was that had Byron lived he would have come back to her, repentant and forgiven, if Augusta had not stood in the way. Of Byron Annabella wrote:

'It is not possible, if I have read human nature rightly, for any one to keep up such bitter resentment without believing in some cause for it . . . Towards the close of his life his feelings towards me were softening—but evil influence had not lost it hold entirely. He *must* have come, had he lived, to the belief that *from first to last* I had been his only truly devoted friend— it was not permitted.' And Augusta was the 'evil influence' who had not 'permitted' this reconciliation. If she could now wring a confession from Augusta of the truth of this, then she would have the added gratification of completely, perfectly forgiving her. That she could persuade herself, and Robertson, of the disinterested purity of her motives is almost beyond belief.

Annabella had decided on a meeting with Augusta, when Emily's letter reached her in Brighton. She sent it on to Robertson on 4th February and requested him to return it, as she wanted to show it to Lord Byron. 'He and Lady B. who spent the Evening here yesterday gave me a frightful description of the hatred now raging between the Mother and her eldest daughter [Georgiana].' She thought the moment was not opportune for seeing Augusta. '. . . how does it appear to you? I would write however to this effect—that I had determined on offering the interview, but felt that in consequence of the application from Emily, it must now be given up . . . It will then rest with her to urge it, and to promise the necessary conditions.' Annabella was incapable of performing an action without an *arrière pensèe*. Robertson agreed that it was not the time 'to be *chosen*', but that she would do well to write in the way that she had proposed.

She wrote on 11th February, giving not her own address, but that of the Brighton Post Office: 'Since the cessation of our personal intercourse you have more than once asked me to see you. If you still feel that wish, I will comply with it. We may not long have it in our power, Augusta, to meet again in this life, and to do so might be the means of leaving to both of us a remembrance of deep though sad thankfulness. But this could not be the effect unless every worldly interest were absolutely excluded from our conversation, and there were the most entire and mutual truthfulness. *No other expectations* must be entertained by you for a moment. On any other terms I cannot see you again, unless summoned to your Death-bed.

'If you decline, these will be the last words of mine ever addressed to you, and as such I wish they could convey to your heart the feelings with which I write them...'

So anxious was she for a reply that when one had not reached her three days later she wrote to Robertson: 'I shall now cease to expect.' However, the following morning she had Augusta's answer: although she was almost 'too unwell' to write, she 'unhesitatingly and thankfully' accepted Annabella's offer. She would write again as soon as her health would admit it—'and I suppose to the same address'—a gentle rebuke.

Augusta's straightforward letter of acceptance was regarded by Annabella as 'heartless'; by the priggish, canting Robertson as 'a *most* unsatisfactory letter ... I certainly was not prepared for anything so deep as this. However, a straight mind must outmatch a crooked one when it declines the task of tracking it through it sinuosities; for then it is lost in the labyrinth and out-witted—I argue well for the interview—so far as you are concerned: but for her—"Can that which is crooked be made straight?"' Annabella waited a fortnight before writing again. She hoped to hear soon of Augusta's recovery, and suggested that they meet 'at the most convenient Hotel on this railway'. Then she raised for the first time a point of some importance: 'I would hear *in Private* whatever you might have to say to me, but should I after hearing it wish to make any observations, you must permit me to do so in the presence of a friend who will accompany me—one who has not been in any way connected with past transactions. The interview cannot but be one of suffering to me, though, as my health is now equal to the effort, I think it right to make it.' Augusta replied, after the delay of a week, that she hoped to be well enough soon to make the journey. She went on: 'There are many things I may wish to say to you—indeed that you may wish to hear, which *could* not be communicated before ANY third person whatever . . .' Indeed, she would sooner forgo the meeting 'than have *any* third person admitted into the confidence . . . ' As it was only Annabella's words that were to be overheard, could not they be put in writing and countersigned by Augusta? 'I feel sure that it never can be your wish to add to my distress and unhappiness, which could not but be the case were *any* other person present . . . and I trust to the generosity of your feelings as to adopting . . . the courses I have proposed respecting your reply.'

Augusta was undoubtedly a little ingenuous in expecting generosity from Annabella on this occasion: nothing was to be allowed to disturb the conception she had formed of her own imperturbable rectitude. Augusta's expedient was quite insufficient; a witness was indispensable, 'a third person whose influence would be the best security against my acting in an Unchristian spirit, if you apprehend my doing so.' Poor Augusta was defenceless against such 'Christian' implacability: 'I can give no better proof of my wishing to see you, than by the sacrifice I make of my own feelings in consenting to see any third person during any part of our interview which must be of a painful nature and may be the last we may ever have in this world—however such are your terms, and be it so!' But Augusta's illness prevented an early appointment, and it was not until 5th April that Annabella fixed for the following Tuesday, the 8th. Augusta was fussed by the thought of the train journey; she had only once travelled in this way, 'and that in 1847'. Annabella gave her minute instructions: '. . . My servant in Drab Livery holding up my card will look into all the 1st Class Carriages, and will have a Fly waiting to convey you to Reigate Town (a mile and a half from the station), where I shall be at the White Hart.'

And so these two ageing ladies met again after twenty years —Augusta, now sixty-seven, timid, frail and ill; Annabella, not yet fifty-nine, equally frail-looking, but supported by the company of a handsome, bewhiskered clergyman. Two private sitting-rooms had been engaged. Annabella arrived first with the Rev. Robertson. Then Augusta was shown in— 'I saw

Death in her face at once', Annabella wrote afterwards. In her hand-bag Annabella had a memorandum of subjects 'to advert to' in her conversation: '1. Elizabeth ... my line of conduct. 2. I have wronged by assisting self-deception [Augusta's, not her own] —will repair it. 3. Questions—*you* kept up hatred—*you* put things in a false and irritating point of view—*you* suppressed what was kindest—most calculated to soften.

We have only Annabella's account of the macabre interview, written up afterwards for the purpose of record and attested as 'most accurate' by Robertson, who, however, was only present at part of it. Annabella, after weeks of brooding on the possible outcome of the eagerly awaited moment, was overwrought. What she thought Augusta was going to communicate is not known; but what she desired was a confession that Augusta had been responsible for Byron's hatred of her. Augusta, for her part, wanted nothing but a full reconciliation, followed perhaps by an offer of financial help. When they were alone, Augusta spoke first. In Annabella's narrative: 'Her communication was very short,—I made no comment *upon it* whatsoever, except, when she ceased to speak, "Is that all?" Had I spoken I must have said "false—false"— There appeared to be no motive on her part but *Self*—no feeling for the nearest of kin to her who was gone—The language (now that I reflect upon it) was studiously *equivocal*—no faltering —I think it had been learned by heart. After this she expressed her extreme gratitude to me for kindness to herself and her family. My feelings then broke loose from all control and I said something about its having been all in vain—I felt utterly hopeless—and asked to be left alone to compose myself.'

After a few minutes Annabella went in to Augusta and Robertson. 'One appeal ... I determined to make to her sense of Justice towards the deceased—I told her that it was not in human nature for any one to keep up such animosity as Lord Byron had shown towards me, unless it had been fed.' Her self-deception could hardly go further; had she not herself kept up just such an animosity towards Byron when living? She wanted to know from Augusta whether she had not fed the hatred in her letters—she added that she 'referred *only* to correspondence subsequent to 1816 when he left England— (for I felt that she was apprehensive) ...' Augusta defended herself (as well she might) against this charge; Byron's letters to her were evidence against it; 'he was very unjust "poor soul" ' towards his wife, 'had said dreadful things . . .', but she had never written anything to irritate him towards Annabella. 'I remarked', the latter continued, 'that there was a difference between exasperating and not softening . . . and that as I was confirmed in my own mind that the truth had not been fairly stated . . . but that I did not speak as her judge . . .'

The matter was then dropped for a short time, and was raised again by Augusta, who declared that the best proof of her standing up to Byron in defence of his wife was Hobhouse's words: 'You not only risked the loss of property, but what was much dearer to you, his affection.' This double reminder was too much for Annabella's overstrung nerves—to be reminded of Byron's affection for Augusta, and in the words of Hobhouse, one, with Kinnaird and Scrope Davies, of the dissipated 'Piccadilly crew'! Perhaps, too, there was a double element of jealousy, for Hobhouse was Byron's most intimate and loyal friend. 'At such a testimony I started up, and all but uttered an ironical answer—but she had *trusted me unconditionally*, and I replied "I don't understand it"— From that moment there was a mingling of indignation with the intense pity I had before felt—and I was afraid of myself—I said, I believe, that I should always wish her the blessing I could not give her, or something kind if my tears did not prevent my uttering it— but the strongest desire to be out of her presence took possession of me lest I should be tempted beyond my strength.' It is not too much to see here the process of her rationalisation: what she was not prepared in retrospect to admit was that at this moment her jealousy, stronger than her sense of frustration and self-pity, flashed out in the most intense hatred.

The meeting had ended in a complete failure of communication. Augusta departed, accompanied in the fly by the servant in drab livery; Annabella left after her in the company of the admiring clergyman. Once home Annabella dictated a brief note to Augusta informing her of her safe return and the state of her health. Strangely, after such an interview, Augusta concluded her short reply on 10th April with the words: 'I am better today, and cannot resist signing myself, Affectionately yours, Augusta Leigh.' A few days later she received another

261

letter from Annabella which must have quickly dispelled any illusion as to the real nature of their relationship: 'Your letter of the 10th affords the last proof that during our Interview, trying and painful as it was to me, I did not for a moment forget the consideration I was bound to observe by your having trusted me *unconditionally*.

'As I have received the communication which you have so long and anxiously desired to make—and upon which I offered no comment except "Is that all?"—I have done all in my power to contribute to your peace of mind. But I remain under the afflicting persuasion that it is not attained by such means as you have taken. Farewell.'

Augusta waited until 26th April before she sent off her dignified and entirely convincing answer:

'I feel sure that you would not willingly be unjust, and therefore, after much perplexing and deep consideration, I have determined again to address you. My great wish for an interview with you arose partly from a secret desire to see you once more in this world, and still more to have the means of convincing you that accusations which I had reason to believe had been brought against me to you were unfounded, and at this, if only from the recollection of the affection that once subsisted between us, you cannot be surprised. I had not, and never implied that I had, anything to reveal to you with which you were not previously acquainted on any other subject. Nor can I at all express to you the regret that I have felt ever since those words escaped you, showing that you imagined I had "encouraged a bitterness of feeling in Lord Byron towards you." I can as solemnly declare to you as if I were on my oath or on my death-bed that I never did so in any one instance, but that I invariably did the contrary. I have letters from him, and of my own to him (and returned to me after his death), which would bear out this assertion, and I am ready at this or any other moment to make the most solemn asseveration of this, in any way that you can desire. I would willingly see your friend Mr. Robertson and afford him every proof of my veracity in my power.

'It was clear that he thought that I was keeping back communications that ought to be made to you, and as your confidential friend it would be a comfort to me to talk openly with him on such points as might tend to convince you of the truth of what I now say—and without which the remainder of my life will be still more unhappy than the miseries, of various kinds, which surround me must inevitably make me.'

Augusta had to wait a week, before she received a response to this moving and truthful letter:

'Madam—Lady Byron has sent to me the enclosed letter which she requests me to transmit to you unopened—Lady Byron considers the correspondence to have been entirely closed by the last letter which she sent—the one, that is, which was written after the interview. I have the honour to be,

'Your obedient servant,
'Fred. W. Robertson.'

As a last desperate effort to secure justice, Augusta appealed to the clergyman—'There was a kindness in your manner which makes me very desirous that *you* at least should know the truth.' She sent the letter returned from Annabella on to him, with a request that he read it. Robertson, though he was prepared to see Augusta, referred the decision to Annabella, who was opposed to their meeting— 'The opportunity for garbled representations could not be resisted.' Robertson wrote a long letter to Augusta, declining— 'The proofs you desire to give could only be given in Lady Byron's presence, and she will never consent to another meeting.'

*

In June Augusta was taken ill; she had been in such indifferent health for so long that at first Emily, her sole companion, was not greatly worried. However, it soon became apparent that her condition was serious; with dropsy and heart disease she was visibly sinking. Lady Chichester called bringing her nourishing dishes and ministering to her wants. There was no money in the house, and Emily was obliged to raise a loan from John Murray, giving as security some of the remaining Byron papers—the bulk of them had already been disposed of. Augusta besought Emily to redeem them, if she could, after her death.

Annabella, when she heard the news, was much affected. 'Be kind to Augusta.' The often remembered words raised in

263

her now a complex of opposed emotions, but the predominant feeling in one not often given to experience such weaknesses was something very like remorse. In her possession was the letter, written by Byron in Ravenna more than thirty years before, thanking her for her promise to provide for Augusta and her children: 'As to Augusta ... Whatever She is or may have been—you have never had reason to complain of her—on the contrary—you are not aware of the obligations under which you have been to her.—Her life and mine—and yours and mine—were two things perfectly distinct from each other—when one ceased the other began—and now both are closed ... It is a comfort to me *now*—beyond all comforts; that A— and her children will be thought of, after I am nothing ... I told you that I was going *long*—and going *far* ... and two words about her or hers would have been to me— like vengeance or freedom to an Italian—i.e. the "Ne plus ultra" of gratifications— She and two others were the only things I ever really loved—I may say it now—for we are young no longer.—'

The poignant irony of her situation was not lost on Annabella: Augusta had had his love—for herself there were only the obligations. And yet she too had loved Augusta. What was there about this 'serpent race' which roused in her such conflicting emotions of love and hate? But at that moment remorse, or affection (her power of self-analysis had failed her), was ascendant. She wrote to Emily to enquire if she 'could add to the comfort or remove any difficulty'. Her offer was politely declined. However, only a fortnight later she received a letter from Emily, saying that 'there was a pecuniary difficulty, which must be brought to her Mother unless provided for'. Annabella settled the matter. She sent regularly and once went herself to the door to enquire for news from the servant.

At the beginning of October Annabella's compunction moved her to make, for her, an extraordinary gesture of reconciliation and affection. She described her action in a letter to Robertson: 'About a week ago I felt so great a desire to send her a message, that after fully considering what might be the effects I determined to disregard all but those which it might possibly have upon herself—I wrote to ask the daughter to whisper two words from me—words of affection long since disused.' Emily thankfully carried out Annabella's request. Bending over her dying mother, she breathed the two words— 'Dearest Augusta.'

Writing to her aunt on Sunday, 5th October, Emily conveyed Augusta's profound thankfulness: 'She desires me to say that the tears which refused to flow from sorrow were produced by the joy of hearing "Dearest Augusta" from you— that they were her greatest consolation—her voice has grown so weak and thick that it is with difficulty that I can make out what she says—she said a great deal to me that I could not hear distinctly—I dare say that she will mention the subject again . . .' But it does not appear that she did, and Annabella regretfully noted: 'A *second* message lost.' A week later, on Sunday, 12th October, 1851, Augusta passed away with her hands in Emily's. On the same morning the bereaved young woman (she was thirty-three) sat down 'alone at the Palace with the Birds and a Dog' and wrote simply to Annabella. 'Poor Mamma died this Morning a little after three, having suffered most dreadfully since yesterday afternoon—it is indeed a most happy release, but her loss can never be made up to me.'

*

It was thought at first that Augusta had died intestate, and on 24th February, 1852, letters of administration were granted to the youngest son, Henry Francis Leigh; but, strangely, after six years (by which time he had died) a will was found and probate was granted in 1858. By this all the real and personal estate and effects (it was filed in the category of wills under £8000) were left to Emily and she was appointed sole executrix. But in October 1851 Lady Chichester considered Emily's state as one of 'complete bankruptcy', yet hardly thought poor Emily could bring herself to believe it. A fund was set up for her by members of the family and close friends. Lady Wilmot Horton wrote to Annabella: 'All I protest against is having to do with any other Members of her Family—they have long enough been "Beggars" to be quite enured to it and I fear worse.' Eventually an annuity of £120 was raised for her, but it was 'not to be considered permanent at present', and she was to have no control over its payment—this was a precaution against the brothers getting their hands on it. (Emily even feared that they would break in to Flag Court and carry off and sell the Byron mementoes) In 1854, when the Byron affairs were brought into the Court of Chancery, twenty-six money-lenders put in an appearance as claimants on all property over and above the capital which secured Annabella's jointure, and even this was forfeit after her death. As Annabella wryly remarked, 'How little was such a result anticipated by the Testator!'

A Short Bibliography

The Works of Lord Byron, Letters and Journals, edited by Rowland E. Prothero, 6 vols., 1898-1901.

Lord Byron's Correspondence, edited by John Murray, 2 vols., 1922.

Byron: A Self-Portrait, Letters and Diaries, edited by Peter Quennell, 2 vols., 1956.

The Poetical Works of Lord Byron, Oxford University Press, 1935.

A short selected list of other works to which reference has been made:

Astarte: A Fragment of Truth concerning George Gordon Byron, Sixth Lord Byron, Earl of Lovelance, 1901.

Byron: A Biography, Leslie A. Marchand, 3 vols., New York, 1957.

Byron: The Last Journey, Harold Nicolson, 1940.

Conversations of Lord Byron, Thomas Medwin, 1824.

In Whig Society, 1775-1818, Countess of Airlie, 1921.

Life, Letters and Journals of Lord Byron, Thomas Moore, 1830.

Lord Byron's Marriage: The Evidence of Asterisks, G. Wilson Knight, 1957.

Lord Byron's Wife, Malcolm Elwin, 1962.

Memoir of the Rev. Francis Hodgson, by his son, Rev. James T. Hodgson, 2 vols., 1878.

Recollections of a Long Life, Lord Broughton (John Cam Hobhouse), edited by Lady Dorchester, 6 vols., 1909-1911.

The Byron Mystery, Sir John C. Fox, 1924.

The Late Lord Byron: Posthumous Dramas, Doris Langley Moore, 1961.

The Life and Letters of Anne Isabella, Lady Noel Byron, Ethel Coburn Mayne, 1929.

Index

268

270

PETER GUNN

Born in 1914 in Sydney, Australia, Peter Gunn studied classics at Melbourne University. A subaltern in the Rifle Brigade during World War II, he was captured in Tunisia and spent time in Italy and Germany as a prisoner of war. After the war, he read Moral Sciences at Trinity College, Cambridge, for three years. From 1949 to 1956 he lectured at the Royal Military Academy at Sandhurst. Married, with one son and four stepchildren, Mr. Gunn now lives outside the village of Great Shelford, near Cambridge, and devotes his time to writing.